THE DATA BANK SOCIETY

THE DATA BANK SOCIETY

Organizations, Computers and Social Freedom

MALCOLM WARNER
MICHAEL STONE

London
GEORGE ALLEN & UNWIN LTD
RUSKIN HOUSE MUSEUM STREET

First Published in 1970

ISBN 0 04 300025 8

Printed in Great Britain
in 10 *point Times Roman*
by Unwin Brothers Limited, The Gresham Press
Old Woking, Surrey, England

To Alan F. Westin

It is the individual man
In his individual freedom who can mature
With his warm spirit the unripe world.

CHRISTOPHER FRY, *The Firstborn*

You argue by results, as this world does,
To settle if an act be good or bad,
You defer to the fact. For every life and every act,
Consequences of good and evil can be shown.

T. S. ELIOT, *Murder in the Cathedral*

Preface

In this book a behavioural scientist and a computer scientist have combined to study the effects on the private citizen of the concentration of massive information search resources by central bureaucracy and large organizations. Both public and private sectors have received attention and are considered in the context of British, European and American experience.

There is an attempt to examine the problem from a social and broadly political standpoint in the knowledge of technical potential and limitations. This relates to the wider perspective of technological pressure on social change and the effects this has on the individual.

We expect the resulting work to interest technologists and social scientists, but we will have failed in our prime intention if the book does not claim the attention of the wider public and add its factual argument to the continuing debate.

Four publications of the US Government Printing Office are referred to, and quoted extensively, throughout this book. Since the titles are somewhat cumbersome, these are given here in full, with the abbreviation which is used in all footnotes:

1. *Hearings*, A: The Computer and Invasion of Privacy, Hearings before a subcommittee of the Committee on Government Operations, House of Representatives, 89th Congress, Second Session. July 26, 27 and 28, 1966.
2. *Hearings*, B: Commercial Credit Bureaux, Hearings before a subcommittee as above; 90th Congress, Second Session. March 12, 13 and 14, 1968.
3. *Hearings*, C: Computer Privacy, Hearings before the Subcommittee on Administrative Practice and Procedure of the Committee on the Judiciary, United States Senate, 90th Congress, First Session. March 14 and 15, 1967.
4. *Hearings*, D: As above, but 'Part 2', Second Session, February 6, 1968.

The great value of these publications is that:

(i) They are the only record of public questioning of private citizens by elected representatives – there is no comparable investigation recorded in this country.

(ii) They include, besides full transcripts of the interrogations, many articles reprinted from other sources, and papers prepared specially for the subcommittees.

(iii) They are a powerful argument for the intervention of the people's elected representatives in a situation which threatens to be disruptive of society if allowed to develop uncontrolled.

The many sources we have used in our research are acknowledged in the body of the book, but we would also wish to thank the staff of the Library of the London Graduate School of Business Studies for their diligent support; Daniel Snowman of the BBC for originally encouraging a paper on the late Third Programme in 1968; and Lance J. Hoffman, of Stanford University, California, for extensive bibliographical advice and information. We have also received valuable encouragement from the British Computer Society in our preparation.

We are particularly happy to record our thanks to Tony Smythe and the National Council for Civil Liberties for positive assistance and use of research facilities.

Contents

Chapter 1

COMPUTERS AND 'PROVISIONAL CATASTROPHE'

Twenty years ago, almost before anyone had built a machine that could reasonably be called a complex computer, George Orwell wrote his novel *1984*. Technology has already outstripped his imagination, with fourteen years still to go. Political reality, fortunately, falls well short of his nightmare. But organizations now have the technical power available to implement his chilling vision of a society under surveillance and control.

A more recent, less polemic study of the future began a few years ago as a continuing exercise. The 'Commission on the Year 2000' brought together under the chairmanship of Daniel Bell a veritable pride of American sociological, political, scientific, literary, and philosophical lions. A transcript of some early discussions of the Commission – together with papers submitted by some members – was published under the title 'Work in Progress', as a special issue of *Daedalus* in 1967.[1]

Two members, Herman Kahn and Anthony J. Wiener,[2] listed in their paper 'One Hundred Technical Innovations' likely to be seen before AD 2000, and included: '29. Extensive and intensive centralization (or automatic interconnection) of current and past personal and business information in high-speed data processors ... 74. Pervasive business use of computers for the storage, processing and retrieval of information'.

These same writers collaborated a year later in a book called *The Year 2000: A Framework for Speculation*, a very detailed survey of many kinds of discernable trends that may be used to provide pointers for the future. In this latter work they describe themselves as 'provisional catastrophists', a description we would wish to adopt for ourselves.

The 'catastrophe' we have in mind is the potential destruction of freedom in our society which the computer may cause; but only if nothing is done to avoid it. There is 'provision' for a lesser degree of upset, because action *can* be taken to avoid the 'catastrophe'. To determine the necessary action demands that an appraisal be made of the computer power which is available now, and still rapidly developing, together with a review of the consequential changes that this power may bring. The potential benefits must then be weighed against what will be destroyed, and society as a whole be allowed to determine the relative values involved. What do we gain; what do we lose; are the changes greater than we can afford to allow?

The choice is there; the values must be weighed. The serious danger is that changes will just happen. On the one hand are the computermen, dedicated to proving their own ingenuity and their machines' versatility; on the other are public and private managements, quite rightly desperate to improve efficiency and economy by using modern tools. Between the two, the side-effects of computer systems which will vastly modify the accepted customs of society could be overlooked. New projects, new ideas, new tools and new techniques may imperceptibly remove the opportunity for choice. Individual liberties are at stake; a large part of our freedom will be seriously threatened if computers take over more and more tasks without serious questioning of the kind of society to which they may be leading us.

Until late in 1968, the ethics of computer usage were rarely questioned in public in Britain. For several years newspapers had been eager to report stories of 'computer errors' (*always*, if one knew the full facts, attributable to a human error at some stage of the process), especially the financial ones. Cheques were sent out for 1d, or for £999,999 19s 11d; final demands were despatched to clients whose account was actually in credit; and so on. These things still happen, and are still occasionally reported. Bold headlines appear, too, bringing us all the latest news of computers that will perform calculations even faster than before: diagnose diseases; design, produce and market new products; plan buildings, roads, and bridges; control air and road traffic; find jobs, and mates, for people; book flights and hotels for a world tour; keep bank accounts; solve crimes. One need only watch the regular current affairs programmes to be persuaded of the ubiquitous role computers play in the modern world.

It is comparatively recently that the known fallibility of the computer, and of its attendant acolytes, has been correlated with its ubiquitous role in organizational life. And as a result, the desirability of 'progress' on all fronts has at last been subjected to informed criticism.

In the electronic computer lies the potential for domination. The degree of control, of surveillance, which our worst political apprehensions can envisage, demands the technical ability to monitor and to record each citizen's actions, transactions, and reactions. And the same machinery must be able to supply this recorded information upon demand – in part, in full, in correlation with other facts apparently relevant, or in whatever form may be desired and selected by that authority whose intent is control and regulation. These things computer systems can do, and are beginning to do.

Will the computer in fact take us into this near-Orwellian situation? Or, to phrase the problem in its mildest form, how near shall we approach to rule by 'computocracy'? These are hard questions, because the trends in technological development cannot be extrapolated with confidence, and because they raise the further difficulties of defining individuality, responsible freedom, and privacy. To some extent we have lived with these values for years in all 'developed' civilizations. Sometimes they have had to be defined and defended against overt attacks. Sometimes, among emerging nations, these values have been set out in a formal constitution. The computer's power brings a new threat, forcing us to new definitions. It offers us much in the way of increased freedom and improved social amenities, yet ironically if it is misused it could deprive us of freedom. It offers men a remarkable prospect of a renewed society, whilst presenting him with almost Godlike choices of what that society shall be like.

Can all this come from what is no more than a few boxes of electronics and mechanics? Yes, all this because these innocuous boxes have voracious appetites, and can digest, churn around, and regurgitate information at prodigiously high speeds. A few of them strung together across the country, linked by telephone lines or radio waves, can become an unprecedentedly versatile storehouse of facts. INFORMATION IS POWER. No country can be run, no business managed, unless its echelons of executives and managers receive a constant supply of information to assist the processes of decision-making.[3] Authority and control cannot be maintained, nor alternative future policies evaluated, in the absence of an information flow. In recent years that flow has increased to a torrent in all channels of administration. Enter the computer, to handle it for us!

'It is an extraordinary era in which we live. It is altogether new. The world has seen nothing like it before. I will not pretend, no one can pretend, to discern the end; but everybody knows that the age is remarkable for scientific research into the heavens, the earth, what is beneath the earth; and perhaps more remarkable still is the application of this scientific research to the pursuit of life. The ancients saw nothing like it. The moderns have seen nothing like it, until the present generation. . . . The progress of the age has almost outstripped human belief.'

The reader may have guessed, perhaps, that the above is not a recent assessment. The words were spoken in 1847 by Daniel Webster, when he opened a new stretch of railway. They serve well to set a perspective for today, and for this comment, by Karl Deutsch:[4] 'We will see the triumph of the computer comparable only to the triumph of the railroad in the past century, or the triumph of the automobile in the first half of this century.' The most significant word in that sentence, it seems to us, is the word 'or'. It could be argued that the railway has been a technological triumph *for* society, bridging distance at speed, in safety and comparative comfort. Neither during its early development, nor in its heyday, did it cause any major interference with the rights of society as a whole – although there were of course a minority of offended landowners who lost ground to the developing routes. It is in this decade, as many train services have been withdrawn, that certain groups of people have been seriously deprived of the valuable liberty they previously had to travel far and fast. And the decline in rail service is to be attributed largely to the advent of the car.

Whilst we should not exaggerate the case, it could even be argued that the car, in contrast to the railway, has triumphed *over* society. The man without one is poor indeed. The man who merely owns one, but takes no pride in it, or in his escapades with it, is a social misfit. Miles of countryside have certainly been carved up, cities, towns, and villages disrupted, for the sake of universal motoring. Vehicle and highway construction, and maintenance, have also assumed a disproportionately fundamental role in our national economy. This egregious self-propellant dominates thinking and planning both personal and social. The artificially stimulated desire for personalized propulsion has been rampant for some years, and the automobile has probably destroyed as much as it has added to society. There are at last some signs – barely more than hints – of a healthy reaction to the destruction of amenities, civic or bucolic, to make room for man and his motor-car. If only the 'provisional catastrophists' of twenty, or even fifteen, years ago had been able to see ahead, and shouted loudly enough, how much of value might have been preserved? Will we even now give more credence to the Buchanan Report than to the blandishments of the Motor Lobby?

The nature of the computer's 'triumph' hangs in the balance. The next few years will determine whether the computer is to be like a train or like a car in its effects – that is, whether it will complement, or annihilate, many of our freedoms. Just as has applied to all other major inventions and discoveries, the computer can be a useful tool for the betterment of man, or it can rock the foundations of modern society. But will we master it, or will it master us?

There is a tale, apocryphal like most computer stories, of the biggest and latest (synonymous, in the degraded verbal currency of our day, with 'best') computer, subjected to the full ceremonial of an official 'opening' by the President of the USA. Formalities, speeches, and switch-manipulation duly accomplished, the honoured guest was invited by the reception committee to submit a problem to the machine. With justified deliberation, unbecoming temerity, and commendable profundity, he fed in the question: 'Is there a God?' With scarcely a blink in its unwavering aplomb, with instanteous reaction, and abysmal theology, the computer replied: 'There is NOW.'

From which tale we might draw many apposite conclusions; we shall take just four points for further comment.

First, we might conclude that we shall eventually be 'taken over' by machines, and ruled by robots. False; the idea that computers themselves will ever manage a business or run a country really should have been extinguished by now. A computer is a machine under human control. People decide and direct its allotted tasks, and always will. They may make wrong decisions, or give the wrong control directions; they may cause significant errors to be made by the machine in its handling of the tasks given to it; but they cannot be directed by the machine. Of all the people who may suffer the trauma of regarding a computer as human, the least afflicted are those who actually make it work – they *know*.

A computer has no mind of its own, no will of its own, no philosophy of its own; it has, to use Hobbes' phrase, 'no artificial life'.[5] It cannot be 'taught', nor can it 'think', in any profound human sense, widely though these anthropomorphic terms are bandied about. It can only be given formalized instructions, within the fixed repertoire of the functions it is built to perform. If it starts to smoulder, or refuses to respond to a push of the STOP button, a human pulls the power plug out. People are in control, all the time.

Second, we might conclude from the story that while the people who work with computers may have a sense of humour – and certainly they have devised many ingenious games of question-and-answer, and all sorts of other entertaining demonstrations – these experts are not highly responsible socially in their concern for the results of their labours. True – they need the sense of humour, for their work is frequently arduous, consuming many hours and much nervous energy. But the computer profession has not distinguished itself in showing a particularly responsible attitude towards the sociological implications of the use of computers. Indeed it is not unjust to say with one critic: 'In a world that many feel more and more impersonal and where the individual is felt to be more and more subject to whims of arbitrary government, where all communication is from "them" to "us" and none the other way, the computing fraternity have earned an unenviable identification with the forces of centralization and faceless authority.'[6]

Computer people have always tended to regard themselves as an elite corps, a minority with exceptional talents. This is, naturally, most notable in those who were among the first small handful in this country to become experts – who are now filling many of the top computer jobs. In the early days certain specialist talents were essential; even now they are desirable. There are very few indeed who have seen that these talents are genuinely rare, with a corresponding responsibility that they shall be used wisely, if not philanthropically. The article just quoted continues: 'It is easy to plead that we are a young and yet immature profession, and to beg for time to assert our responsibility. It is probably truer to say that we are too eager for patronage to finance our latest toy and dare not risk offending the powers that be.'[7] Members of the profession have certainly spent much time in undignified scrambling for personal advantage in an occupation where expertise is sparse and the salaries are high. It is time for them to come out of the sequestered air-conditioning of their machine rooms and see what they are doing to others. This may well be beginning to happen.

The social consequences of the new technology must be faced, particularly by those in a position to understand them. In his Presidential address to the British Computer Society in 1968 (the year in which the Society became, legally and officially, a 'professional body'), Professor Stanley Gill asked: 'To what extent should all of us, who specialize in computing, concern ourselves with what computers are doing to society? This is not a new question. It faced the engineers in the nineteenth century when the industrial revolution began; it faced the nuclear physicists in the nineteen-forties, and now it faces the biologists too.'[8] He drew the conclusion that 'We are surely better equipped than the average citizen – dare I say than the average politician? – to foresee the consequences of our technology and to judge how it ought to be applied . . . there is scope for influencing the course of events. And we have a duty to influence them. How can we exert this influence? Broadly, there are two ways open to us. the first is through the direction of our professional work, by choosing which projects to work on . . . by refusing to implement undesirable features, and if necessary by going on strike.... The second way is by moulding public opinion, through persuasion.'

It is evident that the profession is now, albeit rather belatedly, making a serious attempt to put its technological house in order, to find a new posture of social awareness, to establish an ethical code for its members, to examine the implications of its activity upon the ordinary citizen.

A third inference one might draw from the story is that a computer is a good way of getting questions answered. True – *so long as* it has already been supplied with the answers, or the basic data from which the answer can be calculated or determined (the 'stored data'); and also with the means of performing the necessary calculations, or the searches of its magnetic files, to find the answer (using a 'program' of instructions) by derivation, from examination of the form in which the question was expressed (the 'input data'). More and more, computers *are* being used to answer questions – to act as replacements for filing cabinets, to store information, and allow it to be found and reproduced on demand. The basic changes in computer technology which have transformed the computer from a calculating machine into an information machine will be described in outline later.

Fourth, there is the possibility that ultimate considerations are involved. As another writer has warned: 'A machine with superior intelligence to man could conceivably come between man and God.'[9] From a religious (or even philosophical) standpoint, any suggestion that our technology is outstripping our power to control it and use it for our benefit, or that we are able to create things of a 'higher order' than ourselves, is profoundly disturbing. And similarly, if the computer is leading us into tyranny, any constraint upon man's freedom is a constraint upon a 'God-given' quality, in this view, which insists that each separate person is a unique creation. This view is not only held by 'believers'. Man is to be treated with dignity, respected for his qualities, tolerated for his failings, and *not* to be robbed of that freedom from exterior domination which is his from the beginning. Few humanists, in our opinion, would disagree.

In another critique, it was observed that 'A Big Brother with a nosy interest in your sex life, drinking habits and other private aspects of your existence is rapidly growing to adulthood. This sibling is computerized, and fed with information by many governments, private agencies and businesses. Experts in the field thus consider the demise of traditional privacy in the United States inevitable. The problem, they say, is making sure Big Brother gets his facts straight.'[10]

The problem is more than that. It involves not only making sure the facts are right, but also the *selection* of what facts are put into the record and the length of time they stay there; it includes problems of deciding who is authorized to retrieve this personal data, and who is to base policy decisions upon the information system thus established; it involves the ethics and integrity of those who give directions to the computer experts on what they are to make the machine do with the information, and the ethics of the experts themselves. It entails, in fact, asking society to determine just how much deprivation of privacy it is prepared to tolerate.

As we have observed, there is now a detectable trend towards an increased public criticism of the plans of organizations and their personal records. An early example appeared in the correspondence columns of *The Times*,[11] when a Mr Aubrey Tulley questioned the policy guiding the National GIRO Service, wondering whether this computer system might 'turn out to be an embryo Big Brother'. He asked for assurance that 'safeguards for individual privacy (relating to credit status and transactions) are to be applied to the information which will be stored in the Giro computer complex'. Mr John Grady, Director of Giro at the time, promptly replied the following day on behalf of the GPO. Whilst he gave 'without hesitation or qualification' the assurance asked for, others besides Mr Tulley may not have been entirely comforted, since he appended a portion of the Giro Handbook which said that 'details of your account . . . will not be disclosed to any person except on your instructions or *as required or authorized by law*'. (Our italics; obviously this left the door wide open before the horse was even under starter's orders.)

There are now, in fact, machines in daily use from which computing power is made available on demand to people in places miles away from the computer itself, in ways which begin to look like the distribution of electrical power, and the ordinary communication of the telephone service. The capability for computer power 'on tap', and for information in bulk, will become more widespread very rapidly. When retrieving devices, which need be little more complex than an electric typewriter, are linked to a fact-filing computer, the data from its memory can be sent to the remote devices over telephone lines, radio waves, or even laser beams, at speeds measured in minute fractions of a second. One central source – or, more likely, several intercommunicating computer sources – can hold all the information an organization needs, or a nation needs, and make it available to anyone, anywhere, any time, immediately.

More information, more rational judgements. Better data, better decisions. More facts, more power. The threat to the individual comes primarily from the State, from the increased power put into its hands by the use of computers. Both government and business administration could have instantly available all the recorded facts about everyone, literally 'from cradle to grave'. There is little doubt that technically the State *could* maintain an integrated dossier file on every man, woman and child (and animal too, for that matter) in these isles, using computer equipment which is in existence now. As will be shown later, a number of specialized computer information centres are already in existence, and many more are being planned. Almost inadvertently, a massive integrated computer 'data bank'[12] could come into being, merely by linking the existing smaller centres together.

Here, then is the 'catastrophic' threat to our freedom and privacy. Such a national, integrated, dossier system would, as has been said, 'put your whole life history no further than the push of a button away'.[13] And the development of computer data banks, in one form or another, is quite inevitable, for the pressures of economy and efficiency – especially amongst the bureaucracy in an increasingly legislative society – tend to push all organizations in this direction.

The techniques of computer information storage, and instantaneous retrieval, are already being applied; there are places in this country where a clerk, who once had document files, now types a request for information on a remote retrieving device, and gets what he wants within seconds. As we have already stressed, this facility is devised and planned and made effective by computer programmers, who work some of the longest and hardest hours of anyone today. People are controlling the machine. Is there not some danger, then, that we are allowing programmers to gain a dominant role in society? There has always been the problem of 'Who will guard the guardians?' of any community. *Maybe we should now ask 'Who will program the programmers?*' Who will condition their preferences and prejudices, approve their methods, monitor their actions – all of which can determine the particular phrasing of the questions to an encyclopaedic computer's records? Can we be complacent about their 'span of control', as the industrial sociologists would put it? This question could become one of the basic political issues of the next decade.

Another story that has been told[14] is even more suggestive of the degree of control over people exercised by computers, in its veiled implications. It tells that a hundred of the world's greatest scientists got together and made the 'ultimate' computer, so that there could be a perfect model of society for the purposes of research and planning. As part of the clever devices attached to the main logical elements of their machine, they constructed and connected a large glass sphere, in which were small model men and women – automata directed by the computer logic. Within this glass bowl, they also placed a supply of all the essential resources needed for humans to survive in society. When all was at last ready, the computer was switched on, and all the creators of this wonder gathered around the glass sphere to watch how their 'model society' would behave and develop. It worked perfectly, to the extent that the miniature figures came to life and proceeded to active, apparently purposeful, co-operation. The watchers were, however, utterly shocked to see that the first task, with which the model humans occupied themselves, was the construction of a glass sphere, into which they placed small images of themselves. At this point, one of the more perceptive of the scientists looked around over his shoulder, and realized that they were themselves *all* enveloped in an enormous glass sphere. . . .

The tale is typical of what people read and write about computers, and it is hardly surprising that some genuine fear is created. From inside the computer business it is easy enough to rationalize this fear, to assume calmly that other people will take care of any moral problems, even to dismiss the visible element of public concern as something very minimal when compared with the other traumas of society. It is only too easy for most consciences to shrug off the possibility of social consequences, and blindly to pursue the path of increasingly powerful, imaginative, technological applications. Yet if the populace at large were to take seriously everything it reads and hears about computers, and take to heart the possible consequences of the rumours and half-truths, they could react like the Luddites of old – and the electronic gadgetry could be smashed to pieces. Indeed it has already happened when the students of one university[15] became so incensed about the way its affairs were administered that they broke into the computer building, and wrecked not only all the files, but also the machine itself.

Perhaps it is unfortunate that there remains little real choice as to whether computers shall be used or not. There is no straight case to be made for the quill pen against the computer, as the then Minister of Transport told Mr Edward Taylor, MP, accusing him of a 'Neolithic outburst' for daring to question (in support of Mr Robert Cooke, MP) the proposed centralized computer system for vehicle and driver licensing.[16] The computer is with us, and is essential to modern administration. There is no turning back. The choice is of the specific direction in which we shall go forward in the area of political, legislative and technical safeguards.

When one begins to think about filing systems of any kind, but particularly those containing information in bulk about people, it is immediately obvious that the biggest fact-gathering organism of any kind is the Government. Hence it is in that institution, at all levels, that we may expect to see the rapacious appetite of the computer most welcome for its power to cope with these personal files, to relieve the clerks of an oppressive burden of paperwork. Every commercial enterprise, every household, every individual, knows how the tide rises, steadily and ceaselessly, without a prospect of ever ebbing; There are returns to be made, applications to be completed, forms to be filled up, all the time. Much of this information goes into Government offices, to be filed.

'The gathering of industrial information by the Government is not an exercise in bureaucracy for its own sake; its purpose is to ensure that relevant data are ready to hand to help managements determine their operations in the light of the best information available. Given that a firm knows all about its own activities, our object is to make sure that the relevant facts and figures are fed into the general statistical services, processed and made available in various forms. In this there is a role for trade associations and Government, acting together, to disseminate the information to all industrialists similarly engaged except where it is commercially sensitive.'[17]

It was calculated in early 1967 that on average every citizen of the USA has personal information recorded in the files of *fourteen* different governmental offices. The statistic for this country might not be very different. As Professor Arthur Miller has pointed out,[18] a kind of Parkinson's Law operates: the greater the ability of government to handle information, the more information it demands. Give government the power of computers to handle more information more efficiently, and there is little doubt it will go on demanding more and more.

It is of vital importance to recognize that at present the vast collection of personal and business facts which government has about us is dispersed among dozens of different filing systems in dozens of different places – and much of it irretrievably buried in archives.

But many of the government's files have already been put into computers. We have mentioned the Giro system and the plan for centralized licensing; both have had computer-critical light shone upon them; so have the plans of the Social Security and the Inland Revenue – and rightly so. If all these personal records, and others too, were held in the computers of Central Government; if each Local Authority has its local personal records in a local computer; if in fact *all* the Government's files about people are kept by computer, and the machines are then linked together for interrogation from various administrative offices throughout the land to retrieve instant facts about anybody in any of the files, the long arm of government stretches far indeed. Such a situation may look impossible. But something very like it is now being achieved by the FBI and the State police forces of America, in the relatively restricted field of criminal information. One must say 'relatively', because the files include offences of *all* kinds, suspects as well as proven criminals, so that in practice a wide population spectrum is covered and a great deal of personal data is in records which are nationally instantly available to law enforcement agencies.

The computer has given bureaucracy the potential for omniscience, if not omnipotence, by putting into its hands the power to *know*. No fact unrecorded, nothing forgotten nor lost, nothing forgiven. These facilities may augment the secular horse-power of the present State machinery far beyond the dreams of an administrator of the traditional British Civil Service variety. And while we inevitably tend to think of files and bureaucracy in the context of government, it should not be overlooked that the business organization has its own kinds of citizen-information systems (often overlapping those of Government, and of mutual interest), and its own kind of 'bureaucracy', which will also stand to benefit from computer methods.

It has been suggested by Mr Aubrey Jones[19] that the computer will change the power structure of society in favour of the young – not only because it is the young whose minds are fresh and malleable enough to adapt to both changing technology and methodology, but also because so much information will be 'on tap'. With much readier access to the assembled wisdom of the past, with the facilities to scan it quickly, manipulate it selectively, experiment with permutations of conditions, and extrapolate hypotheses about what *might* have happened in association with the records of what *did* happen, they could build upon the past, and leap over their predecessors.

Certainly the implications of such technological changes as those suggested would be beyond the wildest imaginings of the science-fiction writers. Many of the effects would in fact be what the sociologist calls 'unintended consequences'. That is, effects that were unplanned, or that could be the unanticipated repercussions of something that initially was planned. One cannot say with certainty how our lives would then be altered. But certainly *at the moment* most of us wish to retain our residue of freedom. We do not want to sacrifice it, even if we do become more efficient. Yet it is sadly probable that history might not repeat itself, and the freedoms which grew out of one technological epoch could disappear when a new machine base appears in society. Similarly, the constraints which operate upon the challenges to privacy and freedom, designed for eighteenth-century conditions, may no longer be adequate to protect us.

In the nineteenth century, the new machines which derived from the discovery and application of electrical power opened up new possibilities for invasion of individual privacy. By the end of that century, suitable devices were being mass-produced; and in the twentieth century, in many countries, they have become commonplace. The telephone, for example, brought benefits which we accept as normal for 'civilized' existence; yet this basic application of improved communications has led directly to the further advances in electronics which brought wiretapping, and the menace of sophisticated surveillance methods. These are a reality in some city streets, as the police television cameras scan the pavements – for miscreants today, but for who knows whom, tomorrow?

Of course, it is possible to be paranoid about such inventions. We can overemphasize the prophetic visions of Orwell and others. But examples of the *abuse* of electronic devices for surveillance abound, and have been tested in the courts. Modern totalitarian regimes are based on technology; in earlier eras, the descent of the State into tyranny was always limited by the range of known communications techniques. It was limited, but still bad enough. Eichmann, the master book-keeper, sent thousands (if not hundreds of thousands) to the gas-chamber by way of his filing cabinets. And in earlier pogroms there were thousands who survived – even in Czarist Russia – because the exterminations were less than systematic. It is frightening indeed to imagine what the Nazis *could* have accomplished if they had had electronic storage systems categorizing the whole population, recording its movements and its affiliations and its sympathies; few opponents or 'non-persons' would have survived.

But again, we should not overstress the argument. Technical advance *per se* is not going to bring undesirable effects, however pessimistic we may seem to be. The ominous cloud of surveillance on the horizon is only the strong possibility it provides of dark, unwelcome developments. As several commentators have suggested, the power provided by computers bears comparison with the power in atomic energy; it may well bring a great deal that is good, but it also threatens some of our basic values on a greater scale than ever before.

The possibility that society could be linked up more closely, as an integrated system (or set of systems), has now dawned upon those who think about such matters – and it may be done simply to show that it *can* be done. The cry is heard: 'One Man, One Number'. Let the nation be organized! If there is a law of information-expansion for the bureaucrat, as mentioned earlier, there is also one for his administrative toys. But all this is *not* just play; the State is deadly serious. To give the pluralist system the benefit of what little doubt there is, we might say it intends to govern us more efficiently and perhaps cut the tax-burden, or at least to give us more services and better value for a given amount of tax. But to govern 'more' is, almost inevitably, to increase the extent of domination. Government intervention becomes interference which becomes direction.

With computerized government, we are changing political *space*: the old gaps that once delineated the scope of the separate agencies become built-up areas. This concept of political space, elaborated by the historian of political ideas, Sheldon Wolin, is particularly applicable to an evaluation of the basic and fundamental change which the onset of computerized government will bring.[20] Political time, too, will be modified. The machine operates instantly, or nearly so. While this may bring us our election results faster, it may in extreme times not wait until we have eaten a last breakfast before we are 'liquidated' for this or that political offence. Government by instant referendum may be possible, but this may merely allow the worst whims, of the few or the many, to go against the long-term interest – without a second's interval for sober reflection.

Classical liberalism developed in a political space-time continuum which was bounded by the technological limits of the period. It may well be that the idea of freedom was so endemic in eighteenth-century England that it caused the new economic and technological advances; historians are still battling on that score. But there is no denying that, in certain senses, much technical advance was autonomous, and its effects upon society 'accidental'. A modicum of technological determinism may be permitted in observing how the scope of the free-born Englishman was protected by the very factors which in other ways bound him in industrial chains – we refer here to his concentration in large numbers in factory-units, and urban conglomerations which established the worker as a political force.

The machine, then, shaped the society. It tyrannized, but it also liberated. The train might bring in troops to break a strike; it also brought in the radical newspapers. It brought in cheap goods, food, and information. It might now be argued that the new machines will bring us further liberation, new scope and new outlets in new directions. But this would be to forget that there are discontinuities in technical change, and the idea of persistent progress *ad astra* has only been partially fulfilled – *ad lunam*.

Marshall MacLuhan (of whom we promise to say no more after this observation) glibly glossed over the potential of new machines, like television, for the dictator. Hitler, according to this view, would have come over with too many 'roughnesses, pimples, warts, and everything' like Oliver Cromwell, if he had had TV at his disposal – the argument suggesting that TV is a 'cool' medium, as likely to distract as to convert, opposed to radio which is 'hot'. The prospect of a 'global village', however, is as likely to promote tyranny (or more broadly, oligarchy), as it is to encourage universal Rousseauite hippydom.

The computer, having brought man to the moon, may of course compose its own litany to match the technical achievement. Indeed, will we remain the masters for long? Organizations are notorious for a penchant towards self-maintenance; computer systems may prove to be little different. That is to say, they may 'forget' what they were originally designed for. So, in addition to the obvious fear that they may enable the few to abuse the many – or indeed *vice-versa* – they may in fact enormously encourage electronic bureaucracy as an end it itself. This would leave us with neither democracy, oligarchy, nor polyarchy; in Hannah Arendt's terms this bureaucracy would be the worst tyranny of all, the rule of nobody – as she argued brilliantly in her essay 'On Violence'[21] The computer could become the Master Prefect constantly scanning an infinite number of inputs, the data from personal lives to the *n*th number, setting them against a program laying down the terms of perfection – moral, or ideological, or even just physical. If we transgressed, it would bring down the wrath of the electronic demon, or his agents, upon our heads.

Such a suggestion takes the argument into the realm of science-fiction; but so did the moon-shots. We have already passed *1984* in technological terms; hopefully we have not begun to move there politically. The price of pre-electronic liberty was once eternal vigilance, but computer surveillance may pre-empt all our endeavours.

Notes

1. One of the Commission's working parties is making a special study of the social implications of the computer; no report has yet come from this group.
2. Herman Kahn and Anthony J. Wiener, 'The Next Thirty-Three Years: A Framework for Speculation', *Daedalus*, Summer 1967, pp. 712 ff.
   Also *The Year 2000, A Framework For Speculation*, New York, Collier Macmillan, 1968.
3. See e. g. R. M. Cyert and J. G. March, *A Behavioral Theory of the Firm*, Englewood Cliffs, N. J. Prentice Hall; and Jeremy Bray, *Decision in Government*, London, Gollanz, 1970. See also the following publications:
   H. Sackman, *Computers, System Science, and Evolving Society*, New York, John Wiley and Sons, 1967.

H. Sackman, *The Experimental Challenge of the Information Utility and the Public Interest* – Technical Memorandum TM-L-4293, Systems Development Corporation, Santa Monica, California, 1969.
E. S. Dunn Jnr, *Review of Proposal for a National Data Center*, Statistical Evaluation Report, 6; Office of Statistical Standards, US Bureau of the Budget 1965.
E. S. Dunn Jnr, 'The Idea of a National Data Center and the Issue of Personal Privacy', *The American Statistician*, Vol. 21, 1; February 1967.
C. Kaysen, *et al.*, *Report of the Task Force on the Storage and Access to Government Statistics*, US Bureau of the Budget, 1966.
R. Ruggles, *et al.*, *Report of the Committee on the Preservation and Use of Economic Data*, Social Science Research Council, 1965.
C. Argyris, *Personality and Organization*, New York, Harper Bros, 1957.
R. Likert, *The Human Organization: its Management and Practice*, New York, McGraw-Hill, 1967.
D. C. Pelz and F. M. Andrews, *Scientists in Organizations*, New York, John Wiley and Sons, 1966.
C. L. Schultze, *Governmental and Public Data Needs*, The Brookings Institution, 1969, processed.

4. Karl Deutsch, in 'Working Session, I', *Daedalus*, *op. cit.*, p. 659.
5. Thomas Hobbes, *Leviathan*, Chicago, Gateway Editions, 1956, Preface by Russell Kirk. See Part One, intro., p. 1.
6. H. Baecher, *Computer Weekly*, August 1, 1968.
7. *Ibid.*
8. Reprinted in *The Computer Bulletin*, B.C.S., November 1968.
9. Donn B. Parker, *Computers and Public Concern*, C.D.C. Report TER-09, March 1968.
10. David M. Sullivan, quoted in Parker, *supra.*
11. *The Times*, August 20, 1968.
12. The term 'data bank' is increasingly used to describe *any* (usually still theoretical) aggregation of like data. We use it exclusively as a useful shorthand for 'computer files of personal information, integrated and fully cross-referenced'.
13. Senator Edward V. Long, quoted in *Datamation*, March 1968.
14. See Donn B. Parker, *op. cit.*
15. Sir George Williams University, Montreal, Canada.
16. See *The Times*, December 11, 1968.
17. Anthony Wedgwood Benn, *The Times*, November 17, 1969. To illustrate the *scale* of the operation, consider that the annual farm census (a statutory return) requires every landowner with more than one acre under cultivation to complete a questionnaire of over 170 questions.
18. *Hearings* 'C'.
19. BBC Third Programme, May 26, 1969.
20. See Sheldon S. Wolin, *Politics and Vision*, London, Allen and Unwin, 1961.
21. Hannah Arendt, *On Violence*, London, Allen Lane, The Penguin Press, 1970.

Chapter 2

THE ONRUSH OF TECHNOLOGY AND THE THREAT TO FREEDOM

As we shall show later, the computer has created its own mythology, which has been propagated by science-fiction writers and ill-informed press articles. The myths concern the supposedly 'human' characteristics of 'electronic brains', and have raised their own spectres of the animate being controlled and directed by the inanimate. In fact the dangers which computers pose are not in the least mythical; nor do they derive from any myth-conception. They are real, and urgent, because they reflect the very substantial information-processing power of present-day machinery.

If information is handled as if it were just another automated product, there is grave risk of it being handled carelessly. And if the nation's business and governmental records are handled carelessly, the structure of society, already somewhat decrepit at certain levels, will have lost its firm foundation of organization.

The advance in computer capability over the twenty years or so since the machine's invention in modern form has been rapid, with new techniques and new materials being discovered and adopted. Many even newer techniques, and newer materials, are announced almost daily from the laboratories and the research stations. To predict which of the most recent developments will be adopted for mass production is impossible, and it would be rash even to suggest what the computers of five years hence will look like and how they will be built. Herman Kahn has predicted that 'If, for example, we define the power of a computer as the product of its basic speed and its fast memory capacity, then during the decade of the seventies alone this power should increase, in the largest and most advanced computers, by a factor of 10,000 or so. As a result (and this is one of the most interesting remarks one can make about the computer), many of the seemingly most extravagant technical remarks seem likely to be held to be rather conservative, from the vantage point of 1980 (though as discussed below, such a strong prediction is not likely to be true for the more extremist remarks about its economic impact).'[1]

But it is not necessary to be able to make technical forecasts to see the threat. Computer technology now is quite adequate to cause disruption. As one British legal expert wrote not long ago: '*Modern technology has created means of intrusions upon privacy in a manner so different from conventional invasions that they are best regarded as of a new type*: [our italics]. Let us cite a parallel example. The old necessity for the eavesdropper to approach his subject to within the distance the voice can carry has gone. The modern spy can listen to private conversations from the other side of the street and beyond. In America, this has become so prevalent that important government and commercial business has to be conducted in special chambers erected within the walls of existing rooms – walls within walls. The conception of the modern fiction writer of telephone tapping is too simple. The notorious "two clicks" giving warning of the tap are unnecessary. They relate to a physical interception of the line but electronic interception is now possible. Anonymity in a crowd can be lost by the planting of miniature electronic or radio-active devices on the subject of the surveillance.'[2] This technique is at present used in recording and controlling transport, but obviously there are wider clandestine possibilities.

'Beacons will be fixed to lamp-posts or bus stops, and a scanning device on each bus will record which beacon it is passing. The information will be processed in a computer in a central control room, enabling the controller to watch progress and delays throughout his area.'[3]

Computer technology is as capable as other electronics of assaulting privacy, if personal and private information is handled casually – or is deliberately conveyed to, or by, those who should not have it. The great advantages which a computer offers are its enormous capacity for storage of information and its ability to process it in fractions of a second. Almost any sort of information, whether it consists of numbers, or words, or even coded representations of diagrams, can be converted into electrical pulses and fed into a computer to be stored in a magnetic form. In response to the instructions written in a 'program', themselves coded and fed into the computer, it can be made to extract any specified data from its memory, manipulate it in almost any way that may be required, and display the results either in a printed form or as an image on a small TV-type screen. The results can also, of course, be reconverted from magnetic recording patterns into electrical pulses, and transmitted over any suitable link to activate some remote machinery. A recent technique permits the contents of a computer file to be translated directly into micro-film images by the computer itself, thus providing the cheapest and most convenient form of archival record with no need for intermediate machinery or processes.

In a computer installation full of facts, equipped with links across the country to distant offices, no one knows (literally) at any given moment where information will go next. A lot of people know a little bit, but when the computer is serving the information needs of several users simultaneously, its total activity at any point in time is too fast for human monitoring. Yet when the information is about people, *how* it is manipulated and *where* it reappears in readable form are matters of considerable importance.

The demand continues for bigger and faster systems, to handle more data more quickly. Users want more processing power, and guaranteed reliability, and their pleas are not always balanced by a sense of responsibility for the way they use this power. A brief review will give an idea of the measure of computer 'power'.

Conventionally, this power is measured by the speed at which any two numbers can be added together. Unfortunately, this is no longer adequate by itself. On large systems today the *basic* unit of time measurement is the nanosecond,[4] but the *effective* speeds are faster than the time for any single instruction, since operations are increasingly performed in parallel. One must take account of the degree to which the activities are overlapped – and this is a matter that extends far beyond considerations of instructions and main memory. It must include the fact that input and output units (punched cards, magnetic tapes, discs, drums, etc.) may be operating at the same time as the central processing unit. These 'peripheral' devices may even be transferring information to or from areas of the main memory whilst other areas are being used for other processing. The whole object of this procedure is to get the maximum amount of work done in any given time, and it takes advantage of the vast difference in speed between electro-mechanical equipment and electronics.

The definition of a 'large' computer currently means one with a main memory of 512,000 characters or more – but of course even this is not enough to hold continuously any complete file of information, which may run to millions of characters. Ancillary memory is needed, and for many years reels of magnetic tape have been used to hold data files, but the emphasis now has changed. When tape is used, the recovery of any single record from it is a relatively slow process, and requires human intervention, as a preliminary, to load the correct reel. Users are demanding that much more data be directly available to the system, so that their requests for facts and results can be answered within seconds, without any human intervention. Hence the development of various types of magnetic disc stores, each with the capacity to record several million characters, and to give 'direct access' to any selected record in less than a second.

The expression 'real-time' emerged to describe this instant availability. It is a much-abused verbal concoction, variously applied. In scientific and engineering contexts, it was well defined in the following extract: 'For the first time it became possible to solve complex mathematical problems in time to control or affect on-going phenomena. For example, the calculations needed to direct a missile in flight or a sheet of hot steel rolling through the mill must obviously be completed before the missile reaches its destination or the steel sheet leaves the mill. Manned space flight, therefore, would not have been feasible if it were not for the electronic computer. Many similar technological breakthroughs, although less dramatic, are traceable to this ability to solve problems in "real-time" (i.e. in time to take action in a still-evolving situation).'[5]

When this same ability is transferred from the white heat of action to the white-collar world of administration, we can see that 'solving problems in "real-time"' can mean a Social Security clerk obtaining an instant check, and calculation of amount due, before paying benefit to a client at the counter. It can mean that a traffic policeman is able to radio to his control point, and get a computer-produced check on a car licence number before the suspect vehicle disappears from his sight. Real-time in medicine means that a hospital can feed into a computer all the data about a patient's condition during an operation, and rely on the machine to issue any warnings of danger levels. In commerce it means that a person who presents a credit card for a purchase can have his credit rating checked before he walks out of the shops with the goods. In administration, it means that a manager can get an up-to-the-minute check on how sales are performing against the forecast, or expenditure against budget.

All these things are being done, now. They are examples of a new power which is at work in society.

We have mentioned above that the operations involved in any one computer task may to some extent overlap each other. It is also true that the modern computer may be engaged on several different tasks (or 'programs' of instructions) apparently simultaneously. This is again an exploitation of the significant time differential between even the fastest magnetic units and the electronics. Inevitably, any computer program will reach a point at which it has to 'wait' (in micro-second terms) for the transfer of a record to or from some other unit to be completed. During these valuable fractions of a second the program cannot continue, whilst the electronics wait for the electro-mechanics, but another program can take over. Sophisticated control circuits, and control programs (usually supplied by the manufacturer of the computer), are able to arrange that this shall happen. They are able to make 'decisions' about which programs are to have priority for the time and resources of the computer, and also to control all of the input and output transfers to ensure that there is no conflict between the different programs. This 'multi-programming' ability is already commonplace, and many installations always have three or four programs operating at the same time; a few large computers are able to undertake even more than this.

Speed, capacity and power have all reached the point where any kind of information can be stored, manipulated, and retrieved within seconds.[6] This alone is remarkable enough, and it is complemented by yet another leap forward – in the technology of communications. Information in the wrong place is little more use than no information at all. If all the parts of a computer were still housed in one room, there would be a lot of walking and posting done, and still no sense of *immediate* service to the outside enquirer. Distance is in fact no obstacle now. Communications circuits – telephone lines, radio waves, even laser beams – can be used to carry information in bulk at speeds which can match the computer's own. Cross-country, trans-Atlantic, inter-stellar transmission between computer units is perfectly feasible.

As was said in early 1969, 'Ten years ago it was recognized that it would be possible to connect remote terminals directly to a computer, enabling a number of programmers and users to converse with the machine. Since then, a variety of multi-access computing systems have been developed by universities, research establishments and commercial firms. Indeed, the introduction of such systems at various levels throughout the nation as a whole, and within specific organizations, and their use by people in all walks of life, is likely to be one of the most significant features of computer usage during the seventies. About 70,000 remote terminals are already thought to be in use throughout the United States and it is estimated that this total is likely to rise to between 200,000 and 350,000 terminals by the end of 1972. Furthermore, it is the view of a leading computer manufacturer that by the mid-seventies more than half the value of all data processing equipment being produced will be in terminal equipment.'[7]

The most familiar machine which can be used as a remote terminal for a computer is a simple electric typewriter. With a little extra box of circuitry, and a few wires leading from the back, a typewriter can provide a user who is quite unversed in computing technicalities with the power to enter information directly into the memory of a computer, and to receive results.

Visual display units are becoming equally common. The smallest and simplest of these has a keyboard just like a typewriter, but instead of a printer carriage and type-bars it has a small screen on which several lines of 'typing' can be displayed at once. The principal advantage offered by these units is their speed of response; the reply sent to the user from the computer can be displayed immediately, and probably completely, whereas the typewriter must print it line by line at no more than 15–20 characters a second.

The manager of data transmission services in a British machine company, whilst guilty of the highly tendentious statement that 'The long-term view favours [*sic*] the setting up of a national data bank network', provides in the same article some useful illustrations of the different uses of different computer terminals:

'A ship designer will converse with system A about catalogued methods for shaping metal plates in the aircraft industry, searching for inspiration to solve a flow problem. He will use a video terminal creating no paper and enabling him to flick quickly through pages of computer memory.

'A school teacher will contact system B for statistical trends in GCE A level results in Midland city examination centres over the past five years. He uses a low-cost, slow teleprinter which suits the budget and low-volume use of his school.

'A Tyneside marketing man asks system C for tabulated statistics on consumer spending in the Home Counties. His terminal is a fast serial printer.'[8]

And there is yet another machine that must be mentioned – the so-called 'intelligent' terminal. These are in effect highly complex accounting machines, in which the old electrical and mechanical controls have been replaced by a miniature computer-type store. The device can be applied to a wide range of small-volume office accounting functions, and also be connected at will to a remote computer to take advantage of its filing power, with high-speed transmission of information.

If it is true that 'all power corrupts', it follows that computer power corrupts more rapidly. And each new development adds more to computer power. Harnessed and directed only by men of integrity, honesty, and social responsibility, this power might bring nothing but gain to our national life. It would be put to service in improving the community's health, its safety, its knowledge, its economy. Unfortunately, like all revolutionary discoveries, it also offers the power for a great amount of evil.

As we have said and must continually reiterate in this discussion, all information is *itself* power. When its own inherent power is coupled to computer power, and men have the ability to handle and disseminate information in quantities and at speeds hitherto inconceivable, one may be certain that the lives of private citizens will be affected. The prospect also exists of this double-power being used to dominate and to control. The capability exists and therefore a decision is needed to refrain from using it.

The Computer Revolution has arrived so quickly that the dangers implicit in the misuse of electronic power have come upon us almost too fast to heed. It has taken less than twenty years for the computer to be transformed from a mathematical tool into a massive information-crunching weapon. The development of main computer memory has been counted in *generations*, and although no one is quite sure whether we have now reached the fourth or are still improving upon the third, the earlier lines of demarcation are clear.

First generation computers were built around valves and conventional electrical circuits. In more than one early machine the only memory for working data was a small-capacity magnetic drum, from which only one or two items could be extracted at a time, and into which all results had to be returned. In another, nickel delay lines were the main memory; a train of electrical pulses was 'bounced' into one end and became available again at the other after a known microsecond time interval. With computers such as these, the rated speed of operation was never reached in practice, since everything was dependent upon the programmer's skill in writing instructions that dealt with data at the precise instant when it was available to the logic circuits. This meant that the program instructions did not always follow a natural sequence, but became much more complex so that the delays of drum or pulse rotation could be obviated. One installation, using such a computer, wrote a payroll program which ran initially at 2 seconds per employee; later it was re-programmed for optimum timing and this figure was halved.

A first generation machine could perform about 500 instructions a second.

The second generation came with the simultaneous introduction of transistors (much smaller, more reliable, and not so hot as valves) into the circuitry, and of core storage for the memory. Small magnetic beads, strung on wires, could have their state of magnetism either reversed or examined through these wires, and being built up into honeycomb-like structures could be used to 'hold' coded characters of information and have all of it available for instructions to manipulate. On average some 8,000–16,000 characters could be kept in the memory in this way, and the general speeding-up made it possible for the computer to execute about 5,000 instructions a second.

There were again two features that introduced the third generation of computers. The first of these was micro-miniaturization – the newely-discovered ability to produce a circuit, complete with electronic 'gates' allowing pulses to be stopped, allowed through, or combined and compared, all on a single tiny piece of non-conductive material. The other, which has already been mentioned, was the new inventions put into control circuitry, allowing the peripheral devices of the computer to operate in parallel with the main memory; later it became possible for the memory itself to be effectively divisible between discrete but simultaneous tasks.

A few other figures may be worth mentioning. In 1959, the (first generation) National-Elliott 405 computer read paper tape at 180 characters a second, and magnetic tape at 3,500 characters a second. In 1969, an IBM System/360 read paper tape at 500 characters a second and magnetic tape at a minimum of 20,000 c.p.s. – though the customer could pay more and get 320,000 c.p.s. A popular machine of the fifties, the IBM 650, read punched cards at about 200 per minute and, through a tabulator alongside, printed some 150 lines a minute. Now, with any computer, at least 1,000 cards and 1,000 lines a minute are normal.

In a special Computer Supplement in August 1968, *The Financial Times* reflected that some of the computers used by NASA in its space programme 'are just about 1,000 times as fast as the largest of the so-called first-generation of computers which were first manufactured in 1954'. The same improvement factor of 'about 1,000' can also be applied to main memory capacity; the massive memory of direct access units was not even envisaged in the early 1950s.

We shall have more to say about the power of the machine, and the power of information. Yet all this power is of course only *latent* power. It is released by the skilled craftsmen who direct the operations of the information machine.

In a sense then, the *real* power lies with the computer programmers; the men and women who work hard and long preparing and thoroughly testing the instructions which the machine will eventually store in its memory and carry out, on request, at high speed.

In a perceptive paper David Butler showed how the managerial function in our conventional organization is increasingly being usurped by the computer man. Consider, he says, the 'firms (which) employ research chemists whose skills are a closed book to their management. If the manager can control a chemist, why not a computer expert?' Because, in his postulation, when the chemist leaves his specialist environment, he is bound to interact with his management – directorate, sales force, and so on – on *their* terms, to make himself understood. But the computer expert does not need to explain himself in the same way; when *he* comes outside his own department it is persistently, and rightly, to challenge everyone's assumptions. He is bound to ask, ' "Tell me how you do *your* job. What do you need to know to do it better? Are you sure that the reports you get are clearly related to the parts of your job that really matter? Do you in fact *know* what parts of your job really matter?" These questions . . . go with chilling directness to the heart of the business.'[9]

Power, increasingly, is passing into the hands of these challengers of all assumptions. Who are they? They are clever people, we know; they are young, almost all of them; their major attachment is to their profession, and advancement therein, rather than to any one employer. Having set the fuse for an explosive disruption of established methods in one firm, they may well leave to do the same elsewhere, so that others grasp the smouldering wick and produce a computer system which may be far from perfect in itself, and may be neither what the organization wants nor what it needs. In many, many cases, conventional management has been slow to comprehend the need for its complete involvement in computerization of the office tasks, and the degree of control necessary over a developing project.

Programmers, a new breed of working people, have been too busy to worry about the implications of their work. Like any other piece of machinery, a computer performs nothing other than the functions which it is instructed to carry out. The instructions, however, are mostly contained within the wires and electronics (the control 'logic' circuitry) which has been designed to initiate the necessary impulses for each function to be performed correctly. The sequence of instructions may take months – certainly weeks – to prepare for any job, and will need many trial runs before it can be regarded as reliable. Only at that point can the programmer forget about that program (with the hope that none of the production runs using it will reveal further errors or inadequacies) and turn to another program. Immersed in his own logical exercise, battling to discover which single instruction out of three thousand or more has produced wrong results, working long hours to meet a time deadline, he has little reserves left for moral considerations.

And yet many of the decisions have been left to him, simply because of his hereditary position as an esoteric expert. That firm and fundamental *rationale* that must underline the manipulation of any set of items has been well illustrated by a planning expert:[10]

'Imagine a large pile of all coins, initially in a jumble, placed in the middle of a table, such as might result from emptying several collection boxes. Invite someone to carry out the following task: "Please sort out that money for me." Note that this does not give the "Why" behind the task. One possibility is referred to later.

'In most cases, the pennies will be counted out into shillings and grouped into five shilling sets, the silver coins will be separated into the different denominations and grouped together in 20 shilling piles and then into sets of £5.

'Clearly, familiarity with the routine for banking money will be predominant in the mind of the person doing the job. This method of carrying out the task may bear little resemblance to the type of sorting which was needed to satisfy the purpose behind the task. For example, this might have been to place the coins into date order in their different face values so that the loss of weight resulting from their use could be estimated.'

There is an exact analogy between this example and the process of giving a loosely defined mandate to a computer team. A team will produce results meeting their preconceived notions of what the data is to be used for.

Professor Gill, in the address referred to in Chapter 1,[11] argued the case thus:

'The computer has so far been a comparatively harmless invention, even a beneficial one. Its essential function is the concentrated application of crystallized logic, surely a welcome antidote to the gusts of emotion that have hitherto ruled our collective lives. But it does not ask from what witch's brew did its logic crystallize, and whether the emotion might not still be there, second-hand and soulless, to be propagated from context to context through generations of software. Perhaps this could not happen, because a computer program is an explicit thing, amenable to examination and analysis, to be judged not merely by what it does but by what it is. But explicit to whom? and judged by whom? Only programmers can comprehend it, and even they find its analysis difficult.

'Imagine that you are in charge of the complete suite of software for all the computer operations supporting a manned flight to the moon. Let us not spend time arguing about how all the trivial bugs can be cleared, but when this has been done, how are you to be sure that what remains is pure logic, untinged by subjective and therefore controversial thoughts about how the mission should be conducted?

'Perhaps this is a meaningless question; perhaps we should ask: how can you be sure that the programs faithfully reflect the subjective views of the management? To be more specific: how do you check that, whatever circumstances may arise, the system will behave as the commander would wish? Is this in fact the right criterion? What should you do if you suspect the judgment or the integrity of the authorities? On your answers will depend the lives of men, the prestige of a nation, and the climax of a colossal enterprise. And this is not science fiction; someone is wrestling with this task right now.'[12]

Top management, as data processing men still complain, often is not appreciative of the revolution in methods and power which results from the decision to instal a computer. All too often the purchase is recommended by an accountant, solely to deal with financial work, or by a bright O. & M. man who sees a niche for himself as DP Manager, and provided the installation is 'paying its way' it is left to the middle level of management to run. The men at the top rarely take enough interest to see how the policies of the computer section are determined, nor to see how their own policies can be assisted by computerized information.

In sum, those who could have recognized the threat of the new power had little chance to stand back and view things objectively; those who might have anticipated the impact of the computer were bemused by the apparent maze of technicalities, and opted out. When computer information was made acceptable as evidence in civil cases in the High Court, a spokesman of ICL, the biggest British computer manufacturer, was quoted as follows: 'All information that has been stored can be produced. Increasingly firms are not keeping information in any other way. The possibilities are immense. The people involved in this field do not know themselves what new doors they are opening.'[13]

The Civil Evidence Act of 1968 is already in operation, and allows computer print-out to be used for the first time in civil litigation.[14] This is clearly an important step as a great deal of information is now stored inside information systems, and could not be produced other than as print-out.

Stringent conditions are laid down concerning the admissibility of evidence. Under the Act and the Rules of Court, computer evidence will be admissible (Section 5) provided:

'(*a*) that the computer was used regularly to store or process information for the purposes of any activities regularly carried on by it;

'(*b*) that over that period there was regularly supplied to the computer in the ordinary course of those activities information of the kind contained in the statement or of the kind from which the information so contained is derived;

'(*c*) that throughout the material part of that period the computer was operating properly or, if not, that any respect in which it was not . . . was not such as to affect the production of the document or the accuracy of its contents; and

'(*d*) that the information contained in the statement reproduces or is derived from information supplied to the computer in the ordinary course of those activities.'

The Act declares [Section 5(3)] any combination of computers (or any combination of combinations of computers) to be one computer so that the print-out shall be admissible, and 'computer' is defined to include [Section 5(6)] 'any device for storing and processing information'.

This new development leads to any number of complications, as a legal expert has perceptively pointed out:

'If the information is subjected to a great deal of analysis or processing, questions as to the validity of the analysis will be raised and possibly not answered. It appears therefore that the draughtsmen of the Act did not fully appreciate some of the more complex or advanced applications of computer technology.

'The other main point that may arise under the Rules is that computer people may be called to give evidence as to the proper functioning of their machines and related activities. The notice required to render computer evidence inadmissible must give the names of persons responsible for managing the activities, supplying the information and maintaining the computer. It is quite possible that each of these three could be called in the same case.

'When one considers, for example, how many activities a service bureau firm will be engaged in, it becomes clear that the managers of such firms will be under a considerable likelihood of being called as a witness simply to state that the machine is operating correctly.'[15]

This is just one example of how technology is raising entirely new problems. In fact, these dilemmas are being raised faster than we can ever perceptively react to them. We may be left still looking at yesterday's problem while technology has overtaken us. The information revolution is causing a crisis not merely of anticipation, but also of ability to apprehend the challenge. It is a crisis of intellectual powerlessness, no less serious than the social and political powerlessness many feel in the face of the advance of the technological society. As has been pointed out recently:

'Realistically, the "knowledge explosion" means a few know a great deal about how nature and society "work", while the rest of us are about as ignorant as we have always been. Further, as knowledge has become increasingly refined it becomes more inaccessible to the many, more esoteric, more removed from the world of common experience.'[16] The speed with which the new technology has advanced has been many times faster than the reaction of the public, and even the top decision-makers, to it. We have landed a man on the moon, but his imagination is still earth-bound.

Paradoxically, however, we still overestimate the degree to which technology can perform, in the sense that if some new feat is described as being *technically feasible*, we are left with the impression that it is already operational, or at least could be very soon. We do not wish to fall into the conceptual trap here of arguing that if a new advance is technically possible, it is already a threat.

We deal in this study with the threat that *could* come from the new advances, and the threat which already exists as a result of current technological applications. This is not a work of 'social science-fiction', like H. G. Wells' *Anticipations*, or its successors. A great deal of the phenomena we examine and discuss are at work and enmeshed in the institutional framework of our organizational society.

The historical trend seems to be clearly moving in the direction of the technological society. As Herman Kahn notes: 'It is, of course, now very fashionable to argue that we are entering the computer age. This is clearly correct, at least as compared to the sixties, in terms of an enormous increase in the number, range, and importance of computer applications, in terms of its physical pervasiveness and visibility. It should be noted that already in the United States, 10 per cent of all business expenditures on new plant and equipment is spent on the computer and its input-output or other subsidiary systems. Thus the computer has already become the source, centre and shaper of a significant proportion of business activity.

'This is also beginning – but just beginning – to be true for many other areas of our American society as well – education, scientific research, medical diagnosis, engineering, architectural, and industrial design, information retrieval, and so on. And this is only the beginning.'[17]

These patterns are appearing *now* in most advanced societies. The 'future' is hard upon us; the era of 'big systems' is overtaking that of simple organization. The individual member of society seems puny against these forces, but his right to a personal freedom must be asserted within this structure if the exercise of the resulting power is not to become malevolent.

Notes

1. Herman Kahn, 'Life in 1980. Impact of the Friendly Computer', *The Times*, October 9, 1969.
2. J. Jacob, 'Data Banks, The Computer, Privacy and the Law', *N.C.C.L. News Release.*
3. *The Sunday Times*, November 2, 1969.
4. I.e. 1,000,000,000th of a second. To put this into proportion, 1 nanosecond is to 1 second as 1 second is to 33 years.
5. Boris Yavitz and Thomas M. Stanback, *Electronic Data Processing in New York City*, Columbia University, 1967.
6. On the speed of technical advance and the factors behind it – see W. H. Gruber and D. G. Marquis *Factors in the Transfer of Technology*, M.I.T. Press, 1969, p. 274.
7. *Data Processing*, Jan.–Feb. 1969.
8. *The Times*, November 17, 1969.
9. D. Butler, *Computer Bulletin* (B.C.S.) October 1969, pp. 344 ff.
10. R. A. Ward, 'Planning and the Computer', *Local Government Chronicle*, October 11, 1969.
11. See page 18.
12. Gill, *op. cit.*, *Computer Bulletin*, November 1968.
13. *Sunday Telegraph*, September 28, 1969.
14. See J. Jacob, 'Print-outs may be Used in Evidence . . .', *Computer Weekly*, September 25, 1969, p. 6.
15. J. Jacob, *op. cit.*
16. John H. Schaar and Sheldon S. Wolin, 'Education and the Technological Society', *New York Review of Books*, Vol. XIII, 6, October 9, 1969, p. 4.
17. Herman Kahn, *op. cit.*, *The Times*, October 9, 1969.

Chapter 3

COMPUTERS AND THE STORAGE OF INFORMATION

Before looking in detail at the types of personal information which computers are now storing, and the control over information dispersal, we must consider briefly – if only to dismiss – those many analogies which have made between computers and human brains. We shall also seek to show how, over and above the remarkable increase in power demonstrated in the previous chapter, computing techniques have changed from primarily mathematical and literally 'computational' tools into vastly more efficient replacements for total filing systems over a very wide range of applications.

'Heart' and 'brain' are emotive words. To most people, they represent those anatomical parts of man which, though identifiable physical organs, are felt mysteriously to contain the elements of 'personality'. To transplant a heart is somehow feared to be far more than a merely physical operation. To use surgery on the brain implies the possibility of changing a person's character. Thus, when a machine long since popularized as an 'electronic brain' begins to be spoken of as the 'heart' of a personal, national, information system, it is not at all surprising that rationality is clouded by strong emotions. Mark Twain's dictum is specially appropriate in this context: 'It isn't what they don't know that hurts people, it's what they do know that isn't so.'

People *know* that computers can think. Take this together with the parallel developments in so-called 'robotics' (both factual and fictional) and people *know* that electronic inventions are going to end up as a blend of the worst of Frankenstein, King Kong, and Rossum's Universal Robots – the inanimate usurping man's authority and control. Functions of thought are regarded as the unique province of the human brain, and the prospect of an 'intelligent' machine is frightening.

Man has always personified the machines on which he relies – usually as of the female gender, perhaps to reflect an inbuilt unpredictability! Thus the sailor of his ship, the motorist of his car. Thus too the computer devotee of his familiar machine. In the words of Donn Parker, 'Personification of inanimate objects and the concomitant depersonification of people is a failing of our society. It is so simple and safe to blame inanimate objects for our and other's failings. At the same time, we avoid confrontations with people; thus depersonifying them. In times past we would blame Mr So-and-So at the bank for bank statement errors; then we shifted the blame to the bank; now we just blame the computer at the bank. Mr So-and-So is delighted with this state of affairs, because even though he is responsible for the computer, he now can also blame the computer; and he often gets away with it. The actual culprit may be the system designer, the computer programmer, the computer operator, or the maintenance engineer.'[1]

Things might be a little different, perhaps, if those early experiments in electronics had not been christened 'brains', but 'ganglions' – if someone had realized that they would be a centre of nervous activity both stimulated by, and reacting upon, human brains. But the very 'human' characteristics of 'remembering', 'calculating' and 'decision-making' which were prominent in the earliest machines made the analogy with the human mind inevitable. And some of the early scientists, using computers that we already rate with Victorian antiques (though this was less than 20 years ago), were able to forecast some of the areas in which this machine would outclass the mind of man.

Among the best-known of all the papers written about the concept a 'thinking-machine' is that which first appeared in *Mind*, in October 1950, by the distinguished mathematician A. M. Turing. Confining his attention to a restricted use of the meaning of the word 'thought', Turing was able to foresee that programs would be written to make computers play complex (but logical) games, like chess, by a process of scanning all the possible logical choices of move to establish the 'best' in the circumstances. He also envisaged that a computer would be able to 'learn' – that is to say, programs would be written that were self-adaptive, modifying their own instruction sequence by examination of the relative success or failure of the move in the game when a similar situation had occurred earlier.

Ever since, researchers have experimented with computers to see how 'clever' they could make their programs in simulating activities of the human brain – in playing games, in logic, pattern recognition, problem solving, behaviour models, learning.[2] Amongst those prorams developed to play games, one of the better known is the brainchild of Arthur Samuels, of Stanford University. He chose checkers (draughts) rather than chess, so that instead of having to concentrate on many different rules of the game he could give most attention to building 'learning' techniques into his program. Over the years, with assistance from the author, this program has in fact steadily improved itself, so that it is now good enough to beat all players except the champions. It does not, at every move, scan the full range of 10^{40} possible board positions and situations, but has instead stored away the relative 'values' of tens of thousands of different moves, whilst playing games against itself and against published book plays for hours on end. In each new game it uses this accumulation of acquired experience to determine the value of the possible moves.

If one were playing against this computer program, it would be easy to get the feeling that the machine was 'out-thinking' you – that it was more intelligent. This is not so. The computer is still nothing more than a tool, performing entirely by rote the reasoning already performed by Samuels. It is superior to a man only in the sense that it can 'remember' several years-worth of logical thought processes from the past, and scan these in such a short time as to apply them to the present. Its micro-second speed can be deployed to perform a thorough study of each move, and still respond within reasonable time. The human opponent has only minutes, and only limited memory to draw on, for his own moves. If the human player had unlimited time, and volumes of reference books, he could then compete on an equal basis with the programmed machine.

So this game-playing computer is not *thinking*. It is using its reliable memory, and its vast speed, to rethink (or re-enact) the thought processes of humans. Because the programmer was very clever, the computer appears to be very clever. In any game of this kind, whether it be chess or draughts or even simple noughts and crosses, the computer is merely replaying the method of solution to a problem which has already been devised by a programmer. It does so in a greatly compressed time frame, with greatly increased precision and reliability over any human player. It is making decisions, of a kind, but they are strictly logical decisions whose pattern has been formulated by the programmer – who has also predetermined the course of action to be followed as the result of each decision.

Analogies between the human brain and the computer must not then be pressed too far. Some students of brain mechanisms have found restricted comparisons useful in their own field,[3] but they have to recognize that no machine can match man's versatility. The computer is simply more efficient than man in handling its relatively limited memory, and is never clouded by emotion.

Man will never create a machine to match all the complexities of his own mind, even though he may create wonderful tools to assist his mental processes. But however dispassionate we may all be, we know that the personification of machines will continue, and anthropomorphic metaphor will survive in the world of computers. So we may as well let it have its way, and use it to trace the history of the computer from the early inventions to today's vision of the 'heart of an information system'. Computers can of course have superficial memory disorders too![4]

At its birth, the new brain-child was considered likely to become, when it had grown up, a reasonably useful calculating machine to assist mathematicians and scientists. There was one authoritative prophet who pronounced that just two – or perhaps even three – of these laboratory progeny would be likely to satisfy the needs of the whole of the United Kingdom! But within a few years, there will be nearly ten thousand fairly large machines.[5]

During the computer's early infancy, men came to appreciate that this thriving youngster could be weaned from the pure milk of science and fed with stronger stuff. It would make light work of any calculations, especially those that were purely repetitive, and would be a willing slave for almost any kind of manipulation of figures. Hence the computer began to be used in the financial departments of the larger business organizations, and in America, Federal Government began to take its potential seriously. (Approximately 75 per cent of the world's computers operate in the US.)[6]

In its adolescence, the computer was as wayward as any teenager. Introduced into a catholic variety of *milieux*, learning new tasks of data manipulation, it wandered very far from the conceptions of its progenitor. The guardians and adoptive parents of the machines, and the planners of the new generations of computers, realized that these talented children could be instructed in any logically definable task, and would work away at it for hours without tea-breaks. So the computer got into a lot of new places, covering a wide spectrum of social mores and interests.

Now, perhaps, is the age of irresponsible immaturity. The computer has not yet come of age, but is being tried out in very many forms of employment – and not all the careers chosen for it are entirely suited to its undoubted talents. The salesmen supply quite impeccable character references, but the purchaser does not always get the labour force he really needs, nor does the tool adequately match the task. Many are the tears shed by those, once persuaded that a computer would solve all their problems, who now find that their problems are in fact multiplied by commitment of unsuitable systems to an unsuitable computer.

Most significantly to our theme, the computer's 'brain' has improved vastly since babyhood. The machine's phenomenal memory for facts has multiplied in capacity and been made to operate much faster. And besides this, it has grown arms – ten, a hundred, even a thousand sensitive tentacles can stretch out round the world and out into the universe, sending and receiving coded data far faster than thought. What a marvel is this brain-child of man!

The computer has grown up fast. Paradoxically, it has grown smaller at the same time. Discoveries and advances in electronic and recording techniques have enabled the designers to pack more and more power into smaller and smaller boxes, so that whereas the early machines filled a large room with cabinets the size of double wardrobes, many of the latest computers fit under an ordinary desk-top. (We are considering here only the electronic main memory; not the various devices attached to it such as magnetic tapes and discs, and printers, which are largely mechanical and therefore less subject to miniaturization techniques.) The space programme has not been unimportant in hastening this process of miniaturization, and no doubt the race to the planets will impel the progress further.

In illustration of this point, Murray Laver, who has been involved with the technicalities of computers in the UK since the early fifties, gave the following impression of how small 'memory' may become. 'Nature appears to have left us plenty of scope for the development of storage hardware, despite the information explosion. One hard-to-check estimate has claimed that 10^{15} facts now exist, and that they are doubling every 12 years or so. Consider, as a limit, that these might be stored in binary form by the presence or absence of a single atom in a crystal lattice; then, 10^{15} binary facts could be packed into a cube having a side of 10^5 atoms, that is, a cube of about 1/1000th of an inch side. Thus, even if for protection against accidental damage we were to record each fact a million times, the whole could still be packed into a cube with a side of 1/10th of an inch, which seems compact enough.'[7]

Our concern is with those computers which will be used in offices to replace conventional filing systems. As the heart – or, to retain the anatomical allusion but remove the emotional connotations, the *omphalos* – of an information system, the computer must be able to fulfil all the best features of the best document-filing system. It must also, to pay its way; perform them faster, and require less staff to maintain it. Only within the last three years has this become a genuinely practicable proposition, with the developments in the world of computers. Thus it is that while the fears of 'the machine taking over' have been latent for some while, they become intensely real with the potential that is now revealed for organizations to keep track of all of us, and everything that happens to us.

The developments that have made a national personal record system possible can be briefly traced by outlining, first, the features of the 'conventional' office computer – the machine that we have (extraordinarily rapidly) got accustomed to – which limited its scope as a replacement for efficient document-filing; then by noting the changes in technique which made clerical data the raw material of technology.

As things were (and, to be realistic about the developments, still are in many computer installations), information has been held in a way most unsuited to the rapid retrieval of any required item. Characteristically, each separate 'file' – i.e. a collection of similar or related records – was held on a separate magnetic tape reel. These tapes were not kept loaded on the machine but were stored away from it. Thust to gain access to any particular record demanded first that the righ, tape should be located and loaded on the computer, and then wound until the right section of the file was reached. The recovery of any one single record was always slow, and the total time depended on the relative position of the required data on the tape.

A required record could not, of course, be located by hand. The computer itself had to 'find' what was wanted. Thus, to get any information from his files, an enquirer had to establish a system for doing so. A specialized program – or more likely a large number of programs – needed to be written both for keeping the file up-to-date and for extracting any data from it. To use the most common of business computer applications as an example: a magnetic tape file may be used to record pay details of all employees; programs will be needed to apply changes to this file, to calculate earnings, prepare payslips and payrolls, perhaps produce cheques or bank credit slips, accounting analyses, pension fund analyses, National Insurance information, annual tax returns, and so on. The task of running these programs, as well as any program written to deal with an unexpected request for a printed copy of one employee's details, must be fitted into the overall schedule of the work of the computer installation.

A further constraint upon this 'conventional' computer was that the size both of individual records, and of the files, had a limitation of 'reasonability'. Since all files had to be dealt with entirely serially – i.e. by transferring *every* record through the processing unit of the computer and copying it out onto tape again, whether it was actually changing or not, the time consumed in handling this irrelevant information was an important criterion in system design. The limits of record and file size had to be considered and set, virtually irrevocably, before any programs were written. It was beyond the bounds of reason to contemplate the retention in computer files of large historical records of events and transactions, to be passed regularly through the machine unnecessarily. Only what was absolutely relevant to current needs could be kept in such files.

For similar reasons, it would not be reasonable to file a large quantity of purely textual information, because of the recording space it would consume and the time it would take to handle serially. Therefore, everything had to be rigourously examined by the system designer to see whether its retention within a file could be justified, and whether the data that was essential should be reduced to a coded form – even though this latter course would demand extra programming effort to convert and reconvert the items. The cost for each unit of information was high enough to make such studies essential.

These are, as pointed out, the conditions of planning and of operation that most people in the computer business know at present. But already imminent are changes that remove these restrictions on filing and retrieving information. As the speed of the computer's own internal circuitry is phenomenal, so is the pace of technological development. No wonder that computing is preponderantly a young person's profession; like Alice, computer men must run as hard as they can merely to stay in the same place. Flexibility of mind and constant adaptability to new things are essential. With the removal of the restrictions just listed, new practices, new standards and new techniques must be learned.

No longer need data be confined to files on tape. Computer storage devices now exist which make it entirely practicable to record thousands of millions of characters of information, like the Book of Life, and to have the whole of this always available to the processing unit for instant retrieval, or updating, of any item. No more serial processing; no need, now, to pass through every record in a file so that just one or two may be changed or printed. The system designer, and the programmer, can so arrange things that only the records actually required, for the enquirer or for manipulation, are extracted and used. This flexibility ushers in the new era of mass information processing. Certainly, at present, this type of storage costs a little more for each unit of data than a magnetic tape file – but to balance this extra capital cost there are the daily savings in processing time, allowing more work to be done by the computer. It can be predicted with confidence that the 'direct access' storage device will become both more capacious and cheaper.

The restriction of finding computer time in which to perform an enquiry process has disappeared. The processing units are now designed to permit the computer to be used for several different jobs simultaneously, as mentioned in the preceding chapter.

With the assistance of complex control programs, written for the most part by the computer manufacturers or specialist software organizations, the user can arrange that a random-enqulry program is always present in the computer, just waiting, for much of the time, for someone to feed in a request. Meanwhile, the remainder of the machine proceeds with other tasks. With such a permanent program the normal situation will be for electric typewriters, or TV-type screens with keyboard attachments, to be connected to the computer – so the new computer user may never see the computer itself. To him it will simply appear as a unit on a desk in his office, which he uses to call upon the power of the computer whenever he needs it. He can initiate a job himself, from his remote location, without bothering the computer operators at all. He can get results when and where he wants them.

This kind of equipment is exactly what our society needs in order to keep reasonable control over the rising tide of information. As Professor Arthur Miller observed: 'A glance at the almost geometric expansion of library accessions, publishers' lists, and research projects in recent years confirms the generally held belief that our society is experiencing an information, as well as a population, explosion. . . . In government, academe, and industry, everyone bemoans the information or input overload. Fortunately, a technological revolution, centred around the computer, is in progress and it promises to expedite the accumulating, indexing, analysing, manipulating, storing, retrieving, and transmitting of information. When computer systems are interconnected by some of the modern communications vehicles (television, satellites, and lasers), we will have the capacity to move large quantities of information over vast distances in units of time that are so imperceptible they are difficult to comprehend.'[8] And we shall have more to say about this later.

The computer-to-computer transmissions of data in the course of the American Apollo programme of lunar exploration have demonstrated how entirely possible it now is to move information over distances seemingly without limit, at speeds which are indeed incomprehensible. Yet it is neither distance, nor speed, that forms the primary justification for welcoming the computer to deal with the 'information explosion'. It is its capacity, and ability to manipulate.

Computers remain, of course, naïve creatures in so far as they may only be programmed to deal with simplified categories. Igor Stravinsky has wittily told of how his religious affiliation (Russian

Orthodox) was classified as UNKNOWN at an American hospital, because they only had four categories – this one, Protestant, Catholic and Jewish. It is a cautionary tale indeed. Whereof one cannot classify, thereof one must be silent.

Another commentator has noted that 'In our increasingly complex world, information is becoming the basic building block of society. However, at a time when the acquisition of new scientific information alone is approaching a rate of 250 million pages annually, the tide of knowledge is overwhelming the human capability for dealing with it. So man must turn to a machine if he hopes to contain the tide and channel it to beneficial ends. The electronic computer, handling millions of facts with the swiftness of light, has given contemporary meaning to Aristotle's vision of the liberating possibilities of machines: "When looms weave by themselves, man's slavery will end." By transforming the way in which he gathers, stores, retrieves, and uses information, this versatile instrument is helping man to overcome his mental and physical limitations.'[9]

Two new jargon phrases have crept into the vocabulary of the art. One is the 'automatic office'; an idea that just as automation has vastly changed the environment of the factory production line, the computer can change the entire strategy of paperwork. All original documents would be converted to computer form as quickly as possible, and the machine would then deliver whatever was necessary, – reports, payrolls, invoices, statistics – whenever it was wanted. This idea, however, before anyone attempted to make it come true, has been superseded in favour of the new much-discussed concept of 'management information systems'.

The emphasis here is not upon the routine office work which the computer is presumed to have undertaken already, but upon the usefulness of the wide range of information now readily available from the computer. If the records of all stores items, and sales, customers, suppliers, employees, the whole miscellany of information about people and places and things which is necessary for business, is managed by the computer, then it is simpler than ever before to provide the decision-makers with the facts on which to base their decisions. The business manager, the government administrator, needs to be fed with reports on such things as: What are we doing? How are we doing? What are the current effects of our policies? What is it costing us? What would be the expected effect of such-and-such a change? What should we be doing next week, next year? A natural and continuous demand for better managerial information is the spur to the implementation of computer techniques, which will generate more and better and faster reports – which in turn demand more sophisticated techniques to handle and discriminate upon the information contained in them.

The authors of a study on *Electronic Data Processing in New York City*,[10] offer this as a new principle for survival in the competitive jungle of commerce: 'The combination of internal and external pressures, in a very real sense, confronted the business firms with the constant threat of drowning in a sea of paperwork. Survival was directly dependent on continuous advances in the technology of processing large-volume data, and each new development was eagerly seized upon by the business community. Particular stress was laid on equipment and techniques which could be exploited as a means of mechanizing and speeding up clerical work. . . . Hand-in-hand with mechanization of clerical work, it became evident that computer processing could also yield qualitatively better information which, in form and content, is better suited for management planning and decision-making.'

It seems then that our increasingly complex, increasingly planned, researched, investigated, statistical, economically inter-active society demands the filing and manipulative capabilities of computer information systems. If the most modern methods are not used, the sheer weight – as well as the cost – of storing, processing, and retrieving information will overburden those services which our high standard of living increasingly demands. Details of our health, our education, our employment, our taxes, our income and financial commitments, our pension contribution and entitlement, our various licence holdings and society memberships, our brushes with the law, must be handled by computer. So must the businessman's returns to government of his profits, turnover, exports, labour force, investment grants, etc. – and the farmer's acreage, usage of land, livestock, workers, machinery, trees, subsidies, production and disposal of milk, eggs and broilers.

To summarize the present position: organizations are forced, by the constant search for economies and efficiency, to make use of the best available tools. Until the Industrial Revolution, the only available clerical tools were human minds and hands; until the Computer Revolution, there were such relatively minor (though very useful) extensions to human capability as typewriters and adding machines. Nothing gave any relief from the weight and acreage of paper. Now, as computers have developed, they can take away that burden. With virtually no limit either on the amount of information they can hold, or on the distance over which they can collect and despatch it, thousands of pieces of paper can be abandoned.

The following situation is perfectly feasible today. A travelling representative could return home in late afternoon with his order book. He would telephone a special number, to be connected directly to a central computer, then use a small keyboard to convey details of the orders to the computer. The computer would check from a stock file that the items were available and from a customer file that the order was acceptable. It would then reduce stock balances, transmit the order details to a terminal device at the appropriate depot, calculate the value of the order and transmit this information to the computers both at the firm's own bank and at the customer's for automatic adjustment of the accounts, and also file away the necessary data for calculation of the representative's bonus. Overnight, of course, it would work on all orders received so as to give to each depot the optimum route for its vehicles to fulfil the next day's deliveries. By-product ('managerial') information on turnover, re-ordering, budget, salesman performance, depot effectiveness, vehicle usage, etc., would all be created within the system for use when required.

Such are the possibilities. But this is a cautionary book, and it would be wrong to end this chapter in a glow of euphoria. The computer information network will remove much drudgery, but will introduce new constraints. The American columnist Art Buchwald wrote a piece called 'The Curse',[11] imagining the downfall of a person who dared to fold, bend, *and* mutilate a bill that came to him on a punched card. He found his phone was cut off, then his electricity and gas; he received no salary and his cheques were returned from the bank; all because 'There is a master computer that informs all other computers of anyone who folds or bends or mutilates a card. Our computer is aware of what you did to another computer and it refuses to handle your account.'

Automation of any kind can be planned and implemented in a way that makes no allowance for human foibles, but imposes a conformity upon all. 'Let us be done with cruel efficiency lest we forgo humanity.' It is in the light of its dual potential that we will examine the contribution towards and demands upon society made by the computer's information-handling capabilities.

Notes

1. Parker, *op. cit.*
2. For early work in this field, see E. Feigenbaum and J. Feldman, *Computers and Thought*, New York, McGraw-Hill, 1963.

3. A tabular statement is provided by J. A. Burton, *The Computer Bulletin*, December, 1967. See also G. Somerhoff, 'The Abstract Characteristics of Living Systems', in *Systems Thinking*, ed. F. E. Emery, Penguin Books, London, 1969, pp. 147–202.
4. C.f. George A. Talland, *Disorders of Memory and Learning*, London, Penguin Books, 1968, p. 17.
5. In 1970 there were over 5,000 computers in use in the UK (one per 10,000 of pop. approx.) compared with 60,000 in the US which was three times this number per head (approx.).
6. For future projections see Kahn and Wiener, *op. cit.*
7. F. J. M. Laver, *Datamation*, October 1969, p. 115.
8. *Hearings*, C. p. 72.
9. *Hearings*, A.
10. Boris Yavitz and Thomas M. Stanback, Jr, *op. cit.*
11. Reprinted in *Son of the Great Society*, London, Weidenfeld and Nicolson, 1965.

Chapter 4

THE COMPUTER AND ITS CONTEMPORARY IMPACT ON ADMINISTRATION

There is little doubt that the computer is already a boon to mankind – muffling, though not entirely deadening as some have suggested, the reverberations of the 'information explosion'. We consider now a specific portion of the expanding information business: the collection of facts and figures about people. Some of the real benefits to be achieved from these files, as much by the populace at large as by their actual users, can be seen by a look into the near future, as attempts are made to improve the quality of life for man *as* man.[1]

In the *medical* field, for example: Computer files will contain the latest known data on every identifiable ailment – its symptoms, diagnosis, and treatment – so that the doctor may use a communicating device (a 'terminal') in his consulting room to obtain access to the complete library of medical knowledge. Medical, and computer, techniques have already advanced to the point where a computer is used to *suggest* possible diagnoses from a submitted list of a patient's symptoms. When computers are also used to maintain a complete medical history of everybody from the hour of his birth (and much work is being done in preparation for this, as we shall later see), then a centralized file can be constantly updated through interconnected regional computers, to provide immediate access to records for doctors and hospital staff. This can provide an even better diagnostic service, as symptoms are related not only to the general pattern of illness, but also to the specific health record of the patient. A nationwide record system of this kind could mean that no sick person, wherever he moved, need be out of touch with his records; whenever he needed treatment, the medical staff could access his history, find out his allergies, blood group, immunizations, everything they might need to know.

Profound changes will be seen in *education*. 'Teaching machines' are already helping pupils to learn more readily, and relieve the pressures on over-burdened teachers. Although criticism has been heard that this kind of learning is only 'training', far short of 'education' in its fullest sense, we can expect to see many more teaching machines, working directly from computers. Programmed and operated by teachers trained in the techniques, they will not only assist in problem-solving and provide quick access to vast libraries of up-to-date information of all kinds, but they will also increase the tendency to change the processes of learning. Each student could have his own terminal and proceed at his own pace. As part of each 'lesson', records of the pupil's learning performance could be created within the computer files. At each session, the computer could give him the opportunity to review any areas where he appeared to have difficulty. At any time, teachers – perhaps 'tutors' will become more general usage – could monitor the performance of any pupil. The entire educational experience of each student, from nursery school through university or beyond, automatically assessed as he progressed, could be centrally recorded.

Crime will begin not to pay? Computers will be used by all police forces to maintain their information files of known criminals, suspects, wanted persons, stolen goods and vehicles. Even dogs have their records against theft at the National Pet Registration Centre in Gillette, New Jersey, USA: 'The centre tattoos dogs painlessly and registers their identification numbers on a Univac 9200–II computer, along with the name and address of the dog's owner. The computer, which is owned by the Capitol Data Processing Corporation, can furnish instant ownership data when required. Since the service's inception in 1968, some 10,000 dogs have been registered, and the number is increasing.'[2] Fingerprint files will be held similarly. *Modus operandi* files – police jargon for the recognizable 'style' of recidivists – will be scanned in a way closely resembling the doctors' symptom files, to diagnose likely culprits. The principles are not new; the techniques are, and they will contribute enormously to the efficiency of the police by sifting information in seconds instead of man-hours. Better detection is certain, and so is better crime prevention, as for the first time it becomes possible to analyse thoroughly *all* known offences and offenders. The patterns of behaviour revealed by such analysis will make possible a more skilful deployment of police resources. Anyone in whom the police are, have been, or may be, interested will be remembered in the computer files.

Besides these limitations upon the opportunities for criminal ingenuity, the straightforward acts of banditry for cash in transit should disappear. Large sums of money will simply not be transported. There will be no payrolls to snatch. All our *financial transfers* could be made through a central computer clearing system, to which all banks, governments, businesses, and ultimately private subscribers, might be connected. Wages could be paid, accounts settled, loans and investments handled, without a single 50p-piece changing hands. It is somewhat ironic that the expensive change in our currency to a decimal system may not anticipate by long the time when we hardly need cash in our pockets at all. Our income and expenditure may be handled by updating our personal record in a computer file. In Manhattan already, they say, only the poor carry cash.

If these examples sound too futuristic, based on the network of electronic communication,[3] too Wellsian (if not Orwellian) to be true, consider what is *already* being done in each of the same four areas.

We cite these four because they are among the most private aspects of an individual's life, where he expects – and perhaps is entitled to – confidentiality. He may not get what he expects. There are of course many other areas of impact of the computer: the military situation, for example. But this latter has little *direct* relevance to our theme, which is focused on the individual citizen. Computerized or not, the international tactics of a State are not under the control of the citizen, and *he* does not take the war/no war decision. Using a computer for these affairs does not reflect immediately upon the individual's privacy and freedom.

Three of our examples are only noted briefly here; health records, local government, and credit agencies will be looked at in greater depth in Chapter 9.

Although projects which involve the computer directly in medical systems are being approached with an odd mixture of caution and enthusiasm, it is possible to discern the valid areas of experiment. Many of the people who are involved suffer contradictory feelings because, whilst they have recognized that automated systems have a great deal to offer in improving the care of the sick, they are well aware that all patient data is highly sensitive material, that absolute accuracy is paramount, and that sick people need the mental (or, perhaps one should say, psychological) reassurance that can only be supplied by *caring* fellow-humans. A machine cannot dispense sympathy and encouragement.

It must be noted that the use of computer-based information systems in hospitals, while already extensive, does not mean that computers are running hospitals. This equipment is often installed solely for administrative puposes and may therefore be used only for ordering laundry and simple house-keeping duties remote from the actual treatment of patients.

Nevertheless one of its most important uses is as a tool for doctors and surgeons. Already at the Presbyterian Hospital of the Pacific Medical Centre in San Francisco, IBM is working with leading heart surgeons to use a computer for intensive care. The computer checks the key indicators of the patients' condition on a constant basis and shows them on a visual display at the bedside.

'This sounds as though it could be done without a computer but it cannot. For example, the rate of oxygen intake must be calculated from the patient's breathing rate, carbon dioxide percentage in exhalation and length of breath. Doctors could not make this kind of calculation on the wards, so they have not previously been able to use this type of indication. Other vital factors concerned with the physical state of the lungs and the heart are similarly difficult to obtain without a computer.

'So the Presbyterian Hospital doctors have a new tool which has given them important new insights into what happens to a patient recovering from an operation. Because of the computer's ability to record all the readings as they are made on paper charts, the doctors also have a valuable diagnostic check. In one case, already, this has enabled them to solve the riddle of a patient who very nearly died suddenly and inexplicably with no apparent cause.'[4]

Experimental work has been done in providing a computer service to GP.s. Still in its preliminary phase, this made use of the familiar NHS standard record envelope in the surgery, but after a consultation the details were transferred to paper tape which could be taken to a computer once a week to update the files. 'The main part of this exercise involves the handling of data in the surgery using a machine which is not only easy to operate but which – almost as a by-product – converts the data into a computer acceptable form, i.e. the punched paper tape. We have seen how this is feasible without a marked increase in the work-load of either the doctor or his staff.'[5]

The trial proved to the experimenter's satisfaction that on-line connection with a distant computer was entirely viable, and 'not only would the doctor be communicating with the computer in "real-time" (with editing facilities using the visual display unit and a light pen or keyboard) but that similar terminals in district general hospitals would permit direct exchange of information'.[6]

The authors of the quoted article comment on the problems inherent in converting existing surgery records to a computer format, and the same point has been made by Michael Abrams of Guy's Hospital where work has also been done in this field. He commented that it would be 'almost impossible to take over any GP's records because of their diverse nature'.[7] But it has been done, in part. There are now several local authorities who have successfully translated surgery and clinic records of children's immunizations into computer files, and now use the computer to schedule appointments for the full course of preventative treatment available, thus keeping an up-to-date history of this area of a child's health.[8]

As experimental work develops into full projects, we must anticipate increased centralization of medical records out of the custody of family doctors and hospitals and local authorities. If only to ensure that no patient feels in the least inhibited whilst discussing his ailments with the doctor, these records must be given maximum security. The confidential nature of the doctor-patient relationship is vital. Another computer-minded medical man has expressed the fears of himself and his colleagues very simply: 'The existence of a permanent comprehensive file of linked records might be held to be undesirable for two rather different reasons. The first is that casual access to personal dossiers may be simplified and that this may be contrary to the individual's interests. The second raises a more difficult problem in that such permanent centralized files of dossiers greatly facilitate organized access by government or other central agencies and this also may be deemed undesirable . . . records should not only be preserved from such access but should also clearly be seen to be so preserved.'[9]

With which sentiments we heartily concur.

The possibilities for using computers in the various levels of the educational process are extensive, to say the least.[10] But this is a difficult area of application, because of the serious shortage of programmers who are also knowledgeable in the basic theories of education. The day need not be too far distant, however, when the pupil may be educationally 'untouched by human hands', and almost entirely tutored by teaching-machines.

There is a great deal to be said, from the teachers' point of view at least, for the removal of drudgery from the class-room. For example, if a machine can teach a child to read efficiently, why not use it? At a higher level, there is a lot of basic teaching that bores the university professor, such as elementary statistics. It was recently reported that:

'The University of Texas now teaches entering students the basic mathematics which they need for course qualification by computer. Here the impetus seems to have been the lack of desire among academic staff to take on the chore of teaching elementary and uninteresting classes.

'In Chicago, there is an ambitious project to link several schools into a computer with one or more terminals in each school. Students would be able to use programs which teach arithmetic, say, or perhaps more simply addition and subtraction.'[11]

More tutoring of this kind will most probably be needed when the target 80 per cent of the US school-leaving population go on to higher education.

Although we can be sure Tolstoy would have disapproved, it is by no means certain that teaching by computer is necessarily and self-evidently to be condemned. For one thing, children often take to the new methods with enthusiasm, though whether this is the result of 'novelty' or the 'Hawthorne effect' (that is, being given extra attention by a change in the environment) is difficult to say. None the less, 'The great advantage of the computer over traditional teaching methods is that every child can work at his own pace. In addition, the computer has a diagnostic method which can analyse the child's difficulty in, say, multiplication, to one of perhaps 17 different factors. When it discovers what particularly gives the child trouble, the machine can concentrate on that aspect, and backtrack the child through simpler stages until it learns'.[12]

Even if one is critical of traditional education, there is no reason to believe that computer-based learning is any worse. The intuitive responses of the young are worth using as a yard-stick. They are not yet antagonistic. As the recent report sums up: 'In education, the potential value of computing is enormous. Children seem to be psychologically attracted to the idea of using light pens and television screens, so that even one who hates arithmetic will play for hours and learn at the same time. Evidently mathematics will be the first major area of application. But chemistry and physics are also possible. A computer program can, for instance, simulate a laboratory experiment, showing what happens when chemicals are mixed or when gases are compressed by projecting the picture on to a screen. Even language training is regarded as a possible application of CAI (Computer Assisted Instruction) in the USA, particularly when recorded voices and phonetic recognition capabilities are added to the basic terminal. At present, computer programs for languages are rather mechanistic, merely teaching how to change a French sentence into the plural; yet the prospect of more useful programs is there.

'Real progress in computer-assisted instruction will undoubtedly have to wait upon the technology of cheap terminals and cheap computing time. But in the US this is regarded as being around the corner, that day is being actively prepared for.'[13]

Nevertheless, there are dangers. Given the existence of state systems of education, or public surveillance of private education, every step of the child's development might be easily recorded, collated and evaluated by 'authority'. Not only would we have the power to 'program' the young in a way many times subtler than the Jesuits (and say 'give us a learning-machine for its first decade, and we have its soul for life'), but we would also be able to monitor all stages of pupil's progress, and correlate this with everything else known about him and stored in the various, and co-ordinated, information systems of the State. While the undergraduate can see the threat of technologicalized instruction to *education*, it can be argued that the spread of many new learning-systems is the corruption of innocents. William Blake, who had little time for the class-room as a method of education anyway, would have had an appropriate poetic comment; we can only prosaically preach caution.

The National Union of Students, a body not associated in the public mind with rational and unemotional activities, have, nevertheless, thoughfully considered the possibility of computerized educational dossiers, and objected to the principle. They have asked for the right to examine the records kept by colleges and universities, for as their president said: 'We have no firm evidence that there is any misuse of these files, but there have been suspicions in some cases that information held by a university has been passed on. There have been instances in court cases where the police appear to have had knowledge of non-criminal minor misdemeanours committed in the past by students.'[15] It is salutary to ponder the wide range of personal background information which authority might attempt to justify as essential to an integrated educational record system. Certainly, the disclosure of practices of this kind at Warwick University[16] lent fuel to the fire of student indignation throughout the U.K.

Herman Kahn fails to see the dehumanization involved when he observes that: 'It is interesting to note that in many schools in the United States, children have developed an intense respect and affection for their computer teacher. This is not surprising. The voice of computer has been chosen for its warmth, friendliness, clarity and pleasantness. Thus, the computer is always friendly. It never loses patience; it never gets angry; it is never sarcastic, indifferent, inattentive, or cross. It is always fair; never plays favourites. It greets each student with a friendly "Good morning Johnny" (it always uses the student's name), and ends with an equally friendly "see you again on Monday, Johnny".'[14]

The next logical step, after such electronic teachers, seems the development of computer mothers, for whom of course the innocents could be conditioned to develop 'an intense respect and affection'.

As we have commented earlier, the increasing personification of machines tends to have an unintended and correlative effect of de-personifying people. It could be that the computer-instructed generation will breed increased strain in personal relationships, not only between the pupils themselves but between child and parent.

Let us now turn to computers and crime prevention. One of the advanced police computer systems at present used in the United States is that of the St Louis police department. It is basically employed for the better allocation of manpower resources according to the patterns of crime in the city. A start was made to cover four of the nineteen police districts. Information is fed into the computer about the crimes committed in the areas, and the machine provides a map of crime density so that patrols may be assigned on the most rational basis possible.

'A detailed series of maps and reports is produced by the computer. These include contour maps of crime intensity, comparisons of predicted and actual calls, and "queueing tables" showing the effectiveness in answering calls provided by specific numbers of patrol units.

'The new technique has made it possible for 7–10 patrol cars to handle the same area previously covered by 15 cars. And the time taken to plan the allocation of manpower has been cut from months to hours.'[17]

Another important aspect of the experiment is real-time information retrieval. The computer has much information on store about crimes committed, cars stolen, etc. Instant information can be received by the police stations and radio points by retrieval terminals. A police car can check the number of the car it is tailing, by radio, to see if it has been reported as stolen. Information can also be got on the basis of Field Interview Reports which give descriptions of suspects, and links with certain areas of the city, crimes committed, etc. (Many other cities in the United States have their own police data banks, and these may be linked with each other across the nation, and to the federal National Crime Information Centre in Washington, D.C.)

The St Louis system allows predictions to be made as the patterns projected by the computer follow a consistent shape. Not only information on crime is stored, but items like holes in the highway, cats on roofs, fires, etc., are also sent in, and thus help the planning of many other local government operations parallel to police activities. Traffic-flow prediction, and projection of the demand for hospital services could be a pay-off of such systems.[18]

A systems approach to urban policy using computers is now foreseen as the response of the complex industrial society to its problems.[19] 'In police work as in business, better information networks may make decentralization possible by providing a mode of co-ordination more effective than a monolithic power structure.'[20] This may make the creation of a national police-force – which many associate with tyranny – superfluous, and reduce the cost of what is a rapidly escalating law-enforcement bill. The answer that the systems approach provides is more brains, rather than more muscle. The systems approach using computers allows the traditional values of pragmatism to be combined with planning, and this can cover anything from the number of police cars needed in 1977, to the number of refuse-collection employees required, as well as more spectacular matters like the number of space satellite stations. But the point is that such systems are beyond the drawing board stage, and are actually at work in several American cities, whilst plans for similar support services are well advanced in Britain also.[21]

Our next illustration is from the world of computerized credit. Traders and finance houses naturally want to check the credit rating of applicants for goods, or loans. Big credit agencies have developed in the USA, using computer files to hold a million or more names and credit ratings. It is typical of such files that they include all the applications made by an individual for credit, whether it was granted or not, and the history of the repayments.

Unfortunately, in their endeavours to catch the 'bad risk' applicants, the agencies have found it desirable to go very much further with the data on file. Their 'inspectors' will 'secure details of anything which might have a bearing on a person's current or future financial standing. This leaves them considerable scope and, as a result, files may contain allegations of homosexuality, extra-marital affairs, drinking habits and court records'.[22]

Inevitably, mistakes occur; inevitably, people are refused credit because of erroneous reports on their file; inevitably, 'black lists' appear in places where they should not. Yet again, one must not blame the machine. It is the only way that anyone risking money – be it a bank, a finance house, a local authority housing office, an insurance company – can get a check on the viability of the applicant. When our society increasingly lives on borrowed cash, the computer is the only way to handle the information bulk. But its power can be, and has been, abused by those responsible for setting up the systems.

A common factor may have been observed in the four examples considered. In all of them, agencies of Government are involved in some way. The systems postulated, and illustrated, are the groundwork for a nationally-integrated personal dossier system. And Government, as pointed out earlier, not only takes an increasing interest in the welfare and good conduct of its citizens, but also is most prone to the 'law' of increasing its demands for information commensurate with its capacity to deal with it.

'In our record-keeping civilization, the man whose name is not inscribed on the tab of someone's manilla folder simply does not exist.'[23] To provide a perspective for the problem, try making out a list of all the events, or the transactions, in a person's life which become part of some official file; the list can be very extensive and makes an interesting game.

We start with the duly recorded certificate of birth, and immediately give rise to hospital and other medical records of our ailments, treatments, and immunizations. We represent an extra allowance against our parents' income tax, and are watched to see where the family might settle when we reach the age to need a place in a school. And when we get there, we generate record after record concerning our attendance (and meals consumed on the premises!), I.Q. tests, and our prowess – from 'could do better' to 'couldn't be worse'; much of this we might hope would be forgotten in later life.

As soon as we are old enough, we get ourselves jobs for weekends and the holidays, opening up a new record trail that will be followed for years, of social security, tax and employment. We save up for our first old car, which we have to insure, and be licensed to drive. We become registered electors; most of us will apply for marriage licences; some will later collect divorce decrees – which create voluminous documentation. From house to house, and from job to job, we move; and some aromatic trace of this is left in the archives of the nation.

With luck, we may avoid a criminal record – though even such a minor offence as a parking fine may serve to place us, irrevocably, on the police files. We shall be very lucky to avoid adding to our medical records. Even as we travel, for business and pleasure, we probably need a passport and visas; each airline reservation creates a short record and, as a hang-over from older times of police surveillance, every hotel makes a ritual of preserving for posterity the alleged names and addresses of its guests. In many cases the means come to be taken as ends by the bureaucracy,[24] and instrumental values become terminal ones.

What is the purpose of all this information-keeping? Why is so much recorded? It is not just to keep people busy and happy. There is always the implicit assumption that the records created will sometime, somehow, be useful to somebody (unless means have become ends in themselves). In order that they may be of use, there must be a system of filing adequate to service the interrogator wishing to retrieve the information he seeks. So the game of collecting bits and pieces of personal information has taken a serious turn, involving Organization and Methods experts and filing equipment manufacturers, together with armies of clerks, so that records can be decently interred and readily resurrected, although quite often the organization may over-concern itself with problems which have primarily an internal relevance.[25]

No doubt there are a great number of extremely efficient document systems, which will readily reveal their secrets to the initiated. But the many systems are independent, rather than inter-dependent. They are neither inter-connected nor cross-fertilizing. Each *system* is only useful individually – yet as has been shown, *interests* in information cross organizational boundaries and valuable facts often remain concealed from those who might seek them and profit by them. Thus, here as well as in America:

'An Inland Revenue Department investigator might wish to have access to the tax returns of the associates of a man who is being audited, to check for consistency of financial relationships.

'A doctor may wish to trace the entire medical history of a patient to provide better input to a diagnostic computer.

'The Veterans' Administration [i.e. ex-Servicemens' pensions] may wish to examine a man's complete military record, and possible other previous medical records, to see whether the ailment claimed as being service-connected really is.

'A lawyer for the defence of a man will wish to search for jail records, arrest records, and possibly credit records of *all* witnesses for the plaintiff.

'Professional licensing bodies may want to delve into any records to determine if an applicant has an unblemished character.

'The military [or, we might add, civilian security authorities] in filling extremely sensitive positions may even wish a record of all books borrowed by a prospective applicant, to ensure that his interests are wholesome and he possesses the proper political bias desired.'[26]

It ought to be possible, now, to draw up an impressively detailed personal profile, from files that are ostensibly available for public inspection. The really determined investigator might indeed go further, and exercise his talents for unearthing recondite information from places that would normally be thought secure and confidential. Another view holds that such an assimilation in respect of an individual is already perfectly feasible, although costly, and suggests that 'the easy exchange of information is common even now, before the various investigative agencies have gone very far in adapting to recent advances in the technology of data processing. What the computer now makes possible is a substantial reduction of the time and the marginal cost required for the investigation of any one subject.'[27]

This is a gross simplification of the current situation, although we have found that *some* information is exchanged (see Ch. 8). It is precisely *because* files are well dispersed, and *not* easy to dig into, that individual dossiers are not readily assembled. It is truer to say that it requires a great deal of diligence to get any facts about anyone out of anybody. The official records, whether they are in governmental or private hands, are largely inaccessible to the inquisitive outsider – even if he is known and trusted by the organization.[28] Most information does not even pass readily across the boundaries of the government's own agencies, nor across the functional divisions within a big business. Why else do we hear so much about administration's 'communications problems'? Even where records are supposed to be publicly available, the data will take time and effort to retrieve; where they are not, any inquisitor will (more or less politely) be shown the door.

In sheer practical terms today, if one really wants information from the records that should be around, the only way of getting it is to hire a specialist agency to spend its time, and your money, to do the digging. The costs of spadework in the information field are, in fact, higher than in archaeology – and the finds much rarer.

This situation we may regard as the 'pleasant past'. But what happens when the information that we supply – willingly enough, as we seek a job, a mortgage, insurance; reluctantly as required by statute; or quite unknowingly when our employer fills up some official 'return' – begins to disappear into the gaping jaws of the computer? When these powerful machines begin to take over the chores of filing information in the right slots, and retrieving it on demand to satisfy an enquirer, the investigator can dig with the electronic equivalent of the mechanical shovel, and guarantee a valuable load with every grab.

There are other implications, too. As a first step in automated filing, the data must be converted into a form which the machine can read – i.e. into punched cards or some similar 'input' medium – with some identifier to indicate where it is to be filed. So, while the chances of mis-filing are probably about equal to those in a clerical system, an extra hazard is introduced by the prospect of human errors occurring during the transcription stage from one medium to another. The 'facts' which get into the file stand a greater chance of being wrong from the start.

Second, the data has to be processed by a computer program. This may have been tested and run time and again, to the point of programmer-exhaustion, yet undetected errors may still lurk in it which can cause the data to be inadvertently corrupted. Again, then, the 'facts' may be wrongly filed.

Unfortunately, while the chance of factual error is increased, the reliance placed upon the data will increase as well. The executive who works without making use of the computer system will be inherently suspect for his judgements – where *did* he get his ideas from? Professor Alan F. Westin, of Columbia University, makes this point in his comprehensive study of freedom and technology: 'As our society relies more and more on central files, what is in these becomes the most significant "facts" about an individual in his relations with society. This has a great effect on decision-makers as well. The decision-maker comes to regard making judgements on such recorded facts as the most rational and fair way to make decisions, and will be threatened in his own role within the bureaucracy if he by-passes the record and relies on personal-hunch factors.'[29]

Another commentator makes a similar point. 'If history is recorded on tapes . . . the definition of "what was" will become ever more dependent on how the machine has been programmed and what it is able to retrieve from its memories. As respect for and dependence on the computer increases, it is likely that respect for and dependence on fragile and "ambiguous" paper records will decrease, lessening the ability of the individual to establish a past history different from that jointly provided by the programmer of raw data and the interpreter of processed data. There will be fewer opportunities to derive a public consensus on what the data "is".'[30]

Next, a computerized file has a certain indelible, and thus potentially sinister, quality. Apart from the slight risk of machine malfunction – a risk which is becoming negligible – the magnetic record will be neither lost nor destroyed by accident. The facts in the files are fixed for the future. No longer will the facts in the forms we fill in be subject to incineration or disintegration. They will not disappear into archival vaults with the elapse of time, to moulder and decay. Unless the computer is *specifically programmed* to erase unwanted history, the ghosts from our past may at any time be re-substantiated to confront us. There will be no forgetting nor forgiving, unless the 'computerniks' decide – or are compelled – to build automated obsolescence into the system.

Access to a file-cabinet is achieved by walking to it. Access to computer files is achieved by sending a request to the machine, over a wire or radio link, from a terminal enquiry station – a typewriter or a visual display device. With the proliferation of time-shared computers, multi-file storage devices, and multi-terminal connections, with perhaps dozens of entirely disparate bodies using the power of the same computer, a further danger arises. We must envisage the possibility of one participant in such a scheme, accidentally or deliberately, extracting (or even altering!) information belonging to other participants.

This is an obvious risk, and a danger to our privacy. The citizen's understanding when he supplies information – and this may not necessarily be explicit – is that such information is intended for a particular purpose and will not be exhibited beyond that immediate intent without his consent. The possibility of it escaping to any other party is not something which he should have to envisage. Any such unauthorized use is *misuse*; it is a breach of the privacy we are entitled to expect, and an infringement of such remaining freedom as we have to reveal what we choose to whom we choose.

As one observer points out, 'Private organizations have not been far behind the State. Many employers ask the most personal of questions (although in Britain without using personality tests or polygraphs on any significant scale) before and during employment. They undoubtedly use hidden TV cameras and two-way mirrors to prevent crime by, and to improve efficiency among their employees. Numerous private detectives use the full range of electronic and optical surveillance devices (although such are condemned by the British Association of Private Detectives). Some credit agencies acquire, probably by foul means as much as fair, extensive information as to the financial status of hundreds of thousands of individuals.

'Whilst all this is happening a feeling of the impotence of the individual against the large organization is probably spreading throughout the nation. The totality of the effect of these trends can only be to change radically the traditional concept of the Englishman's liberty.'[31]

There may be a quite general tendency to increase the 'official' sharing of files across the kind of boundaries mentioned above. For the mutual benefit of organizations, without the knowledge (let alone the authority) of the original informant, files may be opened up to widespread inter-functional scrutiny. The pressures of efficiency and that megaton weapon 'the public interest', will break down the barriers when it becomes so easy, technically, to do so. After all, why should the recipient of earnings-related sickness benefit have to tell the Social Security his total earnings in the previous year, when the Inland Revenue already know all about it? There is public money, and private time, to be saved by collaboration. But what else might get spread abroad as these two Government Departments come to share their files? It is an unwelcome prospect that within the admirable contexts of good administration, economy, efficiency, and willing co-operation, appears the spectre of the misuse of information for purposes quite unrelated to the object of its original collection.

A further and similar misuse of data, by its getting into the wrong hands, can be forecast. There are more people handling it now; not just the clerks on the job, with a certain inbuilt 'respect' for their raw material – facts; now the programmers, the punching machine operators, the computer operators, and the engineers who maintain the system will have access to the files. They, as much as users of remote terminals, may be tempted to 'browse' through the files to see if anything interesting turns up.

The next technical stage of growth, beyond the relatively simple connection of remote terminals to a single computer, is (as said earlier) the connection of one remote-access computer with other similar computers. Alongside this will come the new programming methods which will pass enquiries through to the machine that actually holds the desired file, arranging for the answer to be transmitted back to the source of the enquiry (as in the US Police example we noted). Through a nation-wide complex of this kind, any data in any file becomes accessible to any enquirer, *unless the programs are designed to impose restrictions on its release.* An unrestricted system would, all too clearly, lay bare our secrets to the world, and bring us to a situation that would amount to constant surveillance.

Once having committed private data to electronic devices, one must be prepared to recognize the existence of electronic snoopers. Blackmail is a profitable exercise; information is a valuable commodity to the underworld. Wiretapping is illegal – but not uncommon – and the transmissions of data are no more difficult to intercept that conversations. The laser beam, which has already demonstrated remarkable versatility in its applications to the ways of the world, is capable of carrying signals far and fast as well as for focusing to an incredibly small speck. Directed at the window of a room, from any 'straight line' distance away, it can be used to sense the minute vibrations of the glass pane and thus carry the conversation going on inside the room to an eavesdropper. As we improve the techniques of handling information, it is reasonable to assume that the techniques of illegitimate snooping will also improve. One can envisage a small package, secreted in the false ceiling of a computer room, monitoring every bit of data that passes through the electronic circuits.

The criminal is digging for 'dirty' information (known euphemistically in American politics as 'negative research') to use for nefarious purposes. Today, it costs a lot to get anything useful out of other people's filing systems, clean or dirty. The costs of excavation are high, as we noted, and the rewards few. But pile up all the dirt under one corner of an electronic carpet and the 'cost-per-unit-of dirt' falls dramatically. 'Negative research' will pay off handsomely.

Not only should we fear individual misuse, and criminal misuse, but also sociological misuse of the new file structures. One can see a new vista opening up for the construction of inferential relationships. The researcher, the economist, the planner, the social scientist, the statistician, those who revolve in high Ministerial circles, can play for hours, matching the records of any person, organization, or event, with any other person, organization, or event, to see if any trends turn up.[32] Who knows what profound (and almost irrefutable) conclusions they may reach about the moulding and directing of society and its citizens?

It has been argued that the tendency towards computerization encourages the 'de-personification' of individuals. To encourage this unwelcome tendency, the integration of the dispersed files of a nation demands a consistent method of identification. Computer filing systems work much better if every record carries a code number; names and addresses are highly unreliable factors where the matching of different records must take place entirely logically. The computer is *too* logical for this problem. Human intelligence will make the very reasonable assumption that a 'Mr A. Blogins of 2a Carlisle Gardens' in one file, is almost certainly the same person who appears elsewhere as 'Mr A. J. Bloggins of 2 Carlyle Gdns.' The computer much prefers to know him consistently as EJGZ2163. This is an emotive possibility: reducing us all to 'mere numbers'. It is redolent of the conditions of war, when the necessity of greater *control* of individual movement and action is accepted as an unfortunate necessity. We in Britain may use credit cards, but identity papers are still taboo.

For inanimate objects, standardization of description is rapidly on the increase, because *the computer needs it*.[33] All new books published now bear a standardized number; a Danish system for identifying all building components by unique number is gaining acceptance here; the National Computing Centre reported, in November 1968, on research into standardized coding of all 'Commodities'.

It can always be argued that to allot numbers to people is in fact *not* destructive of individuality in any way, and the apologists for such a position point to the proliferation of numbers we already carry – Social Security, National Health, Tax Reference, payroll, Armed Services, and so on. To agree on one single number for all systems is no more than rationalization. They can also instance the European nations, where a common identity numbering method was introduced wherever Napoleon went, and has remained an operative system ever since. They can tell us that the recent introduction of person-numbering in Scandinavian countries was accomplished with very little objection from moralists, humanists, or psychologists – even though in all three countries (Norway, Denmark, Sweden) the method of allocating numbers makes it possible to derive the person's age directly from the number.

To us it appears inevitable that national numbering will come. What is therefore important is to ensure that, although we each have a unique number, and may be asked to quote it from time to time, it will be used merely as a convenient associative tag to our personal particulars, not as our *primary identification.* It need not, and must not, become so important that we feel reduced in dignity to mere parts, instead of persons. Computer systems designers *can* arrange things this way – provided they, or their managers, have the social conscience to recognize the unpleasantness of the number becoming dominant. It has been suggested that the student resentment in the USA is in part fostered by the computer-grading of examination papers, and all the associated documents showing the student's identification number twice as prominently as his name. In this, the seeds of so-called alienation might lie.

To preserve the continuity of the strain, all pedigree animals – horses, dogs, cats – have to be registered. The 'Somerset House' of equine genealogy is maintained as a 'Stud Book' by Messrs Weatherby & Sons in the UK and by the National Jockey Club in the USA. Both use computers. Every thoroughbred horse can be traced back to about 1730. Changes of ownership, all breeding mares, all newly-born foals, are entered into the system – using a standard numbering scheme, which has not involved any kind of 'de-equinisation'; indeed, one of the tasks of the system is to ensure that horses' names are not duplicated. The US Jockey Club, in Lexington (Kentucky) runs a data bank of all horses foaled in the USA and Canada since 1927. The file is kept up-to-date with all performance statistics and new foaling to keep trace of pedigrees.

The Club is on record as saying that it 'hopes to be able to assist in the *selective breeding* [our italics] of race horses to produce winners instead of also-rans'.[34]

Another system is run by a computer at Amarillo, Texas. Every day, information from racetracks is used to update individual horse records, and the revised data transmitted back to print in next day's race cards. The service is run by the American Quarter Horse Association, for the benefit of punters and owners. Besides performance data (number of races, position, winnings, track conditions, wind direction and velocity, jockey weight, etc.), full bloodstock data is held with performance records of sire, dam, and maternal grandsire.[35]

A privately sponsored scheme in this country is also interesting, because of the analogy with integrated personal files. With an international market for racehorses, bloodstock and performance records are of increasing importance, but the present UK organizations attempting to provide this kind of information-service do so with a very small experienced staff who carry out the necessary research on a manual and visual basis. But it is hoped to be able to produce, from a computer, the pedigree and performance details of any registered thoroughbred horse, including a complete analysis of the racing record back through three or four generations in the female line, and the breeding record of between 50 and 150 fillies.

Ancestry, and performance records, available on demand. And with horses, no one would question the ethics. But what can be done for the friends of man can be done for man himself – ancestry, and performance in the human race, up-to-date and available on demand. What possibilities this raises! 'One of the many interesting matters . . . is to see whether any female bloodlines have definitely proved more successful when mated to certain types of stallions. If any such "nicks" are discovered, the "type" of stallion must be defined. Apart from the qualifications of soundness, conformation, temperament, speed, and race record, every horse has other qualifications such as his female line, his sire line, and his maternal sire line.'[36]

Society must always ask whether what *can* be done *should* be done. The scrutiny of race-horse dossiers in order to develop planned breeding, and the 'perfect' animal, may itself be a questionable process. To apply the same techniques to humanity would be catastrophic tyranny. 'This human instinct to preserve the mystery and privacy of procreation has had profound *political* consequences. There is no example in human history of even the most depraved tyrant seeking to impose a pattern of procreation by social dictate. Every other human act has been subjected to political control – except the act of procreation.'[37]

Yet human dossiers there seem certain to be. As a prescient critic foresees: 'When technological efficiency is coupled with the government's ever-increasing demands for special information, the prospect is one of a formidable dossier on every member of society. Information may initially be collected for relatively innocuous purposes such as income tax, social security, special aid programmes, and special support for education. One can also anticipate increased interest in testing competence, aptitude, and personality. At some happy future moment, all this information could be combined with the F.B.I. files so as to produce a devastatingly detailed and accurate profile of each member of the society. The disturbing result could be that everyone will live burdened by an unerasable record of his past and his limitations. In a way, the threat is that because of its record-keeping ability the society will have lost its *benign capacity to forget*.'[38]

Ironically, the very inefficiency of government and commerce, their inability to collaborate and share information effectively, has been a safeguard of our liberty. That vast army of clerks who record our movements, our vicissitudes, our wants and our woes, is an army of independent platoons, communicating, if at all, by unreliable field telephones. Even within organizations, communication is sub-optimal.[39] The computer puts into its hands the power of modern weapons, and the position is radically changed.

In the past, the power of the bureaucracy was in effect limited by the enormous problem of processing enough information about a given subject, and then acting upon it in relation to certain policy goals. In the near future, this inefficiency will be markedly diminished. If one central source has all the data concerning our life-history, and is bent on regulating our behaviour to conform with the prescribed goals of the society, how can this be opposed? Only by the society demanding that sufficient thought be taken, before the threat becomes a *fait accompli*.

As we have defined earlier, the generic term used for a mass-file computer is a 'data bank'. A *national* data bank puts our whole life history, easily and cheaply, into a vault that can be thrown open by a few taps on a terminal keyboard. In the plans for establishing personal data banks, small or large, the crucial question is whether, by not taking sufficient thought for the future, the implementers are allowing technology to get out of hand and simply ignoring the hazards to human values. If one thing is certain, it is this: because of the complexity of the programming needed to set up these data banks, it will be quite impossible to 'patch in' modifications at some later stage to place restrictions on the inflow and outflow of data. The safeguards must be determined whilst the whole project is still only a mental concept; they must come *first*; the protection which is essential for individual privacy must be programmed into the data bank computers before the doors open for business.

A Canadian journalist living in Britain emphasizes one of our national characteristics in the following extract: 'Adherence to the usual British custom of refusing to recognize a problem until it is fully developed could do incalculable harm. By the time any computer-based system is in operation a substantial investment – often of public money – has been made in hardware and intensive human effort. This, allied with purely technical considerations, will make it difficult to effect any major changes in design.'[40]

If the safeguards are left out (or are inadequate), and we discover that the deposit boxes which we thought were private to us – the knowledge that organizations have about us – is *not* remaining in one place, but being used to affect our lives in some entirely different connotation, we will become (quite rightly) much more wary about what we say to anybody. A society in which each member is fearful about revealing anything of himself to anyone is not a viable society. It is almost axiomatic in these times that politicians are not to be trusted; if distrust of, and alienation from, the bureaucrat increases through breaches of presumed confidentiality, there will be a decline in the quality of our civilization.

Some disagree: a British observer recently pointed out that 'in worries about computers, people have overlooked that in Sweden the future is here. Computers scan the whole society. There are huge gains and privacy may even survive'.[41] He points out that every Swede has a number based on his birthdate and area of birth, and that numbers are better than names, because the latter are often shared, or even changed over the course of a life-time.

'Every Swede, or settler in Sweden, knows this number as well as his name; because he quotes it constantly, in every single transaction with the state, or increasingly in most transactions with private organizations too. One advantage accrues to the individual: he isn't cluttered up with a whole string of code numbers issued to him by different organizations, as in Britain. His birth number is his, and his alone, and it serves him wherever he goes.

'From this, the Swedes are able to build up one of their basic information registers, containing information about people: name, address, marital status, nationality, residence code, and taxation district. This register is updated once a week in each province of

Sweden, once a month in the case of the central nation register in Stockholm. This is only possible, of course, because as in other European countries Swedes are expected to register with the police every time they change address.

'The basic population register is, however, only the centre of a whole series of special registers, all of which provide information about people's more specialized attributes. They include educational registers (for students in schools and colleges, people with university degrees, people with government scholarships, teachers), tax records, medical records, employment records and crime records. In all these files, individuals can be identified, and tied back to the central population register, by use of the personal birth number. Thus it is possible to discover, almost instantaneously, a very large amount of personal data about any individual [see chart overleaf].'[42]

The author of this article is a little too sure that there is little danger to privacy:

'In a sense, this problem is less in Sweden than anywhere else in the world. First to have a modern census (in the mid-eighteenth century) the Swedes have a long tradition of publicity in personal information. Personal numbers, marital status and number of legitimate children are all public data. So, perhaps more surprisingly, are all income data, as well as examination marks. For decades, any Swede has been able to obtain all this information about any other Swede if he had the mind to do it. The new computerized methods merely make it easier. But . . . the publication laws make it possible for any Swede to control the release of his data, and this right is now in effect part of the constitution.

'The Swedes gave us the Ombudsman. Perhaps, too, they will give us the clue to control over the all-seeing computer eye.'[43]

We would suggest a more positive approach, and are not prepared to wait until the situation deteriorates.

National numbering has of course been talked about for such a long time that it is a severe indictment of the body known as the 'National Suggestions Centre' that it awarded a £50 prize to a lady who suggested that we all have a single number. To be fair, though, in its magazine (called *What*) the comment was added that such a suggestion added to the threats of over-efficient bureaucracy.

The report of this easily-earnt prize[44] brought a reminder from that vigilant warrior who has appeared elsewhere in these pages, Mr Joseph Jacob, a legal expert, that all was not benefit in such a scheme. He referred[45] to the American experience of computer files, the dangers of error and abuse, and the work of the NCCL 'to prevent the authorities *lapsing into bureaucratic efficiency* (our italics) without the safeguards that are needed to prevent us living in a transparent

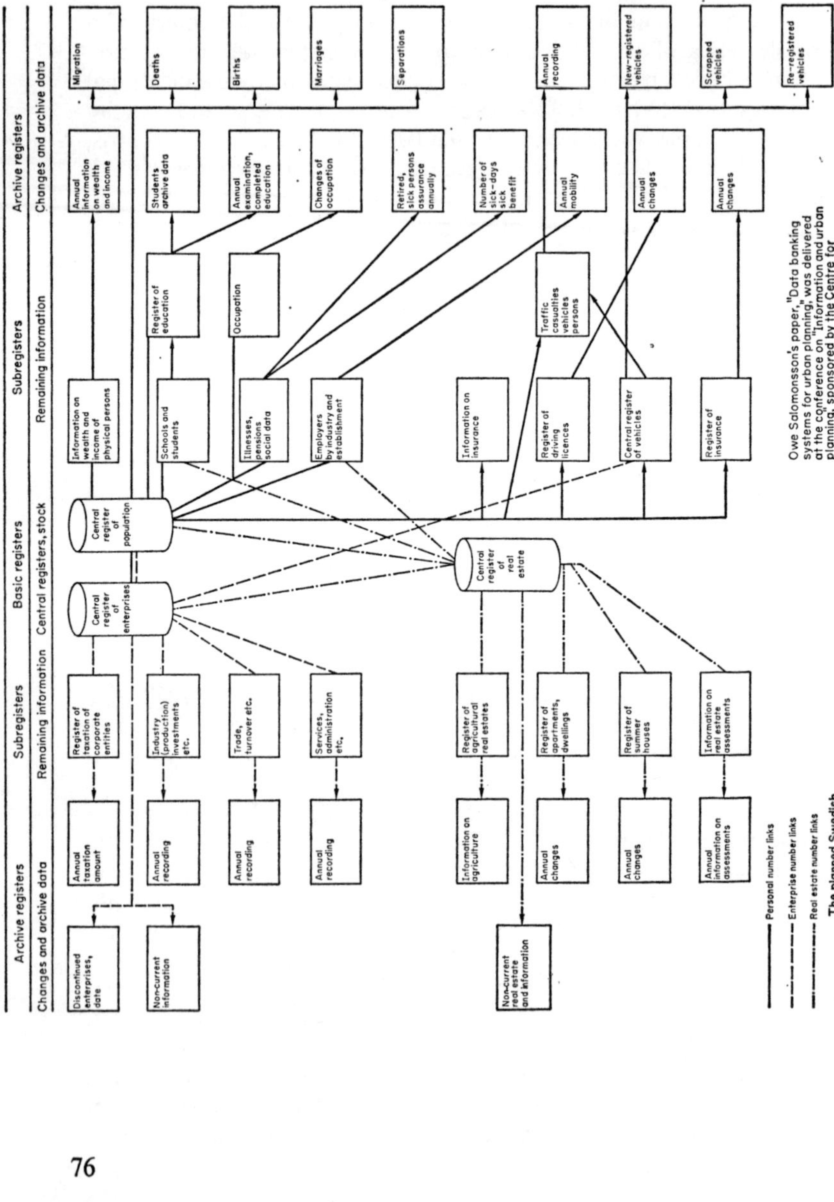

The planned Swedish data registers and their linkages

Owe Salomonsson's paper, "Data banking systems for urban planning," was delivered at the conference on "Information and urban planning," sponsored by the Centre for Environmental Studies world where anyone except the citizen can find out anything about him.'

Probably a unique number would mean that there would have to be an issue of identity cards – to be carried at all times so that the number could be quoted at all times. That seems harmless, but once you make any piece of paper obligatory it is a very easy step into tyranny – witness South Africa. If you haven't got it, it's a crime; if it is taken from you, you're stuck – you become a 'non-person'.

Another everyday application of computers relates to the collection and processing of news. Reuters use a computer to collate and assemble their news reports from all over the world. Two and a half million words of news pass through it every day. All we get is a selected version, distorted and restricted by the medium in which it is eventually displayed. The world is full of voices, and nine out of ten of them are the voices of Government, telling us what we are wanted to know. When even translation from another language can distort, interpretation is impossible. There is no such thing as a neutral or objective record of 'the facts' in any situation. With more and better means of communication, distillation, manipulation, synthesis, and integration of 'facts', come more and worse deceptions. The scales become weighted increasingly in favour of the official, bureaucratic sources, *vis-à-vis* the individual. The management of news is no novelty, even in the so-called free societies of the West. Even John F. Kennedy was not averse to it during the Cuban crisis. One does not dare to imagine what might happen when newspapers are printed by one's personal living-room computer-Telex, which is predicted as a norm before very long, the efficiency of the Japanese electronics industry permitting.

Personnel records are being controlled by computers. A recent television documentary observed that: 'In one factory we visited, a central computer keeps an eye on every single member of the staff. It is the computer that records every rise and fall in a man's productivity and decides whether he should be moved to a more demanding or a less demanding job. The computer decides whether a man is redundant or too old. The decision is final. One firm transferred all its 50- to 60-year-olds to so-called courtyard units. We were told of firms where skilled workers were demoted from one day to the next to jobs which meant that they lost up to 30 per cent of their wages, and their self-respect.'[46]

This is industrial bureaucracy at its most advanced, and insensitive, stage. 'The decision is final'. It is a more ruthless system than even the one Charlie Chaplin satirized in his film *Modern Times*, or René Clair, in *À Nous La Liberté*.

As we mentioned earlier, computer people and computers are closely identified with the faceless names, the nameless faces, of bureaucracy. And the public does not like it at all.

> A charitable action I can skilfully dissect;
> And interested motives I'm delighted to detect;
> I know everybody's income and what everybody earns;
> And I carefully compare it with the income-tax returns;
>
> To everybody's prejudice I know a thing or two;
> I can tell a woman's age in half a minute – and I do!
>
> Yet everybody says I am a disagreeable man!
> And I can't think why![47]

Some may wish to object at this point that surely it is only the social non-conformist, the criminal, the deliberately fraudulent, etc., who need have cause to fear the increased monitoring, and inter-relating, of personal data. But as we have shown, the potential ready availability of information reduces everyone's privacy; as will be shown later, the retention of privacy is essential for personality to flourish. And three small instances of the 'innocency' of computer records may be apposite here.

1. Consider a record tagged 'Divorced'. To one enquirer, this may be no more than a simple fact for statistical purposes; to another – perhaps a prospective employer – it may carry an entirely different, and harmful significance.

2. The computer does not forget. It has happened already, that an applicant for recruitment to one of the more selective branches of the US armed forces was turned down on account of a 'criminal past'. Further investigation, after pressure by the applicant and others on his behalf, showed that the 'offence' for which he had been so labelled was pilfering from a shop when he was ten years old.

3. Books borrowed by a student in his period at university may be recorded for posterity (and future security probe), and certain required course reading – say Marx, or Marcuse – may be held against him by government departments or certain unreasoning future employers.

These examples exist, here and now. In the case of the third, we have been told that checks of this kind are made, by the FBI and even by large commercial firms. It is not fanciful to dream up further examples. Who knows what travesties the year 2000 will bring? By this time all records may be on computer direct-access devices; the clerk replaced by the coder, punch-operator, and programmer; it may happen well before 2000. It is prophesied by one of the contributors to the *Daedalus* issue that, by that date, privacy will be at a premium, even if it has not entirely disappeared.

The four areas we mentioned earlier will be dominated by the computer, almost entirely. Medicine, crime-prevention, education, and credit, are all now well on the way to having their records handled by electronic systems. But this is only half the story. Soon, not only can the data be linked nationally, but also *between* countries.[48] It will be easy, by communications satellites and land-lines, to have 'world-systems', to check the medical data of a patient, for example, against all stored knowledge of similar cases in the world. Similarly, for crime-prevention, the print-storehouse of the globe can be scanned for warnings and identifications of potential suspects.

In education, the learning systems could operate on a world-wide basis, giving the less developed countries the benefit of the 'libraries' of data held by the information-fat countries of the West – or rather, of the North, as the geographical and cultural split in the world is increasingly moving this way.

The advantages of linking up all the credit and finance systems are too obvious to labour here. A world market will become a reality in any area where there is buying and selling, without any money say, through a multi-national corporation having to change hands, or bills to go by mail. It is to be hoped that as information flows more evenly, there will be a greater degree of one aspect of the economist's characterization of 'perfect' competition: that all buyers will know of all sellers, and *vice versa.* We fear, though, that there will be information monopolies, and inequalities of data-processing facilities. Already, the US has more computers than the grand total of those installed in many of the advanced countries.

The spread of cheap terminals, and cheap computing time, could however be to the advantage of the less privileged areas. Technological innovations, like the rapid spread of the inexpensive transistor radio in the recent past, will make the problem less severe. *Already*, the Japanese are producing very cheap desk-top computers, and there is a thriving market in second-hand computers.

The huge size of the Indian and Chinese populations assures them of a large absolute number of geniuses, according to Karl

Deutsch.[49] Given a reasonable level of science education, he argues, this will provide a considerable pool of programmers, and computer scientists, which – given the ancient skills of science and mathematics these two nations once had – assures them a good potential. Given a genetic bank relating intelligence to numbers, the nations concerned, if they have an educational system which gives minimal opportunities for all, will have millions of 'geniuses.' This may well enable them to make some short-cuts; say, in computer design. One may be sceptical here, but the Chinese have already accomplished something similar in the production of thermo-nuclear fusion.

Whatever the specific outcome, the onset of world systems in each of the four fields we mentioned, and no doubt others too, could be a reality before very long. It is in the very nature of the expanding process that the dangers will lie, as the very totality of such systems will constitute an even greater threat to freedom and to privacy. It will be *impossible to exist* outside any of the basic world systems; this is obvious if we consider the examples which involve economics. There will hardly be a bank which will be able to function *at all*, if it is outside the national financial system; and no national system will be able to do so outside the international one. The prospects for 'one world' may be enhanced – but in direct proportion to the threat to individual freedom. The steamship and telegraph created the British Empire, and the law and order it brought in its train – but the colonial peoples lost their liberty in the process. Will the new imperialism of advanced technology bring such mixed blessings accompanying its expansion?

Within a few years, you will be able to dial any number in the world from your desk; in fact today you can reach most European telephone numbers without using the services of an operator. An agreement has been reached over the distribution of standardized numbers for all the receivers in the world; as we have already said, it will soon be necessary to do the same for all individual identity numbers not only in one country, but world-wide. Just as 'One man, one vote' has spread to most countries, so 'One man, one number' may spread. This sort of reflection makes Orwell's picture of a future society seem like a nursery tale, and we are sure that one could readily construct an elaborate scenario for the worst electronic inferno the imagination could produce.

If this is possible, then the most Utopian outcome could also be imagined in some detail – but even the potentiality for this would contain the seeds of its own antithesis.

'Man was born free, but everywhere he is on tape! Workers of the world unite; you have nothing to lose but your IBM cards! '– there is the political slogan for the future. We suspect that the technical advance, which we have reluctantly admitted to be inevitable, has a built-in anti-libertarian bias. We are not constructing a plea for retrogression into an earlier state of innocence and ignorance. We can see that, before the abacus, as it were, life was nasty, short, even brutish. Yet strong and impenetrable barriers must be erected to avert domination by a machine which makes the process of institutional and personal domination (and destruction, for that matter) any easier.

Public opinion in Britain has until recently been complacent, even somnolent, about the implications of computer technology. In contrast, there has been considerable discussion and public outcry in the USA. The next chapter will discuss these developments at some length, and later we shall see what can be learnt from them.

Notes

1. See Hudson Hoagland, 'Biology, Brains and Insight', *Columbia University Forum*, Summer, 1967.
2. *Computer Weekly*, January 15, 1970.
3. See Kenneth Boulding's development of this theme, in his 'Expecting the Unexpected', *Prospective Changes in Society by 1980*, New York, 1960.
4. See *Financial Times*, August 5, 1968.
5. A. H. Clarke, *et. al.*, 'Practis', *Journal of the Royal College of General Practitioners*, 1969, Vol. 17; p. 60.
6. *Ibid.*
7. 'Computers in Medicine', BBC Third Programme, May 19, 1969.
8. See e.g. 'The Health of West Sussex', Annual reports of C.M.O.H. 1963–68.
9. Prof. Alwyn Smith, 'Preservation of Confidence at the Central Level' in (ed. E. D. Acheson) *Record Linkage in Medicine*, London E. S. Livingstone, 1968, pp. 338 ff.
10. See Z. Brzezinski, 'America in the Technetronic Age', *Encounter*, January 1968, p. 22.
11. *Financial Times*, August 5, 1968.
12. *Ibid.*
13. *Ibid.*
14. *Op. cit. The Times*, October 9, 1969.
15. *Daily Telegraph*, November 17, 1969.
16. See *The Times*, editorial, February 28, 1970.
17. *The Times*, June 12, 1969.
18. See Timothy Johnson, 'Print-out from Computer City', *Sunday Times*, June 16, 1968. Also James Ensor, 'Computers Versus Crime', *Financial Times*, July 10, 1970.
19. See M. Ways, 'The Road to 1977', *Fortune*, January 1967.
20. *Op. cit.*, p. 385.
21. We touch on this in Ch. 6.

22. *The Sunday Times*, July 7, 1968.
23. *Hearings*, C, p. 175 (Kenneth L. Karst).
24. See Robert K. Merton, 'Bureaucratic Structure and Personality', *Social Forces*, XVII, 1940, pp. 560–8.
25. See the description of P. Selznick's view in A. Etzioni, *Modern Organizations*, Englewood Cliffs, New Jersey, Prentice-Hall 1964, p. 12.
26. *Hearings*, A and C, with slight variations; (Paul Baran).
27. *Hearings*, C, p. 175–6 (Karst).
28. Organizations resent outside investigation in detail. (See A. Downs, *Inside Bureaucracy*. Boston, Little Brown, 1966, p. 266, proposition 14.)
29. *Privacy and Freedom*, Atheneum, New York, 1967, published in London, Bodley Head, 1970, with a Preface by Louis Blom-Cooper; (quoted here from *Hearings*, D, p. 300).
30. *Hearings*, A, p. 184; (Donald N. Michael).
31. J. Jacob, *op. cit.*, p. 4.
32. It is alleged that Barclaycard holders are unaware that their consumer habits are being constantly inferred from their pattern of purchases (see *Observer*, October 26, 1969.
33. Carrying further the process of bureaucratization classically described by Max Weber in (trans. T. Parsons and A. M. Henderson), *The Theory of Social and Economic Organization* (New York, Oxford University Press, 1947).
34. *Datamation*, March 1969.
35. See *Computer Weekly*, September 18, 1969.
36. Private letter to Stone from Mr Robin Radclyffe, to whom thanks are due for detailed information on computers and race-horses.
37. Peregrine Worsthorne, Birth of a Test Tube Nation, *The Times*, March 1, 1970.
38. *Daedalus*, p. 877 (Harry Kalven).
39. See A. Downs, *op. cit.*, pp. 112–131.
40. Laura Tatham, *The Times*, August 14, 1969.
41. See Peter Hall, 'Computer Privacy', *New Society*, September 31, 1969, pp. 163–4.
42. *Ibid.*
43. *Ibid.* For earlier, largely Scandinavian work in this area see, e.g. T. Hägerstrand, 'Geographic Data-Banks and the Use of Computers in Research', paper given at Regional Studies Association, London, October 1967 (mimeo). S. Norback, 'Location of Areal Data for Computer Processing', *Lund Studies in Geography*, Ser. C, No. 2, 1962.
    W. R. Tobler, 'Automation in the preparation of Thematic Maps', *The Cartographic Journal*, June 1965.
    W. R. Tobler, 'Numerical Map', Michigan Inter-university Community of Mathematical Geographers, Discussion Paper No. 8, 1966 (mimeo).
44. *Observer*, April 27, 1969.
45. *The Times*, April 30, 1969.
46. *The Listener*, May 22, 1969 – from a West German documentary shown on 'Europa' BBC 2.
47. Thanks to Dr P. Samet for retrieving this data from the file on King Gama, in Gilbert and Sullivan's *Princess Ida*.
48. Already airline reservation systems operate across national boundaries.
49. Paper (unpublished) to a Columbia University Seminar on Technological Innovation and Society, Winter 1966.

Chapter 5

THE AMERICAN SCENE

As may be expected, the nation most technologically advanced in the world has been the first to be forced to attempt a reconciliation of the conflicting demands of progress and civil liberty. Evidence of distress about the use of computers became evident in the USA during 1966 – the two-year time-lag before warning voices were heard on this side of the Atlantic is a fair reflection of the time-lag in technical development.

For the most part, this chapter is devoted to re-sounding the alarms which have been heard in America. There are two points to make clear as preliminaries:

1. The American system of government is based on a written Constitution, and some of the arguments concern the possible amendments of this to deal with a twentieth-century situation that the original framers could not have foreseen. Also, the system tends to require Federal Departments to obtain specific authority for their every action from the full assemblage of the Congress and the Senate – there does not exist our structure of devolved Ministerial responsibility.[1] Hence the specialist committees, able to summon witnesses both from the Civil Service and from backgrounds of expertise, and to interrogate them under oath.[2]

2. Although the Congressional special Subcommittee on Privacy, under the chairmanship of Cornelius E. Gallagher, was established in 1965, its initial concern was with the multiplicity of intelligence and personality tests being applied to recruits for various government, and government-sponsored, jobs. It was not concerned with computers, nor fears expressed in other public statements, until a specific proposal was brought before the committee by the Bureau of the Budget. This was a plan to establish a vast computerized National Data Centre.

No such explicit proposal has been made in this country. But that does not mean there is no possibility of it happening. No doubt somebody in the Ministry of Technology, or the National Data Processing Service, or the General Register Office, has thought about it. They may even be planning it; until some MP frames the right Parliamentary question to the right Minister, and gets a complete and truthful answer, we shall not know.[3]

It could happen only too easily. All the components of such a system already exist, and as we have shown, the interconnection of the separate computer files, which is already more than a possibility, implies that data can be readily transferred between them. Thus a national data service could come about almost by accident, as the computer installations proliferate and begin to collaborate. In a small way at first, perhaps by linking a Local Authority to the Department of Education, or one of the Inland Revenue machines to the Ministry of Social Security, the network could be imperceptibly established. Anyone hooked on to the system could get any information from any computer within the complex. There is no need to establish a *centre*, or even to *plan* from the centre, to provide such a system. We could find that, like Topsy, it 'just growed', and society has been turned topsy-turvy. America has already faced up to some of these problems, or at least has acknowledged their importance. For this reason a review of the American discussion is relevant to our theme.

Thus we might begin these extracts with the chairman's (Congressman C. E. Gallagher) introduction to the subcommittee on July 26, 1966. 'We do not want to see the intended good use of a data centre distorted so that it simply makes confidential information more readily available to more people. Nor do we wish to see a composite picture of an individual recorded in a single information warehouse, where the touch of a button would assemble all the governmental information about the person since his birth. . . . The presence of these records in Government files is frightening enough, but the thought of them neatly bundled together in one compact package is appalling. We cannot be certain that such dossiers would always be used by benevolent people for benevolent purposes.'[4]

And whilst the first target of the citizen's watchful eye must always be the encroaching activities of local and central government, it is reasonable to assume that first the public utilities and later the larger people-processing organizations (banks, insurance companies, building societies) would add their pool of files to the national data reservoir, and draw their supplies from the one source. Mr Gallagher said later:[5] The 'exchange of file information between outside data-gathering organizations and agencies of the Federal Government needs to be explored. . . . A transfer of hundreds of records can be carried out now by merely taking a tape from one computer and putting it into another. It is the conviction of the chairman and the subcommittee that a long, hard, and close look must be taken at the manner in which information is gained, the restrictions against unauthorized access, the assurances of accuracy, and the possibility of legislation aimed at preserving a measure of privacy and dignity in our data-rich society.

'For we must not become data-rich by becoming privacy-poor.

'There is a growing compulsion today to make each action by every single American a permanent record. Once it is known that this record exists, there is a tendency for some person, inside or outside the Government, to discover another purpose for that record. Because his goal in using the data frequently may be noble and public-spirited, he will not consider confidentiality to be an over-riding concern. He will ignore the fact that the data was originally gathered and used solely for administrative functions. Idle curiosity or illegal purposes will, of course, completely eliminate any compunctions about confidentiality.'

Both Raymond T. Bowman in 1966[6] and Charles J. Zwick in 1967,[7] Assistant Directors from the Bureau of the Budget, insisted during their respective cross-examinations that the Data Centre proposed was intended only as a central processing-facility, and archival storage-facility, for *statistical* data, not for the creation of personal dossiers. The plan, it appeared, was to centralize the accumulated data collected by twenty different Federal Departments, including the Internal Revenue, Census, Education, Labour and Health.[8] The declared purpose was to rationalize the collection and manipulation of national statistics.

The following extract describing the plans is chosen to illustrate how essentially rational and desirable (and therefore ultimately inevitable) is the concept of a nationally integrated data base. It is from a paper prepared by the Council of Social Science Data Archives:[9]

'In its survey of twenty Federal agencies the Committee (on the Preservation and Use of Economic Data, under Richard Ruggles) found over 600 major bodies of data stored on 100 million punch cards and 30,000 computer tapes. The decentralized nature of the Federal statistical system makes it extremely difficult to know what data exists on various topics and how to obtain access to it. Different agencies have entirely different policies with respect to access and outsiders must know exactly whom to contact for each kind of information. Most agencies . . . find it inconvenient and costly to respond to requests for information which might disrupt or delay their own work.'

'. . . The Committee . . . recommended that "a Federal Data Centre be established by the Federal Government to preserve and make available to both Federal Agencies and non-governmental users basic statistical data originating in all Federal agencies."

'. . . The proposed Centre would provide servicing facilities so that Federal agencies and individuals could obtain specific information directly and it would publish descriptions of the data available. In this sense the [Centre] would serve in somewhat the same role as the Library of Congress in providing a systematic and comprehensive coverage. . . .

'. . . Mr Dunn [a Bureau consultant who examined the Ruggles report] points to records which are missing in the Federal system. He says these are "records that enable policy makers and planners to understand adequately how people, households, regions, activities, enterprises, and administrative units are functionally related and how they change over time". These "are the most relevant information sources for policy making and program evaluation in these areas". He indicates that potentialities for system development . . . are being missed, and that "it is particularly important, therefore, that improvements in the Federal program lay the groundwork that will permit effective integration of the Federal file with other sources as they emerge".'

In summary, the case was being made for a completely open-ended system to be set up, which would take all the data which could now be recognized and identified and computerized, and still leave scope for the additional information files that would derive from local State sources, from industry, from commerce, or anything else that could be grabbed and put into the gargantuan Centre.

During the hearings, however, the proponents of the system (including Ruggles and Dunn) were thrown on to the defensive by the strong Subcommittee questioning, and the powerful arguments of adverse witnesses. Mr Gallagher, reporting to Congress on his Subcommittee's initial hearings, said:[10]

'Spokesmen for the Bureau of the Budget came to the subcommittee to discuss . . . the Data Centre. Yet, under extensive interrogation, the witnesses proved to be at a distressing loss of words when pressed for a detailed explanation of the system and for specific safeguards that could be built into the centre to provide for the protection of the individual's right to privacy.

'They seemed unable to comprehend the ease with which a statistical data bank could be converted into a possible dossier centre, and they failed to realize the potential power of such a centre. This is, we believe, the crux of the problem with which we are faced. . . .

'. . . The *New York Times* of August 9th in commenting on our hearings and expressing their concern over the National Data Centre summed it all up in two lines:

' "Perhaps in the long run the fight to preserve privacy is a vain one. But, like the struggle to preserve life, it must be continued while any shred of privacy remains."

'In the future no responsibility of our Government will be greater than the preservation of privacy and the protection of our fundamental human values. Like the problem of nuclear warfare, it is a time to reflect on how far we have come before we drift into a course that is beyond our capacity to navigate.'

The 'two lines' cited from the *New York Times* were the conclusion of an editorial worth reproducing in full:

'Can personal privacy survive in the ceaseless advances of the technological juggernaut? Many in public and private life now fear to use telephones for conversations they would keep confidential, while the variety of electronic "bugs" available to eavesdrop on even whispered communications staggers the imagination. And young lovers would be well-advised to remember that the skies are increasingly full of sputniks equipped with cameras capable of taking extraordinarily detailed pictures of what transpires under the moon as well as on it. George Orwell foresaw the logical end of this trend in a device that would enable "Big Brother" to keep an eye on everyone anywhere.

'The Orwellian nightmare would be brought very close indeed if Congress permits the proposed National Data Centre to come into being. We already live with the fact that from birth to grave Federal agencies keep tabs on each of us, recording our individual puny existence, monitoring our incomes and claimed deductions, noting when we are employed or jobless, and – through the FBI and similar agencies – keeping all too close watch on what we think or say, what we read and what organizations we belong to.

'If this situation is still somewhat tolerable, it is because each agency keeps separate files and it takes some considerable effort to find and bring together all that is known about a particular individual. What is now proposed is the amalgamation of these files, and the creation of a situation in which the push of a button would promptly dredge up all that is known about anyone.

'Understandably, this idea has brought about vigorous protest, in which we join. Aside from the opportunities for blackmail and from the likelihood that the record of any single past transgression might damage one for life, this proposed device would approach the effective end of privacy. Those Government officials who insist that the all-knowing computer could be provided with safeguards against unauthorized access are no doubt of the same breed as their brethren who "guaranteed" that last November's electricity blackout could never occur. Even the Swiss banks have learnt to their own and their client's sorrow that the device of numbered accounts is inadequate to frustrate determined would-be blackmailers.

'Perhaps, in the long run the fight to preserve privacy is a vain one. But, like the struggle to preserve life, it must be continued while any shred of privacy remains.'

The controversy centres on this proposed data bank to serve twenty Federal agencies, originally mooted in 1965,[11] and the primary issue from the outset was protection of individual privacy and 'the threat to civil liberties'.[12] It was hoped that the data bank would save public money – the US government was spending $178 million on statistical activities in 1967.

Those who proposed and defended the National Data Centre sought to make a fundamental distinction between purely statistical data, and personal dossiers – but since their evidence revealed that even 'statistical' data would carry a personal identifier (so that later data could be related to the same person's earlier record), criticism was strong – sufficiently so indeed to cause the scheme to be abandoned.[13]

Meanwhile, isolated developments by separate agencies of the Government have gone ahead – not without a steady flow of public criticism. The Police, in St Louis, in California, and other places, as we have already seen, each have computer files of wanted persons and suspects, and stolen vehicles. And we can recall that these are linked by land-lines to the National Crime Information Centre of the FBI in Washington. In each case remote terminals are linked to the local computer, giving the policeman instant information; there are something like 26,000 computer enquiries a day handled by the Washington centre.[14]

Information files on the non-criminal population are not so advanced, yet Alameda County, just across the bay from San Francisco, (the first to implement a police information system) has extended its files to deal with a social service index handling welfare, hospital, health and probation data. Thirty miles south in San Jose, work is well advanced in putting the whole population into a computer register. Within a decade 'it will be impossible to move far into an American city without being on-line to City Hall. Central computers will stretch out their tendrils to detect the movement of the citizen's car, record his borrowing of a library book, his parking ticket and his children's exam results'.[15]

'Perhaps the most important development of all [in the United States] is the use of computers as a new tool for doctors and surgeons.'[16] More and more medical information can be recorded by computer, directly monitored if necessary from intensive care patients via electrodes, and can rapidly indicate critical changes in condition – as well as providing vital data on blood groups, allergies, and so on for the occasional patient who may be unconscious and need urgent attention.

These things did not happen without public fear. Throughout 1967 and 1968 many anguished voices were raised about personal privacy. As one newspaper commented on the US police systems, 'some pertinent questions on the privacy and personal freedom issues' are raised by the project.[17] Charles P. Lickson found that so many questions were being raised in public that it was worth the attempt to review what is meant by the right to privacy,[18] and discovered that in some states specific law attempted to protect the citizen's right. 'Ironically, in England, the land from which the United States has drawn her common law, the right to privacy, *per se*, does not exist today,' as noted earlier.

Professor Arthur Miller, who provided a cogent and disturbing statement to the Senate Subcommittee, wrote earlier: 'With its insatiable appetite for information, its inability to forget anything that has been put into it, a central computer might become the heart of a government surveillance system that would lay bare our finances, our associations, our mental and physical health to government inquisitors or even casual observers.'[19]

All American commentators seem to agree that, whilst the computer men have some responsibility for respecting confidentiality, the real burden lies with Congress to formulate the appropriate legislation for the protection of information. Miller says 'Congressional action is necessary to establish the appropriate balance between the needs of the national government in accumulating, processing, and disseminating information and the right of individual privacy. This legislation must be reinforced by statutory civil remedies and penal sanctions.'[20]

We consider it worthwhile to cite further examples of the apprehension the problem has aroused in the United States. It does not necessarily follow that everything which happens in that country will similarly come to pass in other societies, but there is some probability. We recognize that there is possibly some over-statement of the dangers in the American evidence, but we feel it is better to err on the side of emphasis, considering the magnitude of potential dangers.

There is more discussion of the problem in the US than in Europe, so we consider the choice of materials broader and therefore more illuminating. A recent RAND bibliography cited 300 books on privacy and the technological challenge. The *New York Times* files hold records of at least 3,500 references (books and articles), excluding many more news items on the problem of computer privacy alone (up to 1969).[21]

The broad implications of the issue were spelled out by another expert, in his verbal evidence. He stressed that the menace was not necessarily less without a central data archive. He had little faith in the soothing words of the pundits:

'The problems of the invasion of privacy are, in my view, significant, and they will exist whether or not the central data bank is created by the Government. Individual data systems, both public and private, now being developed, can be tied together eventually into a network that will present essentially the same problems.

'Every time someone proposes a system that handles embarrassing information, we are commonly reassured by the words "only those having a legitimate need to know will have access to the information" While the statement rings seductively of safety and is granted in good faith, its validity is sometimes overstated – particularly when such systems are interconnected. As one familiar with the inherent weaknesses of both our computer and communications systems, I am less sanguine about these assurances.

'My remarks are intended to raise a healthy scepticism to this soothing syrup. While our computer and communications systems are foolproof, they are not smart-proof. These sytems are wide open to tampering by anyone sufficiently intelligent and motivated enough to take advantage of their weak spots.'[22]

There is little doubt that the American public has been exposed to extremely sophisticated public relations exercises by the computer industry. Large data-processing Corporations have spent millions of dollars in assuaging public fears, and stressing the promises of abundance to come from the application of computer technology. The involvement of the industry in the defence and space programmes runs into further thousands of millions of dollars. The stakes are extremely valuable, and the expenditure on public relations has been more than offset by the returns to the large corporations involved. The public has no way of judging the claims of the interested parties; many have benefited from the rapid growth in the value of investment in computer industry stocks and shares, and have not been too eager to ask too many questions.

The dangers stemming from the growth of systems cannot, in any case, be anticipated in advance. It is difficult to know how technological developments, apparently isolated, can become an integrated system. As can be pointed out:

'Our first railroads in the 1830s were short routes connecting local population centres. No one sat down and laid out a master plan for a network of railroad rails. With time, an increasing number of such separate local systems were built. A network gradually grew as economic pressure caused the new links to be built to span the gaps between the individual routes.

'We didn't start to build a nationwide telegraph network in the late 1840s; only independent telegraph links. But it was not long before we had an integrated nationwide network. Even the name, Western Union, recalls the pattern of independent links joined together to provide a more useful system.

'We didn't start to build a nationwide telephone system in the early days of the telephone in the 1890s. Yet, today we have a highly integrated telephone network.

'Such patterns of growth are not accidents. Communications and transportation are services that historically tend to form "natural monopolies". The reason is well understood. It's cheaper to share use of a large entity than to build your own facilities.'[23]

We can see that the reaction may be *ex post*, and it often takes time before remedial legislation can be implemented. Even today anti-monopoly laws are not always as effective as we might like. The added problem, in dealing with the growth of information systems, is the degree of complexity we shall have to deal with, which dwarfs past experience in earlier communications systems like the telephone networks. The growth of computer systems will be unparalleled, and we shall find it difficult to develop adequate policies to regulate them in the public interest.

Another witness sets out the 'total' nature of the threat. We do not consider his view of the world in any way paranoid. In a paper submitted to the subcommittee Professor Miller set out his apprehension more fully than in the article quoted earlier:

'On the opposite side of the ledger, the new technology poses a grave threat to individual freedom and privacy. The computer with its insatiable appetite for information, its image of infallibility, its inability to forget anything that has been put into it, may become the heart of a surveillance system that will turn society into a transparent world in which our home, our finances, our associations, our mental and physical condition are laid bare to the most casual observer. The same electronic sensors that can warn us of an impending heart attack can be used to locate us, track our movements, and measure our emotions and thoughts. The identification number given us at birth might become a leash around our necks and make us the object of constant governmental surveillance. Even the idea that there is no place in the world where we cannot be reached through our number is somewhat frightening. Finally, a high degree of information centralization gives those who control the recording and preservation of data a degree of power, which, if abused, might make the alleged "credibility gap" of today look like a bridge table bidding misunderstanding.'[24]

Some may say that this view is over-reacting, that the observer is obsessed by his pessimistic vision. But he is not to blame if so; we have all too often heard the extraordinary technical claims of the computer scientists, but rarely anything about the constitutional guarantees to deal with the new technological matrix of civil society. Can we really believe that the political system will be able to take the strain, whether through its written, or unwritten rules? There are those who believe that even without this problem the American political system is unable to accommodate the new demands being made upon it. The system can put one man on the moon, but cannot take another out of the Black Ghetto.

Another contributor to the debate takes us into this very area – the legal concepts we need to develop to accommodate the strains on the social system in the coming technological age:

'We have concepts of business information rights and proprietary rights, we have concepts about circulating information that does harm to people, in the libel and slander sense, but we have not developed, because the computer age was not yet upon us, the idea that personal information given to one person for one purpose should not be circulated further in ways that administer us, regulate us, and so forth, unless we consent to that further circulation or have notice that the information is being used against us so we can challenge any bit of information built into these enormous evaluation systems through large-scale computer centres.

'I think we need to recognize that the essence of privacy, in every definition that I have seen, is the right of the individual to control the information about himself that he chooses to share with others, how much he gives, when he gives it, and so on. . . .

'. . . it is a special problem when the Federal Government takes information from a citizen for one purpose and then uses it without his permission for another purpose, either commercial or governmental.

'I hope we can develop some kind of legal concept that sensitive information about the individual is a part of his personality, in ways that the courts will recognize, and that will operate as the standards that could be used for various kinds of administrative and statutory rules.'[25]

There has been some advance in recent years concerning the rights of citizens not to be 'bugged' electronically. The Fourth Amendment of the US Constitution has been invoked; but this is not really going to be sufficient. In the US and beyond, special constitutional revisions will be necessary to deal with the oncoming technological society – perhaps new political systems. This is a topic that the 'futurists' have sadly neglected in so far as they have not got beyond the stage of suggesting vague generalities. Whatever the academics have attempted,[26] informed public discussion has not gone beyond platitudes about participation.

But let us return for a moment to the problem as it faces us *in the short term*. An important area which was discussed in the US debate concerned the interest in private information by people outside the organizations collecting the data. As the American economy is based on credit to a degree unmatched elsewhere, with its reliance on credit cards and hire purchase, etc., business has not been slow to use computers in the area of assessment of credit-worthiness. Without assured foundations of consumer credit-worthiness, modern American capitalism would collapse. Thus there is a great deal of money to be made by selling data, whether authorized or not, to interested parties. Vance Packard, well-known for his popular books documenting the social phenomena of America, pointed out in verbal evidence that:

'Many of the filekeepers have been quick to learn that the records they control may hold considerable interest for people outside their own organization. Years after our birth, for example, an interested party such as a lawyer may be happy to pay $50 for information from our birth certificate, which officially is confidential information. And in a number of cities there are entrepreneurs happy to obtain and sell the information, as well as hospital records, police records, immigration records, passport records, and so on.

'Then there are the legitimate organizations engaged in selling personal information about us. The credit bureaus circulate to members the information that we give a store when we seek credit; and if there is any interest the same information may be passed on to curious Federal investigating agencies that inquire. Also there are the giant investigating enterprises such as the Retail Credit Co. which has openly assured prospective clients that it can strengthen any report it makes by drawing from its vast file of investigations made in previous investigations. The investigative firms making reports for insurance companies on insurance applicants have often felt free to sell the same information to non-insurance clients.

'Within the Federal Government, agencies have increasingly been developing systematic patterns for exchanging information. When a Federal agent makes a national agency check on a person, it customarily involves checking the files of at least eight Federal agencies.

'The individual citizen who is concerned about the erosion of his privacy has up until now had some consolation in the knowledge that all these files about his life have been widely dispersed and often difficult to get at. Digging up a sizable file of any individual has been a time-consuming, expensive proposition.

'This is changing with the advent of giant computers with their capacity for instant recall of a great variety of available information.'[27]

The reduction in cost of security checks makes this development particularly attractive to government. At the moment, a security clearance for military purposes could cost over 10,000 dollars. The point is that once the State enters the field with a new technique, *it will exploit it to the full*, in the absence of effective checks. Intolerance of deviants – the tyranny of the majority (in de Tocqueville's phrase) – makes the authorities over-zealous in their pursuit of personal information.

The penchant for 'witch-hunting' has perhaps abated, but the fear of new heresies and scandals presses the authorities to seek out attitudinal skeletons in cupboards. Even with the constitutional checks on electronic surveillance, the Federal authorities were none too fussy about 'wire-tapping'. Later, restrictions were made effective and the practice was restricted to cases involving the country's security. But recently, national security has been re-defined to include threats to internal order, such as relate to protests against the Vietnam War, student radicalism and black militancy.[28] It is worth pausing before condemning the sub-committee evidence we have presented as being merely the product of paranoid over-statement. Even at the *prima-facie* level, the television news media have been under attack by the US Vice-President for exercising their freedom of expression. We argue that all these questions of liberty and privacy are indivisible, and that the trend of governments is to present challenges to them.

The problem concerns every citizen, and impinges upon his everyday life, as Professor Westin told the sub-committee. The impact of credit-surveillance by computer systems can adversely affect the innocent consumer in the following way:

'If you think for a minute about a technological society in which individuals move from one place to another, you must realize that wherever an individual moves a credit corporation will be able to print out his record from the former community which will be a vital aspect of his life in the new community.

'Let me give one example of the kind of problem that you have here. Suppose somebody buys an appliance from a department store, becomes concerned about whether he has made the right selection or whether the appliance is working properly, and then decides his only leverage to get either service or action on his claim that the merchandise is bad or working improperly is not to pay the balance or payment on the bill. The department store will most likely put him down as a slow payer or bad payer. At that point the individual can be seriously damaged in all of the aspects that I have mentioned, even though it isn't a question of being truly delinquent but rather a question of the bargaining relationship between the individual and the seller. At the present time this can create a bad credit situation for an individual bacause the individual doesn't know that he had been put in as a bad payer. It can haunt the individual time after time then as as he seeks loans, mortgages, employment and so on.

'How does an individual learn about the decisions that are being made about him by these giant organizations collecting these data pools so that he can challenge the rating that is given to him, explain it, and in some way have the feeling that he is getting the due process that our society expects him to get?'[29]

We are beginning to see the reaction of the student to the technological society, with its consequent feeling of powerlessness.[30] Imagine the impact on the average citizen, 'the little man', as he begins fully to realize the way in which large organizations are increasingly going to frustrate him. The political consequences could be exceedingly dangerous.

The psychological pressures have already shown themselves in the 'grass-roots' reaction in favour of ex-Governor Wallace of Alabama, and equivalents in other countries. Like fascism in its earlier form, the political response is a populist revolt against technological modernism, and its social implications by a blind, anti-rationalist, rejection. When the full impact of automation is felt in the employment situation, the response of the working and lower middle-class could be most unpleasant.[31] There is also the vicious circle effect, by which populist discontent could be used as an excuse to suppress dissent.

Even the present liberal custodians of society could have the means to control the population to a degree which make a mockery of their ostensible credo. We may indeed be warned that:

'. . . The very existence of a National Data Centre may encourage certain federal officials to engage in questionable surveillance tactics. For example, optical scanners – devices with the capacity to read a variety of type fonts or handwriting at fantastic rates of speed – could be used to monitor our mail. By linking scanners with a computer system, the information drawn in by the scanner would be converted into machine-readable form and transferred into the subject's file in the National Data Centre.

'Then, with sophisticated programming, the dossiers of all the surveillance subject's correspondents could be produced at the touch of a button, and an appropriate entry – perhaps "associates with known criminals" – could be added to all of them. As a result, someone who simply exchanges Christmas cards with a person whose mail is being monitored might find himself under surveillance or might be turned down when he applies for a job with the government or requests a government grant or applies for some other government benefit. An untested, impersonal, and erroneous computer entry such as "associates with known criminals" has marked him, and he is helpless to rectify the situation. Indeed, it is likely that he would not even be aware that the entry existed.'[32]

This may be even worse than the 'guilt by association' smear technique which was at least *openly* practised during the McCarthy era. This, on the other hand, would be *covert*, and unbeknown to the 'smeared' individual—thus, in our view, a much greater evil. Kafka's *The Trial* comes to mind here, and the mental anguish of trying to find out the nature and origin of the accusation.

We have tried to show the issues being debated in the United States, and the dangers felt to be around the corner. On the other hand, the very fact that the hearings were held has shown the anxiety and concern felt in influential places like the US Congress, and in important publications. One most significant effect has been to alert the public to the dangers; but in addition action has been taken, and legislation is in the pipe-line. In the California State Legislature a Bill was presented (No. 1381, April 3, 1968) specifically recognizing (*a*) an individual's right to privacy as a direct right, and (*b*) computerized data as 'public records' – i.e. to be available for public scrutiny. Even so, two months later, one well-known computer scientist lamented the lack of adequate protection in the California State Social Welfare Data Bank[33] – this in a County which prides itself in blazing a trail in computer safeguards.

Since the hearings took place in 1966 and 1967, raising the issues involved, there has been no comparable furore, although some reaction has occurred, cementing the gains made *vis-à-vis* the issue of a national data centre. As the *Economist* recently reported:

'A fuss about confidentiality of data has been blowing pretty strong in the United States now for about two years, ever since a proposal was made to establish a huge national data centre. Dr Carl Kaysen prepared a report on the proposal for a Senate sub-committee which emphasized the dangers of misuse. The notion was dropped. But in the backwash, there have been many attempts to curtail the questions asked in the next United States population census, to be taken on April 1, 1970. Although almost every decennial census in America has raised some protests, this time there has been a real storm. Although the outcome may not, in the end, be all that restrictive, the Bureau of the Census has refrained from including some questions which it would have liked to do. The proposal, for instance, to include the social security number, even on a sample basis, was dropped after considerable opposition in Congress and elsewhere. Now new legislation is being sought which recommends that techniques and procedures be developed which will, in the next but one decennial questionnaire, lead to greater Congressional control over the questions asked and, in the meantime, asks that the gaol sentence penalty provisions, currently applicable to both individuals and organizations, for either refusal to answer questions or wilful falsification of the answers, be withdrawn.'[34]

Several commentators have shown that an American citizen's

Social Security number, originally established with a firm guarantee that it would not be released or required for any other purpose, has in fact become the common reference point for a host of returns and services.[35]

Given the sophistication of sampling techniques, one might ask whether a comprehensive census is needed anyway. Congress is certainly moving in the right direction.

It must be made clear that the function of this chapter has been to show the way in which the issue of computer privacy was first raised in the United States – understandably because there are more computers there. Secondly, it has shown the discussion which was cited in the later British reaction to the problem – with a time-lag of two years intervening.[36] And thirdly, it has demonstrated the successful arousal of public opinion to vigilance, and Congress specifically to action, on the vital issue of the national data centre.

Since the Congressional Hearings were held, there has been much public discussion. The computer manufacturers have had to soft-pedal; the largest credit bureau association has promised to set its house in order; but the use of computers has proliferated even further. There is the possibility that there will be 250,000 computers operative by 1975 in the US (employing 3 million computer people), compared with 60,000 in 1969, (operated by nearly a million people). Britain had under 10 per cent of this number of machines (about 4,000) in the latter period. These are only broad estimates, but a group of UK local authority chief officers visiting some US State and County computer installations in mid-1969 found that an average 1½ per cent of the annual budget was spent on computers – approximately six times that of a typical English county. One point is clear – the threat to privacy will continue to exist on both sides of the Atlantic as government becomes increasingly computerized. The search for cost-efficiency in Government will accelerate this trend, as the overhead costs of the advanced industrial society soar, and impel the use of computers in public administration. In a recent lecture, Alan Westin significantly emphasized the trend in American thinking, which is to realize that the questions of data banks and privacy are thoroughly political, rather than technical. He said: 'What computer data systems offer government is a virtually irresistable temptation, in the absence of restraints, to unite Rational Government, Social Science and Social Reform in a "total information attack" on the pressing problems of our society. It is an article of faith by Rational Government that what we are missing in the policy-making process is better information.'[37] He is hopeful that since the debate has become largely a political one, some constructive proposals may begin to emerge. Certainly, the *New York Times* announcement (March 12, 1970) of a nationwide investigation into computers and the growing threat to individual freedom, to be headed by Westin, sponsored by the National Academy of Science and financed by the Russell Sage Foundation, gives encouragement.

We do not wish to go into further detail on American developments,[38] although this cannot be totally avoided, as a great deal of the material available to illustrate our argument comes from the US. We would like to use the American discussion and developments to lead us to an examination of what has been happening in the United Kingdom. The two-year time-lag is an interesting phenomenon, and we should like to see the linear connection between the American and British discussion. The emphasis on computer privacy in 1968–70 in Britain resulted from the beginning of several new computer projects, particularly in the field of government, which were not on the scene at the time of the American hearings, so that they did not have the chance of becoming newsworthy.

Another factor is the improved reporting of technological developments in the serious British newspapers, so that there was more information available over here on American developments, as well as the 'issues' raised for public policy-making. There was little of this available in the early sixties, and the Congressional hearings we have quoted were not given prominence in the British press. Neither radio nor television went into the questions in any depth, and it has only been recently that the topics have been minimally aired. The broad question of privacy has been a delicate subject anyway, as far as newspapers, and to some degree TV, have been concerned, as quite often journalists have been accused of excessive invasion of privacy in the search for news.[39]

Thus, we have looked at the United States. 'We have seen the future, and it computes' (to paraphrase an oft-quoted observation on the effect of the Russian Revolution). We have seen that there is a threat that privacy as an individual freedom could be invaded in no small way, and that American expert opinion was worried.[40] We have also seen that some steps to deal with the problem have been suggested.

We must look now at the situation in the United Kingdom: the steps being taken to introduce computer systems in ways which could limit our privacy, and the degree to which this has been discussed, and made plain to public opinion.[41]

Notes

1. See for example J. C. Wahlke and H. Enlau, *Legislative Behavior*, Glencoe, Illinois, the Free Press, 1959.
2. See G. Goodwin Jnr, 'Sub-Committees: the Miniature Legislatures of Congress', *American Political Science Review*, (LVI), 1962, pp. 596–604.
3. The National Council for Civil Liberties is at present engaged in pressing Ministers concerned for statements of policy.
4. *Hearings*, A, p. 3.
5. *Hearings*, B, p. 2.
6. *Hearings*, A, pp. 49 ff.
7. *Hearings*, C, pp. 37 ff.
8. On the role of these Departments in the US System of Government, see David B. Truman, *The Governmental Process*, New York, Knopf, 1953.
9. Julian Nixon, reprinted in *Hearings*, C, pp. 199 ff.
10. *Congressional Record*, August 18, 1966, reprinted in *Hearings*, A. p. 315.
11. See American Report from Brandon Applied Systems Inc. 'The National Data Center Controversy', *Data Systems*, March 1969, pp. 20–4.
12. *Ibid.*, p. 20.
13. See L. J. Carter, 'National Data Bank: Its Advocates Try to Erase "Big' Brother" Image', *Science*, Vol. 163, January 10, 1969, p. 160.
14. *The Sunday Times*, June 16, 1968.
15. *Ibid.* See also Gordon Milliman, 'Alameda County's "People Information System"', *Datamation*, March 1967, p. 28 ff.
16. *The Financial Times*, June 5, 1968.
17. *Daily Telegraph*, June 20, 1968.
18. *Computer Group News*, January 1968. Reproduced in *Spectrum*, I.E.E.E., October 1968.
19. *Atlantic Monthly*, December 1967. For a fuller and later expression of Professor Miller's views, see the book-length article 'Personal Privacy in the Computer Age: The Challenge of a New Technology in an Information Oriented Society', *Michigan Law Review*, Vol. 67, 61, April 1969.
20. *Ibid.*
21. See for 1968, e.g. *New York Times Index*, 1968, p. 350, p. 1208, and for 1969, e.g. *Index*, June 1–15, 1969, p. 67.
22. Paul Baran, *Hearings*, A, p. 120.
23. *Ibid.*, p. 121.
24. Miller, *Hearings*, C, p. 72.
25. Westin, *Hearings*, D, p. 292.
26. See 'Working Session II: Four Futures', *Daedalus*, pp. 948 ff.
27. Packard, *Hearings*, A, p. 8.
28. See the recent sentences in trials in Chicago for Conspiracy and the anxiety about the persecution of the Black Panthers, e.g. in *The Times*, February 17, 1970, February 18, 1970.
29. Westin, *Hearings*, D, p. 287.
30. See for example Bruno Bettelheim, 'Obsolete Youth', *Encounter*, September 1969, pp. 29 ff.
31. There is little evidence that the entrenched labour bureaucracy would not take advantage of it. See issue on the American Labor Movement, *New Politics*, Vol. VII, No. 3, summer 1968.
32. Miller, *Atlantic Monthly*, *op cit.*, December 1967.

33. L. P. Deutsch, 'Snooping by Computer', *San Francisco Chronicle*, June 19, 1968.
34. *The Economist*, September 6, 1969, p. 53.
35. See e.g. C. E. Gallagher, 'Dangerous Datamania', *San Francisco Chronicle*, August 3, 1969; also Judith Moss, *Confidentiality and Identity* (Lockheed Government Information Systems, Report GIS-83), September 6, 1968. This document concentrates on the problems of ensuring that the computer has 'got the right person', either to update or display a record.
36. Early British attempts to consider the social implications of the computer have been largely micro-sociological in character, for example Enid Mumford and Olive Banks, *The Computer and the Clerk*, London, Routledge & Kegan Paul, 1967, which describes the reactions of the staff to the introduction of automated techniques in two firms. These, while thorough, have not raised some of the broader questions relating to freedom and privacy, and were not intended to do so, we must add. For an early American study see I. R. Hoos 'When the Computer Takes Over the Office', *Harvard Business Review*, July–August 1960, Vol. 38, No. 4, p. 102–12.
37. *Datamation*, February 1970, p. 16.
38. See e.g. J. Rosenberg, *The Death of Privacy*, New York, Random House, 1969, for recent American discussion.
39. The end of 1969 and the start of 1970 saw an increased focus on privacy and individual freedom in Britain. See special supplement on Liberty and the Individual in the *New Statesman*, February 6, 1970.
40. See an unpublished paper; 'Resources for the Future', Inc. Washington, December 17, 1969, by Edgar S. Dunn, author of a report in 1967 recommending a National Data Centre, who has recently called for a more realisitc dialogue between the proponents and opponents of databanks, which would consider certain *specific computer filing systems* rather than perpetuating the philosophical (and emotional) tone of the last three years. He calls for a 'national information policy' commission, which seems a very practical proposal not only for the US but also for the UK.
41. It should be noted that national data-banking is very advanced in Belgium, and at least in the police field in France. There is however some public concern, see the recent series of articles in *Le Monde*, in May 1970, e.g. 'Les Français Devant L'Informatique', *Le Monde*, May 29th, 1970

Chapter 6

THE BRITISH CASE

Having discussed what is already happening in computer technology – much of it admittedly in the United States, but setting a pattern for advanced societies – and the American concern about its implications for individual freedom and privacy – we now turn our attention to Britain. We hope to discuss recent British experience both of the applied technology and its social implications, and also the relatively limited amount of public discussion and concern about its consequences.[1]

The *Financial Times* of January 10, 1970, reflected:

'Partly this concern stems from the fact that the Government's policy seems to have been deliberately obscure; the awards of contracts have not always seemed to square with the policy as explained by Ministers, and many people within the industry are baffled as to the precise guidelines used by the Government. They are equally concerned that British use of computers in Government-sponsored areas such as medicine, and education, and within Whitehall, is lagging badly behind not only the US but most of the advanced European countries as well. Again, there are many users and manufacturers who feel that the Post Office has seriously underestimated the likely demand for data transmission facilities.'

The public sessions of sub-committee D of the House of Commons Select Committee on Science and Technology are further evidence of the strange, and apparently impenetrable, procedures surrounding the acquirement of computers by Government.

In the United Kingdom, 'the computerization of society has reached only a modest scale'.[2] However, 'modest' should not here be construed as 'negligible'. The visitor to I.C.I., Vauxhall Motors, British Rail, Barclay's Bank, and the Greater London Council (to name only a few representatives of major organizations) will find acres of office space devoted to computer equipment. In many smaller firms, too, smaller computers are at work, whilst virtually every University and College has its machine and appropriate courses. At least one large union, the Engineers, has its own computer, and several others participate in time-sharing arrangements. If the scale is 'modest', it is only so to the extent that the computer is not yet entirely all-pervasive; by comparison with America, we are still some way from the situation where it becomes axiomatic for every corporate body, large or small, to possess computing facilities.

Yet both public and private organizations are rapidly expanding their 'banking' of information. For example, several Ministries now have extensive data-storage plans, and perhaps chief amongst these are the Ministry of Social Security and the Post Office. Soon, thirty million social security records will be stored in computers, and the Ministry will handle fifty million enquiries per year. The Post Office is moving ahead with its National Data Processing Service – whose aim is to establish a linked network of regional computer centres serving government and commerce alike on a service-industry basis – and considers this to be one of its major developments over the next few years. There is even a Working Party specially engaged on the topic, acting as a subcommittee of the Post Office 'Little Neddy' (Economic Development Committee), because it would not be in the national interest if demand out-stripped supply in relation to this very important service.[3] There is also an Electronics 'Little Neddy' on the topic of computer and associated developments.

But there is no Working Party studying the national interest in relation to the very important data which will be held in National Data Processing Service computers. In 1967, Parliament made it an offence to divulge information gathered by the NDPS. The Act was not discussed before Parliament.[4] The legal implications of it are complex, and one expert discusses them as follows:

'It is said that the 1967 Act lays down an obligation of absolute secrecy so that not even the Postmaster General can get at the information. Section 2 allows disclosures only for purposes of the NDPS or "in such cases as may be required by law". "In view of our long reputation for confidentiality and of the new safeguards (i.e. electronic storage) there is no need for any fear on this." The provisions of section 2 are backed by the Official Secrets Act 1911 as amended and each employee of NDPS at the commencement and termination of his employment is informed of this. Further, the physical arrangements . . . render it impossible to obtain access to the information except in circumstances where such would most probably be discovered. The information is therefore reasonably safe against espionage.[5]'

On the other hand, he is unsure as to what is meant by 'in such cases as may be required by law'. If this refers to the Civil Evidence Act of 1968, there is no harm in the phrase. But if it is to read as a reference to a requirement of law enforcement officers, on terms and occasions that have not been prescribed, he is less at ease, and raises strong objections. 'The information to be stored will contain much that is of a sensitive nature and dependent upon third party evaluations; and at present if such officers want the information they must ask the owner of the information. The mere fact that it is kept by a public corporation should not make their task easier. If it does, the odds are that some of the potential use of NDPS will be lost. There are therefore no reasons why it should be removed. Similar considerations should apply to the security of information in private computer bureaux.[6]

This comment merely raises some of the implications, and is by no means a complete exposition of all the dangers. We shall revert to the specific question of legal protection in a later chapter, and proceed now to illustrate some of the other UK developments.

Only a few of the developments towards data banks, which are so extensively planned, are already in operation. Although we understand that procedures have changed recently, visitors to the London office of an airline were able to see a flight-booking terminal demonstrated, working on the live computer-held files in New York, and from time to time interesting passenger lists were displayed with no attempt to disguise the names. This was, at the least assessment, thoughtless – and thereby serves to pinpoint again one of our main arguments: that systems are not *automatically* secure, but have to have security built in.

Several of the major banks in this country have begun to connect their branch offices to the computer centres where the accounts are kept. It might not be so easy for a stranger to gain illicit access to the terminals, and thence to the files; but armed robberies of banks are not unknown, and we do not consider it fanciful to prophesy that bulk information on clients' accounts will be of more value to a criminal than straight cash – so there will be 'bank data bank' robberies. In fact, it would be very simple, and most enlightening, to wire-tap the banks' communication circuits, and attach a terminal of one's own.

A claim that their computer service can give 'immediate data on over 200,000 businesses in the United Kingdom' is made by Dun and Bradstreet.[7] This data comprises: 'name and address of prospect organisation, number of employees both in the section concerned and the group as a whole, credit rating, volume of sales, year the business was established, registered capital, line of business, standard industrial classification codes'. Although not strictly within our definition of a data bank (i.e. *personal* information on individuals), we are bound to wonder at the origin, reliability, and range of destinations, of this data – and ask how it is protected.

International Data Highways operates a service for stockbrokers, which though again not based on personal information is sufficient evidence of the fact that data banks and remote links are not only possible, but operational, now. The exchanges made daily at the Stock Exchange are fed into the computer, which in return for this diet produces quotations, valuations, and portfolios for its clients.

Fortunately, in the light of our theme that privacy must be planned, most of the UK computers that will hold and deploy personal facts are still in the design stage. The next two years will see a large number of them in operation. Scarcely a week passes without some announcement, of which the following is typical: 'A massive computer-based information service for south-west London is being designed to unite the intelligence systems of the hospital service, general practice and the community health service.'[8]

Local authority departments for vehicle and driver licensing are preparing to shut up shop. This work, which has been done in the Town and County Halls of 183 authorities, will be centralized by 1972. It has always been strictly a Ministry of Transport function, and the local Councils have always had their costs fully reimbursed by the Ministry. Now a computer at Swansea will take over completely. The centre will cost £6 million, and from an initial 16 million vehicles and 20 million drivers is expected to deal with 25 million, and 33 million, respectively, by 1980. There will be about 500,000 actual transactions a day, and a vast number of enquiries, processed from the remote terminals which the Ministry will establish in its own local offices. Enquiries must be answered 24 hours a day, for it is vital for the Police to be able to trace the owner of a vehicle quickly. The suggestion has been made that links will be established between the projected national police computer network (see below), and the licensing computer.

In the Parliamentary Standing Committee which considered the Bill authorizing the Swansea centre, the then Minister of Transport (Mr Richard Marsh) appeared to have little sympathy with two other Members who questioned both the wisdom of the scheme in particular, and the potential for the future of computerized licensing.[9] Mr Robert Cooke, MP, was one of the challengers, and 'pictured the stage being reached where a button was pressed and if the computer gave the "thumbs down" sign he would never get a licence'. As in a credit-granting situation, this is a specific example where the computer is in fact producing a decision – a straight 'yes' or 'no' to an application – according to the data it is given and the criteria written into the programme.

How long will it be before this Ministry renews its close association with local authorities, to keep up to date on population movement – that is, to keep tabs on the drivers? Worse, how long before licence applicants are not simply asked to declare their state of health, but find that the information has been automatically extracted from their (computerized) medical record? Just how much freedom will remain for the individual in a fully data-banked society? How is he to know what is happening to his vital records? It is of course perfectly feasible to control the granting of marriage licences by computer, given merely a file of all single persons over eighteen, and from thence not too great a step – given perfect birth-control methods which cannot be far away – to 'licence' families to have children. This might appear a highly desirable objective in an over-populated world.

The new Civil Service Department, which plays a co-ordinating role in the staffing and methods of Government departments, is concentrating on the encouragement of exchanges of data. 'With one exception it is co-ordinating schemes rather than developing central systems. There is no plan to establish any "Big Brother" data bank of personal information on members of the public.'[10] The article quoted does not reveal the 'exception', and we are left guessing – and aghast at the unprecedented dissemination of personal information implied by creating 'the conditions for the interchange of data between departments in machine-readable form so that . . . a magnetic tape from one department's computer can be used on another's'.[11] We are bound to demand clear legislation to control this flow, and also to emphasize that if the Government's computers are sufficiently compatible for *this* kind of interchange, one of the technical difficulties in linking the machines directly to each other over communications circuits will have been removed.

The Labour Government's revised earnings-related pension scheme was announced provisionally in February, 1969, and during the long delay before the full plans appeared in a second *White Paper* there was a mighty outcry. This came, though, not from the computer privacy interests but from those who saw another freedom threatened the right to enter employment providing a good (i.e. substantial and actuarially sound) occupational pension scheme. These people saw themselves threatened in two ways; either with a diminution of their expected retirement income or, if 'modified contracting-out' were to be allowed, further enforced deductions from their pay in addition to their present superannuation deductions, to prop up the financing of the State scheme. It seemed quite possible that they would lose both ways. It was not surprising that this affronted section of the population – the middle-age-group, middle-income-group sector – shouted loudest. Yet there were some who noticed that the whole scheme was going to be run by a computer, and a broader and possibly more important issue was involved. What *did* this mean? That the *whole working population* would be in the files of a single computer. 'There is a danger,' pointed out the observant *Computer Weekly*, 'that the system will not be adequately protected by legislation, nor will it be technically infallible . . . A catastrophic failure could disrupt or destroy all the data of contributions made or benefits due.' [12] And, of course, given such a comprehensive system, it would be delightfully efficient to blend into the pensions records the whole of the tax system – not to mention medical or criminal records, both of which are distinctly relevant to the scrutiny and detection of potentially fraudulent claims.

It is salutary to be reminded that computers *do* disrupt data. The RAF Records Office machine, holding personnel information for the whole Force, made at least two crass errors because of programming mistakes. It discharged one airmen on the grounds of pregnancy, and awarded a flying badge to a carpenter.[13] These things will happen. The more we rely on computers, the more error-prone society could become. In August 1970, there was the Post Office *Telephone Directory* furore, due to computer type-setting.

Soon, £57 million will be spent by the Inland Revenue to supplement the existing regional computer centre at East Kilbride, enabling a further eight computers to gradually assimilate the PAYE and other routine tax affairs of 25 million people. The scale of expenditure must be expected to ameliorate the lot of the genuinely over-burdened local office staff, but offers no guarantees of more accurate or quicker assessments. In the experience of one of the present writers, it takes an average of three attempts annually to arrive at a correct PAYE coding, and one can only wonder how much tax is erroneously deducted from those with insufficient knowledge to challenge the local Inspector. Shall we be able to challenge the computer which makes mistakes? All the evidence suggests that the bureaucrat will take the line that 'the computer output must be right'. And a report by the TUC has pointed out that whilst fears of large-scale redundancies following the introduction of computers have proved unfounded, 'many companies (have installed) computers without giving staff sufficient training in how to operate them. The result is unnecessary work from feeding in inaccurate information'.[14] Also,

'In one nationalized industry, the computer takes two weeks longer than traditional methods to prepare and send out bills to customers.'[15]

The SAYE scheme – Save As You Earn – is another recent development, introduced in October 1969. Any person may enter into a contract to save a maximum of £10 per month, *either* into a Trustee Savings Bank *or* into the Department of National Savings. Clearly, there is going to be sharing of records between all the TSBs and the DNS, to spot the people who have taken out separate contracts for more than they are 'allowed' to save. Consequently, a government department is going to be getting its hands on (private) savings account records.

Worse than this, anyone is allowed also to take out a contract (with a similar maximum of £10) with a building society – but only one at any time. Who is going to police and detect the over-enthusiastic saver amongst the proliferation of building societies? A government department again, doubtless, since it is Treasury money that will be paid to the societies to finance the high interest rates on these contracts. This will all go on to the NDPS computer in Leeds, and will be 'live' during 1970.

In December 1969, there were nearly 240 computers in local government service, and 187 in the Civil Service with a further 76 on order. Some of the plans for their use, other than those already mentioned, include a register of blood donors run by the Department of Health and Social Security; the administration of legal aid; and medical records. Before long, data banks will cover all important areas of central and local government. Just how this will finally be worked out is obscured in the variety of plans still being formulated. It is certain that the Local Authorities (Goods and Services) Bill will make legal the sharing of computers between authorities,[16] and perhaps of information as well.

Another certainty is that we shall see the influence of a major data bank upon law-enforcement in Britain. The National Police Computer, planned by the Home Office together with the Metropolitan Police, will have some 700 terminals throughout the country. According to Lord Stonham it will be a major innovation: 'A large number of forces are using local authority computers for payroll and other administrative work and for statistics, and in some cases they are processing statistics for the regional deployment of manpower . . . But . . . the really exciting project that we are now planning is a national computer to process operational police records for the whole country, so that every force, and divisions within the forces, will have direct and immediate access to the information about the "m.o." – the *modus operandi* – of criminals, the names and previous convictions of criminals and the main fingerprint collection. It is an immense concept, and will entail storing far more information than any comparable project in the world. Although planning has reached an advanced stage it is still too soon for a final decision to be made, but if all goes well as we hope these plans will become a reality within the next year or so.'[17]

News reports on the computer centre to be established for use by all British Police Forces are very scanty, and the Home Office seems reluctant to divulge details of its plans. What is known is that the computer has been ordered, for delivery in the spring of 1971, and will cost about £2 million. Central files will be set up on stolen vehicles and property, and on missing and wanted persons; the centre will also take over the files of Scotland Yard's national criminal records – about 2 million people have dossiers in this system. Initially there will be 9 remote terminals, in Regional crime squad offices, then a further 47, one for each of the main force areas in Britain; and eventually some 800.[18]

It seems important to us that this system should *not* be developed under the cloak of Official Secrets[19] – just as important as that the actual data *should* be kept confidential. The methods of administrative and technical protection of the data, against both infiltration and distortion, are matters of public concern. So, too, is the content of the files in broad terms – e.g. will anyone who spends a night in detention remain in the file as a 'known offender' even though the next morning's magistrates' court decides he was an innocent bystander at a riotous demonstration?

The policies can only be effectively challenged through Parliamentary action, and it was encouraging that this very issue was to be raised in Sub-committee D of the Commons Select Committee on Science and Technology, whose task (before the general Election) was an investigation of the computer industry and Government as a user.

The system can be seen to inaugurate 'a new era of police surveillance'[20] and while seeming admirable on the face of it should not be immune from challenge. The computer will certainly store data on people with *no* criminal record, who are vaguely classified as suspects, or sometime associates of criminals. Lord Denning, Master of the Rolls, has said in the Appeal Court that 'The police must never invade the privacy of an individual or deprive him of his liberty of movement except for the most compelling reasons.'[21] The particular case concerned the impounding by the police of passports, a topic on which a Professor of Law had earlier written at length, noting that 'Passport control seems to be an exceptional area in which the Government claim a free power to restrict personal liberty without reasons given . . . there is virtually no law about them. (Passports) are granted, withheld or revoked under the royal prerogative – that is to say, at the discretion of ministers; no one has a legal right to a passport; reasons for refusal or revocation will not be given; the passport itself remains Government property . . . elementary rights are conspicuous by their absence.'[22]

We may presume that the National Police Computer's advice will be taken when an application is made for issue or renewal of a passport – and in the light of the foregoing its ruling would appear to be unchallengeable. In this way too, many of the other 'facts' and inferences in the machine may be used to inhibit our liberties in many areas.

The London Boroughs' Management Services Unit produced a report (see Ch. 9 for a fuller discussion) as the first phase of a long-term study into the computer needs of Haringey and surrounding Boroughs. It concluded that the sensible and most economic approach was to obtain a large computer with ample direct-access space, to be shared by six or more authorities, and to establish completely cross-referenced files about all the people and all the properties or plots of land, with enough computer power to manipulate these files from remote terminals in all the appropriate offices.

Other local authorities had previously been thinking of similar developments, and approaching this degree of integration in a rather less direct way without such bold commitment to a specific plan. To them it must appear that many of the detailed estimates of required computer filing capacity listed in the Haringey document are extremely optimistic, and that the costings of the hardware are correspondingly low. But the report remains an important contribution to development throughout the country, not only as the first comprehensive study of the electronic possibilities for inter-relationship between the departmentalized functions of authorities, but also as the first occasion on which a published data bank proposal contained a reference to the problems of personal data protection. It is nevertheless only a mention, passed off quickly, and does not reflect that serious thinking found in many American local authorities.[23] Indeed, in March 1969, one of the present authors had criticised the then prevalent situation: 'It is distressing that there is not yet one computer manager . . . who has gone on record with a public announcement to the effect that "we are planning a real-time/data bank system, and these are the safeguards we shall build in to protect the deliberate or inadvertant misuse of the information . . ."'.[24] Apart from Haringey, this remains true. It is impossible to avoid the conclusion that the majority of those responsible for installing computers are *still* not willing, or able, to consider the social consequences.

The shape of computer systems to come will be affected by the coding structures adopted, and coding methods are under review in many areas. The National Computing Centre published a booklet on the standardization of Commodity Codes in early 1969, for the benefit of those considering computers to handle supplies. In a review of this publication, one critic[25] postulates that coding structures have a significant effect upon the company which uses them. Indirectly, the nature of the coding employed may well decide which departments become more important, and which less; what tasks become redundant; and how policy will be formulated in certain aspects. He notes that certain recommendations are deliberately omitted from the N.C.C. report, because they are 'largely the concern of government departments', and comments on this omission: 'I would dearly like to know what the gentlemen in Whitehall are concocting; their decisions on code structure will certainly influence economic thinking – this will have a very real effect upon the *organization* of government in the UK.'

Of course, the British public is insulated from the planners in the Ministries by the Official Secrets Act. At least the Swedes are better off in this respect.[26] The Civil Service can be very touchy at times, however and by whomsoever it is approached. A request from the National Council of Civil Liberties and the B.C.S. Privacy Group for full information on the type of computer system to be used by the Ministry of Health and Social Security has so far been turned down. (Within that same Ministry, an employee was in fact sacked, for writing an *anonymous* article revealing the incidence of fraudulent claims for benefit.)

It may be thought ironic that during the same week of 1969 in which Lord Wade was telling the Liberal party Conference of the need for legislation to protect the individual from 'intrusion into privacy by modern technological developments – particularly computers', the formation of a Business Statistics Office was announced. This new government body, operating as an ancillary to the Board of Trade but closely linked with the central Statistical Office, would employ over 2,000 Civil Servants – and a computer – at Newport. Its first major task would be to set up a central register of businesses – running to over two million entries – and from these samples would be subjected to much deeper survey so as to feed back yet more and more information into the data bank.

What is it all *for*? To avoid confusion and duplication, to improve current statistics and future prognostications. Where will all the data go? To anyone who asks for it, in government departments, universities, and industry. In one light, the more statisticians willing to use the data and carry out research upon it, the better for society. On the darker side, what right has this new office to redistribute the private information it can gather (whether its surveys will *demand* a reply under threat of penalty has not been made clear) to *anybody*? That national administration requires nation-wide statistical evidence is not in dispute; that those who administer may distribute their gleanings to others certainly should be.

There is a question of principle involved here which should be debated in Parliament (and the press). One trouble with the modern legislature is that it is inadequately filled with those expert enough to understand some of the questions and their implications. Nor do the qualifications of the non-scientific Civil Servants involved in this and the projects mentioned earlier seem adequate to an understanding of the issues involved.

On the other hand, it is gratifying to see that the hands of the bureaucrats are not entirely free in the matter. As a recent report in *The Economist* noted: 'In Whitehall it is felt that this storm in the United States which has grown out of the debate over data banks, may have put back progress there in official statistical inquiries several years. It is anxious to avoid a similar setback in Britain and will therefore try to keep the computer people in check. Mr Moser's main concern at present is to build up respect for his organisation among businessmen. Inevitably, however, this means that researchers outside government departments are deprived of valuable material; in Britain they are more handicapped in this respect than in either America or Scandinavia.

'Less attention has been attached to the confidentiality of non-official statistical inquiries, such as market research surveys, presumably because no one need take part in them unless he wants to. But commercial and central banks take elaborate precautions to prevent the unauthorized extraction of information about their client's monetary affairs, with, in computer operations, the use of remote enquiry terminals, such as passwords necessary to extract data.'[27]

The nonsensical conclusion of this extract shows that the writer and/or subeditor is as inadequate in computer understanding as anyone, and thus it is no surprise that the piece should glide too glibly over the difficulties involved in 'elaborate precautions' – which we shall discuss in greater detail later.

The 'Mr Moser' referred to is actually Professor C. Moser, the head of the Government's Statistical Service, and it was later pointed out that 'His department is also working on a multi-purpose social survey delving into family spending, people's buying habits, housing, education and spare-time activities. The social survey, which will supplement the ten-yearly nationwide census, is to be carried out four times a year and its questions will be "flexible".'[28] One need hardly look further for evidence in support of the earlier proposition that the demands of Government agencies for information increase commensurately with its ability to process the information. Before such a survey was even contemplated, there should have been the opportunity for public discussion of the propriety of adding further burdens of compulsory returns to those we already suffer; we hope that before any action is taken to implement the project it will be carefully reconsidered, for the collection and computerisation of 'incidental' and highly personal matters would be intolerable. In saying this, we fully understand the need of modern government for accurate, up-to-date information about social and economic activity. We are merely seeking adequate protections for existing civil liberties, both *de jure* and *de facto*. We may add that neither of the present writers are members of the 'Monday Club'!

The computer used by the Universities Admissions Clearing House has come in for some justifiable criticism from students, not because of its methods of allocation, but because it is also used to hold an 'Individualised Data System'. This euphemistic title – and with what scorn would Quiller-Couch have reacted to the adoption by academics of the linguistic perversion 'individualised'! – covers the multitude of school leavers, trainee teachers, and all school and further education teachers; the data bank will be extended to include the records of all students. It will prove extremely useful, no doubt, to the authors of Papers both White and Black, for reviewing the policies that underlie our educational system. Analyses of selected groupings, comparing personal histories right through from infant school into employment, will be a fascinating study. Anyone will be able to prove anything – according to the presumptions made by the computer programmers.

Speakers at the National Union of Students conference in November 1969 alleged that records are already falling into the wrong hands and being abused. They 'conceded the necessity to maintain factual records [but] raised the spectre of *1984* and the misuse of intimate personal or political details in the records by university and college authorities, especially in references for employers or after student disturbances'.[29] A year earlier, when the system was announced, an editorial comment had wisely noted that 'The records will include examination failure and the source of students' support; and there is something highly distasteful about the idea that a man's standing should be shaped by his antecedents'.[30] Indeed there is, and this is a fundamental criticism of all 'historical record' data banks. The basic, apparently objective, facts recorded will always be liable to varieties of interpretation. *Why* did a student fail his degree? Perhaps because some parental circumstance caused distress and then, being forced to work and support a widowed or separated mother he was unable to re-sit the exam. Will *that* be in the file? What explanatory, or justificatory, data will be? No wonder the NUS resolved 'that every record . . . should state when the information was acquired and the name and position of the person who gave it; and that no person outside the academic staff or any institution should have access to records without written permission from the student'.[31]

Any computer archival system can so easily provide a frame of reference for many years to came, so that time will inevitably distort whatever there may have been of 'objectivity' in the original collecting of the information. With manual methods this was never a danger, since the old files simply mouldered away – and in any case the original data was rarely updated by newly-occurring incidents. Modern researchers can find a few of those who in earlier years fitted a particular category: as recent 'follow-up' studies (for public entertainment, rather than serious sociological purpose) have traced the Whiz-Kid Battle of Britain pilots, and the post-war Teddy Boy phenomena. Some of the former are apparently still living on the strength of their wartime glory; some of the latter are still 'anti-social'; the majority of both have settled to conventional domesticity, standards, and mores, within their abilities and environments – and what they once were is virtually forgotten.

The researcher of tomorrow will have no problems in isolating his group for study. They will all be recorded and known. So, the student who today marches outside embassies and disrupts lectures and demonstrates for and against many causes will probably be a very different cast of person in fifteen years' time. It is dangerous for the future of society that we should stack up knowledge of people's present, for potential use when it has become their past. Every record is a potential threat to present privacy and future freedom; every item of alleged statistic is a weapon that may be turned against the individual.

There is an immensely valuable freedom in *not being known*. But everybody is known, everyone is on somebody's mailing list. Computers are also being used for mailing lists, as many recipients of unsolicited rubbish will have realized. *The Sunday Times* carried one of the first significant complaints, with the experience of musician Steve Race who, being a postal subscriber to a magazine, discovered that the distribution list was also being used for the despatch of advertising matter – and that even when he cancelled his subscription, the computer still refused to forget him.[32]

The columns of *The Times* were soon busy with this topic after a letter appeared alleging 'an intolerable invasion of privacy by the tyrannical computer'.[33] The complainant's eleven-year-old daughter had been sent some unsuitable advertising matter, and the firm responsible had maintained that the name could not be removed from their mailing list. Subsequent published correspondence[34] revealed that the example was far from unique, and that although any individual prepared to be persistent enough, belligerent enough, and even abusive enough, *could* succeed in halting a specific abuse of his name and address, there is no general remedy against the buying and selling of such information.

With the computer's aid, this process is becoming increasingly sophisticated. Although a list starts as nothing more than a name and address, it soon begins to accrue other background information on the person, correlated both from such responses as he makes to the material he receives, and also from any other source that can be found (e.g. other data banks). This harvesting of incidental data means that the 'aim' of any circulation campaign can be made much more selective; the amount of matter that you receive may begin to decline, but that which you do get is likely to prove most tempting – because it will be directed at your known income, habits, interests, and sympathies. This we consider to be a contradiction of the citizen's right of privacy.

Such computer mailing lists also have produced the 'inertia sale' – unsolicited books, magazines and even more ambitious hardware, which arrive on 'free trial', to be paid for if retained. These deliveries have been followed up by letters threatening to 'blacklist' the recipient as a debtor if payment was delayed. Such unsolicited goods may soon be dumped in the dustbin with impunity, leaving no redress for the originator.[35] But the basic problem of access to lists of identifiable persons remains, and the recourse to dumping such goods is a bother that could be avoided and tackled at the root. If something is not done soon, we will be inundated with advertising material and unwanted goods, particularly if we belong to the professions or the income-bracket the advertisers most eagerly pursue. There is a relentless pursuit of the recalcitrant re-subscriber; often twenty or thirty special offers are repeated, tempting and begging him to renew his annual order for an international news magazine, for instance.

Further pursuit ensues, applying pressure to buy later special book publications.

During 1968 only a very few consciences in the computer community were alert to the possible effects of the technology upon personal privacy,[36] and even after public comment and political concern in the UK to date, there remains only slender evidence that the computer users themselves, and their policy-makers, are alive to their responsibilities in this respect. The main inpact upon the general public has been from press commentators who (pardonably) love such headlines as 'Fighting Computer Tyranny'; from the National Council of Civil Liberties who (quite unjustly) are bracketed by many with the 'irresponsible and fanatic' pressure groups; and from a few politicians – in an age when there are few of these whom the public trusts and respects.

It is becoming clearer now that there are more people who *do* care – perhaps they will always be a minority, for when a Liverpool police van started making furtive video-tape recordings of bad drivers, eventually stopping the driver and playing back the tape to show his errors, 'only 5 per cent of those stopped found the technique objectionable.'[37] It would seem that most people do not realize how each small new process of surveillance adds to the power of officialdom, and subtracts from human personality.

The computer press, on the whole, has taken a responsible attitude, though in December 1969 one of the less notable trade publications, possibly reflecting the ostrich-like attitude of many in the profession, could say that 'only the odd megolomaniac may set up models of the voting population of every street in a district and work out how people will vote . . . unless (national data bank) information is allowed to fall into the hands of large scale sales organizations it is unlikely to be of much use to any individual'.[38] Such comment is blind to the models already set up, and apparently regardless of what organizations may do with information *contrary* to the interests of 'any individual'.

More typical is the *Computer Weekly*, already much quoted in these pages, from which comes the following sober report: 'The decision as to what goes into, and perhaps more importantly, what comes out of a data bank should be taken out of the hands of computer professionals, and regulated in some legislative manner.' This was the basic message of addresses by Charles Ross, a director of IDH and Professor John Anderson, of Kings College Hospital Medical School, to the Parliamentary Civil Liberties Group.

'The meeting provided an opportunity for two computer experts, who are both strong advocates for the protection of the citizen's right to privacy, to address a basically non-technical group of MPs on this vexed subject. Weight was added to the viewpoints they put forward in the subsequent discussion by Mr. Peter Wyatt, of SPL, and Dr. G. B. F. Niblett, of the UKAEA, both commitee members of the newly formed BCS Computer Privacy Specialist Group.

'It was not the purpose of the meeting to reach any conclusions; instead it aimed at providing an opportunity for dialogue. . . . The real problem of the meeting was in making clear the potential of the computer as opposed to manual methods of record keeping, and even more fundamentally in deciding whether the regulation of the use of computer records is a subject in itself or merely a facit [*sic*] of man's overall right to privacy.'[39]

The Parliamentary Civil Liberties Group sponsored and prepared the Data Surveillance Bill (see Appendix for text) which was introduced as a Private Member's Bill in the Commons by Mr Kenneth Baker, MP, on May 6, 1969, and in the Lords (in virtually identical terms) by Lord Windlesham on June 26, 1969. Mr Baker claimed that 'this is not a Luddite Measure which seeks to inhibit and prevent the use of computers. . . . I am not leading a campaign to restore the quill pen. My Bill seeks to establish a code of conduct, backed by legal sanctions, for computer operators operating these personal data banks. . . . When records are computerized in this way no specific decision has to be made as to whom information can be passed'.[40] He went on to point out that, in his view, 'Bureaucracy . . . is tolerated because it is relatively inefficient, but when it has the opportunity to become highly efficient we have to examine again the checks and balances that may be required,' and that 'there is increasing recognition of the need for some new protection of individual rights and protection against an over-zealous State intruding too much into individual people's privacy. In the changing conditions of contemporary society we need the right to be left alone.' The Bill had all-party support in the Commons, but failed on its second reading on June 13th.

The House of Lords returned to the subject on December 3, 1969. In the course of a 3½-hour debate, Lord Ritchie-Calder caused some laughter – though rather nervous laughter, one imagines – by mentioning that 'during the war, he had accidental access to his police dossier [and] read it with fascination, thinking: "What a sinister, exciting character this Calder must have been. I wish I had known him." '[41] He continued: 'One episode, the real circumstances of which I had practically forgotten because they were so unimportant, assumed the glamour and deviousness of a really exciting James

Bond. But *I did not recognize myself*, and could not have given completely simple explanations of incidents which had acquired suspicious significance.' [42]

As one Peer commented during the debate, it is unfortunate that not many of the public read *Hansard;* all who study the days' proceedings on December 3, 1969, must be impressed by the responsible tone of the debate, and the informed sense of urgency felt by all the contributors, 'to reconcile the more efficient handling of personal records by means of computers with individual freedom and privacy.' [43] Only the Lord Chancellor, presumably inhibited from demonstrating an excess of concern by his task of providing reassuring Governmental noises, failed to sound the call either for speedy study in depth leading to comprehensive legislation, or for brief enabling legislation to admit practical cases of intrusion and abuse into the Courts. For the rest, there was unanimity with Lord Byers, who emphasized 'that it is a political decision that is required. In a matter such as this Parliament cannot "pass the buck". There is a tendency for people to say: "Leave it to the programmers, to the manufacturers, to the people who handle these machines." This . . . is wrong and unfair. This is a political decision'.[44]

Fortunately, the President of the British Computer Society for the year was the Earl of Halsbury. His presence, and speech, during the debate augurs well for a useful dialogue between the profession and the Legislature. It was he who sounded the warning note that 'It is extremely important not to get starry-eyed about the security provided by the security system. These systems can be beaten . . . (they) are proliferating throughout the United States everywhere, and not one of them has not been beaten within six months by somebody clever enough to do it.' [45] In his view, the difference in *degree* of information-power represented by the computer (equated by another speaker to the thermo-nuclear device as against conventional bombs) compels society only to put on to computers those records which it is prepared to allow the individual affected to inspect; if data is secret, it must be kept by conventional methods. 'The administrator cannot have it both ways . . . we cannot mix the two.' [46]

This principle was welcomed by the Earl of Lauderdale, in whose view we are already not far from tyranny – 'not the tyranny of the old tyrant; it is the tyranny of the busybody society. . . . It is, in effect, the busybody society – not the efficient society – with its cloak of doing good and its pretence at bestowing compassion, with which we are dealing.' [47]

The consensus of informed opinion seems to agree that the benefits and economies for the administrator, and the advantage for the individual citizen, are sufficient and just causes to continue to apply electronic technology to record-keeping. There is, of course, nothing wrong with putting information into a computer. The problems are, as we have said, how it is manipulated, where it comes out again in readable form, how much of it comes out, and how it is used or abused for the manipulation of persons. And above and beyond all these is the problem that many of the intending beneficiaries are not yet taking account of the problems.

From within the Civil Service, J. H. Robertson has written with admiration of the vision before us – the 'large, integrated information systems for planning, *controlling* [our italics] and operating . . . recording . . . transmitting to a central record, for keeping this record up to date, for analysing it'.[48] He does not mention that there may be dangers for the populace inherent in such a system, and this omission is characteristic. It seems clear that we cannot rely upon senior management to see further than the end of its organizational nose, nor upon the computer profession to apply the maximum checks and safeguards without suitable direction (and authorization, to take account of the higher costs of protection). Thus, only legislation can satisfy the growing desire to find means of protecting the citizen from unreasonable infringements of his privacy.

The Parliamentary activity is encouraging, for the anxieties are manifold. They have been summarized most succinctly by an American commentator upon the National Data Centre controversy:

'1. The Centre will contain information that should not be in it.
2. The information can be improperly used by those . . . who have access to it.
3. The data "bank" will be subject to cracking,[49] so to speak, and data on individuals will be used to their detriment in any way from blackmail to gossip.
4. An enterprise of this sort is inherently expanding in nature, and no matter how modestly it begins, it will grow to include more and more, and eventually too much.
5. It both represents and encourages medling and paternalistic government, trying to do too much in controlling the lives of its citizens.
6. At a deeper level, it stands for the notion of an omniscient government, which is in some fundamental way inconsistent with our individualistic and democratic values.'[50]

One American professor, himself a computer expert, has called for a new Bill of Rights to deal with the situation, on the grounds that constitutional provision designed for an eighteenth century civilization may not be adequate to deal with the new state of information-processing technology.

In this country, a Draft Bill of Rights was introduced in the Commons on April 23, 1969. Moving the First Reading, Viscount Lambton, MP,[51] appreciated that he was being anachronistic – for it was the *previous* year that had been ostensibly 'supported' by the British Government as Human Rights Year. Yet during 1968 little had in fact happened, nationally or internationally, to promote human rights; indeed, much of the legislation passing through Westminster had precisely the opposite effect. All the provisions of the famous Bill of Rights of 1680 had been effectively eroded. As long ago as 1884 Herbert Spencer had written that: 'Regulations have been made in yearly growing numbers restraining the citizen in directions where his actions were previously unchecked and compelling actions which previously he might perform or not as he liked.' Much recent new law, and even more still of the anticipated legislation, would further curtail freedom; the all-powerful State was certainly approaching.

Viscount Lambton's Draft was modelled on a Canadian enactment of 1960, which obliged the Minister of Justice to examine all newly proposed legislation, to ensure that it was not in conflict with the provisions of the Bill of Rights. Despite the votes of 137 Members for the Bill, there were 161 who apparently agreed with Mr Alexander Lyon, MP, (himself a great sympathizer with the cause of individual rights and freedoms) that the Bill as Drafted would inhibit the right of Parliament to remain supreme and to change any law; and that the House of Commons is itself an adequate instrument for the preservation of liberty and justice in the nation.

We hope it is. Perhaps in this case, we should try for the adoption of a new legal principle. Dr G. B. S. Niblett, a barrister and senior scientist with the Atomic Energy Authority, has even originated a formula of *habeas scriptus*, which would state that 'every man has the right to know what has been recorded about him on any . . . electronic information files.'[52] This would be a considerable advance, and has been advocated by both the NCCL and the late Minister of Technology.[53]

We should at this point, like to delve a little deeper into what is at stake – that is, the nature of that area of social freedom covered by privacy. This will constitute the focus of our next chapter.

Notes

1. For a broad picture see Lord Robens, 'People and Computers', *Computer Bulletin*, April 1969, pp. 112–17.
2. *The Sunday Times*, March 2, 1969.
3. See Data Processing Supplement, *The Financial Times*, August 25, 1969.
4. *The Sunday Times*, March 2, 1969.
5. J. Jacob *op cit.* (N.C.C.L.), p. 6, imbedded quote from *Hansard.*
6. *Ibid.*, p. 7.
7. See 'The Information Industry' special Report, *The Times*, November 17, 1969.
8. *Local Government Chronicle*, December 7, 1968, p. 1939. Also on the new Land Registry data-bank, see *New Data*, July 21, 1970, p. 16,
9. See *The Times*, December 11, 1968; and *Computer Weekly*, December 19, 1968.
10. *The Times*, December 2, 1969.
11. *Ibid.*
12. *Computer Weekly*, February 6, 1969.
13. See *Daily Telegraph*, February 19, 1969.
14. *The Times*, December 1, 1969.
15. *Ibid.*
16. See *Computer Weekly*, December 4, 1969, p. 3.
17. Cited in J. Jacob, *op cit.*
18. *Computer Weekly*, February 19, 1970.
19. Cf. A Spokesman 'at Hendon . . . said "I cannot tell you anything. This comes under the Official Secrets Act"'. *Daily Telegraph*, December 18, 1969.
20. *The Sunday Times*, March 2, 1969.
21. *Daily Telegraph*, October 30, 1969.
22. H. W. R. Wade, *The Times*, August 7, 1968.
23. E.g. Michael S. Fogarty, *Issues of Privacy and Security in the Urban Information System* (N.W. Regional Educational Laboratory, Portland, Oregon; February 1969).
24. Stone, *Computer Weekly*, March 13, 1969.
25. Derrick K. Hearne, *Computer Bulletin*, February 1969.
26. See Peter Hall, *op cit.*, also Andrew Shonfield, *Modern Capitalism*, Oxford, O.U.P., 1965, pp. 385 ff., on this theme.
27. *The Economist*, September 6, 1969, p. 53.
28. *Daily Telegraph*, December 10, 1969. cf. Artemus Ward, 'The Census': 'Did you ever have the measels, and if so how many?'
29. *The Times*, October 24, 1969.
30. *Sunday Telegraph*, October 20, 1968.
31. *The Times*, *op. cit.*
32. *The Sunday Times*, June 9, 1968.
33. *The Times*, February 10, 1969.
34. See e.g. *The Times*, February 18, 1969 and February 21, 1969. *Los Angeles Times*, September 3, 1969. An article by Noel Greenwood shows how direct mail firms can send a magnetic tape to the California Department of Motor Vehicles, and receive it back with a copy of all registered drivers' names and addresses.
35. Under the provisions of the Inertia Selling Bill, introduced by Mr Arthur

Davidson, MP, which has Government support, and received its Second Reading on January 30, 1970.

36. Notable exceptions were John Hargreaves, Director of Public Relations for I.B.M. in the UK, Charles Ross, of I.D.H., and those members of the B.C.S. who responded to the invitation to form the Privacy Group. See also Stone, *Computer Privacy*, Anbar Monograph No. 13, 1968.
37. BBC TV News, December 2, 1969.
38. *Dataweek*, December 3, 1969.
39. Computer Weekly, May 1, 1969. See also *Data Processing* editorial page, November–December 1969.
40. *Hansard*, May 6, 1969, col. 286.
41. *The Times*, December 4, 1969.
42. *Hansard*, December 3, 1969, col. 126 (italics added).
43. *Ibid.*, col. 103.
44. Col. 116.
45. Col. 120, 121.
46. Col. 122.
47. Col. 153.
48. *H.M.S.O. Occasional Paper* No. 1, Centre for Administrative Studies, H.M. Treasury.
49. Adopting the same metaphor, *Business Week*, January 13, 1968, said: 'The professional criminal of the future will be a fully-fledged programmer . . . the Mafia will have gigantic recruiting problems. However, some penitentiaries have begun offering their inmates courses in programming. Crime's headhunters might seek their talent there.'
50. Carl Kaysen, *The Public Interest*, Spring 1967.
51. *Hansard*, April 23, 1969, col. 474.
52. *The Times*, August 6, 1968.
53. Anthony Wedgwood Benn, 'Maintaining Human Supremacy', *New Scientist*, August 7, 1969, pp. 274–6. See also articles by the present writers in the *New Scientist*, May 1, 1969, the *Guardian*, May 6, 1969, and the *Political Quarterly*, June 1969.

Chapter 7

PRIVACY, FREEDOM AND SOCIETY

British society has a tradition of freedom, and an international reputation for individual reserve and aloofness, even if it has no supporting doctrine of privacy. The tradition of freedom, in theory, allows almost anybody to do almost anything which does not violate the freedom or the privacy of somebody else. Yet our civilization, claiming to honour the freedom of the individual, is in practice heartily resistant to the *single* non-conformist and only allows free expression when it clearly represents a consensus.

Privacy, as a value, is hard to define, but we may begin by tracing its development briefly. In less civilized, more tribal societies than our own, no notion of a recognized right to privacy exists. The life of the individual is entirely bound up with the life of the community. So it has been for thousands of years. For most of history, privacy has simply not been possible, either at a man's place of living or of work. Everything was corporate. To be physically alone was out of the question, and the impossibility of physical isolation was matched by unacceptibility of mental isolation.[1]

Though we may have cause to lament the consequences of permitting free expression of personal opinion in modern times, we must recognize that privacy of neither belief nor opinion was respected until the last few centuries. In his moving play *A Man for All Seasons*, Robert Bolt gives these words to the doomed Sir Thomas More: 'What you have hunted me for is not my actions, but the thoughts of my heart. It is a long road you have opened. For first men will disclaim their hearts and presently they will have no hearts. God help the people whose statesmen walk your road.'

The classic works on the problem we are facing, on the nature of freedom and privacy, are the famous essay by John Stuart Mill, 'On Liberty', and the monolithic study by Professor Alan Westin already quoted. Mill wrote that:

'There is a limit to the legitimate interference of collective opinion with individual independence: and to find that limit, and maintain it against encroachment, is as indispensable to a good condition of human affairs, as protection against political despotism.'[2]

Westin, in verbal evidence to the Senate Sub-Committee, said: 'I think we need to recognize that the essence of privacy . . . is the right of the individual to control the information about himself that he chooses to share with others, how much he gives, when he gives it, and so on.'[3]

Many others would agree that a structure of privacy has grown up. It has been nourished by the industrial revolution, laying on mains services to individual homes, making absolute physical privacy possible in our isolated, separated dwelling-places; by political revolution, as the principles of democracy endue every individual, separately, with personal worth and significance; and by Judae-Christian influence which emphasizes in the major societies of the West the importance and dignity of every person as a unique creation. As a result society has come to assume that each citizen has a right to some degree of privacy, and the computer revolution could be allowed to destroy it, by the return to corporate ownership of personal information on a hitherto unimaginable scale.

Privacy, to many, means the right to be let alone. It can be contrasted with the state of the common soldier, who never knows when he may be caught by the eye of some NCO or officer for the performance of unpleasant fatigues, or guard duty, or some other interruption to the ordering of his own life. Give the administrator in government or business the use of an integrated national population file, with leave to browse through these for selected abstracts of persons in certain income areas, with certain health patterns, education, hobbies, family circumstances – any parameters he wishes – and you provide him with a powerful tool for interference in private lives, to manipulate, to sell more, to condition, to coerce.

Paradoxically, privacy also means the right to communicate, secure in the knowledge that what we say will not be used against us. We are each aware, in our introspective moments, that we are ambivalent beings possessing a gregarious instinct matched by the desire to retreat from the world. We need to communicate, and even while doing so to hold back. We need both to share and to withhold, but to share with whom *we* choose.

There are constant tensions in our environment, between the need for matters to be openly known, and the need of industry, government, and the individual for secrecy. But since this does not apply to more 'primitive' societies, privacy is demonstrably not a value to all mankind, nor of equal importance in all communities. The basic human instinct may, then, be recognized as gregariousness, rather than solitude; community, rather than privacy. But as all the social scientists of the 'civilized' world recognize, mutations in our physiological structure have been necessary adaptations to fit us to our developing social structure, so that each of us has not only a desire but an absolute *need* for a core of privacy into which no-one else is admitted. The recognition that this is so, and its corollary – that private personality forms a part of our morality – is a relatively recent phenomenon. The growth of a doctrine of private personality can be traced to the formal recognition of private property, around which grew a legal system concerning matters of trespass, theft, copyright – even squatters' rights. Such indeed has been the concentration upon the protection of property that injury to personality – except insofar as it is caused by defamation – has largely escaped legal constructs.

In practice, there has been little need to analyse the concept of private personality, for the assaults upon this privacy have been few. It is within our own lifetime that the agencies (sometimes suspect of being the *agents*) of news have reached more intrusively into private lives; that government, simultaneously regulating more and becoming more paternalistic, has vastly extended its scope and its interference with private affairs; that technology has given to the intrusive ample power for surveillance without physical trespass.

So it is only in very recent times that privacy has become a problem. When people begin to complain that their 'right to privacy' has been invaded, then that 'right' must be examined. When psychologists tell us that we all need to withhold certain things from certain people at certain times, we must look to the defensive mechanism. When the weight of public opinion swings to the view that some intrusions are intolerable, then the definition of privacy is a prerequisite to the essential legislation.

Privacy is an extremely slippery virtue – intangible, hard to define and harder still to measure. There is a danger, in hedging it with formal constraints, that the inhibitions will give more offence than their absence allows. A 'right to privacy' is not and cannot be some immutable statute. To different people it means different things at different times. It is closely allied with our sense of anonymity. We may commute for years – same train, same compartment, same fellow-travellers – and yet the man to whom we reveal our hopes, our opinions, our beliefs, our business and domestic joys and crises remains 'The chap who gets on at Dorking with *The Times* and a pipe; I don't know who he *is*'. And he does not know who we *are*, because we have never exchanged names, and thus the necessary communication and release of our private concerns is accomplished without violation of our privacy. *In our anonymity is our security.*

The close association of a name with a personality can, of course, be traced back into antiquity and is rooted in the tribal 'totem', although we do not give such formal expression to the bond as was, for example, characteristic of the ancient Hebrew. The student of the Old Testament knows that the word 'Jahweh', or 'Jehovah', is a transliteration of something never pronounced by the Jew because, being the *name* of God, it embodied all His most holy characteristics and was too sacred to be used. In Shakespeare's *Othello*, Iago would sooner lose his wealth than his 'good name' ('Who steals my purse, steals trash,' etc.); and Surtees' Jorrocks lived up to his own aphorism: 'Three things I never lends – my 'oss, my wife, and my name.' We will tolerate considerable intrusion, and even volunteer supererogatory circumstantial detail of our lives, if our anonymity is preserved.

The problem today is the intrusion by people who *do* know who we are, and a consensus may well be developing as to what right of privacy we can and should retain. This will not remain stable however. In any particular grouping at any time a definition of privacy may be attainable, but inevitably it will be a fluctuating value simply because of the opposing requirement of an organized society to know in order to plan.

John Stuart Mill, in his essay, held an essentially pessimistic view: 'the practical question, where to place the limit – how to make the fitting adjustment between individual independence and social control – is a subject on which nearly everything remains to be done. . . . Some rules of conduct, therefore, must be imposed, by law in the first place, and by opinion on many things which are not fit subjects for the operation of law. What these rules should be is the principal question in human affairs; but if we except a few of the most obvious cases, it is one of those in which least progress has been made in resolving'.

Not only is the nature of privacy itself intangible, but part of the defence against unwarranted intrusion upon privacy must lie with our definition of consent – another intangible.[4] Any probe into personal behaviour, habit, history, or opinion, might be justified by the researcher if the subject's 'consent' has been obtained. But such a justification begs vital questions: was the consent freely given? how was it given? was the subject conversant with all the implications when he gave it? who, in good law and ethics, is entitled to give consent? The continuing controversy over the transplant of organs from the recently-dead is a good case where 'consent' is a blurred area.

In some situations, we are right to imply that consent to personal scrutiny has been given. The candidate for public office, for example, and the latest pop record idol, must expect public discussion of their strengths, weaknesses, foibles and proclivities. Comparably, the person wanting a cash loan, or the parent seeking educational advice, is voluntarily and by implication offering himself and his affairs for scrutiny. What of the client who seeks psychological help, however? If consent is to be implied, he has given it. But was it *freely* given? A learned paper suggests not:

'Torture is an old and well-tried technique for extracting private information – and torture need not be physical. Mental anguish can be just as searing and difficult to endure. The prospect of release from suffering, therefore, is a powerful lever for access to the private area. Its uses for the manipulation of behaviour or the probing for knowledge are not unknown to sheriffs or prosecutors, to personnel directors, school teachers, and parents – indeed, to virtually anyone who has experienced authority. Conversely, its uses are very well known by the jobless, the hungry, the homeless, the ambitious and the young. The obvious cases of physical, mental, economic, or social duress are readily identifiable; but when does a subtle inducement such as the regard of your boss or even of your peers, or some inducement, not quite so subtle, such as an extra point added to your college grade in return for participation in psychological experiments – when do these become tantamount to duress? . . . It is all too apparent that the distinction between consent and concealed coercion may often be difficult to establish.'[5]

A similar danger was recognized in the bill, passed by the United States Senate in September 1967, which stated in part:

'It shall be unlawful for any officer of any executive department of any executive agencies of the United States government, or for any person acting or purporting to act under his authority, to do any of the following things:

(G) To inquire or request or to attempt to require or request, any employee of the United States serving in the department or agency, or any person seeking employment in the executive branch of the United States Government, to submit to any interrogation or examination or to take any psychological or polygraph test which is designed to elict from him information concerning his personal relationship with any person connected with him by blood or marriage, or concerning his religious beliefs or practices, or concerning attitude or conduct with respect to sexual matters.' This bill had been proposed by Senator Sam Ervin, Chairman of the Senate Subcommittee on Constitutional Rights (S1035), and was sent to the House Post Office and Civil Service Committee.[6]

Ruebhausen and Brim (quoted above), fully aware of the conflict between the value of privacy and the value of information, set out a seven-point code of ethics for the practitioners of Behavioural Research (whom, they note, cannot refuse to disclose intensely personal clinical data under subpoena, and whose clients are therefore subject to no statutory protection). The seven points are interesting for anyone who is concerned to restrict unjustified, unwarranted, and indeed unhealthy intrusion, and are therefore given here in full.

'*One:* There should be a recognition, and an affirmation, of the claim to private personality.

Two: There should be a positive commitment to respect private personality in the conduct of research.

Three: To the fullest extent possible, without prejudicing the validity of the research, the informed, and voluntary, consent of the respondents should be obtained.

Four: If consent is impossible, without invalidating the research, then before the research is undertaken, the responsible officials of the institutions financing, administering and sponsoring the research should be satisfied that the social good in the proposed research outweighs the social value of the claim to privacy under the specific conditions of the proposed invasion. These officials in turn are responsible, and must be responsive, to the views of the larger community in which science and research must work.

Five: The identification of the individual respondent should be divorced as fully and as effectively as possible from the data furnished. Anonymity of the respondent to a behavioural research study, so far as possible, should be sought actively in the design and execution of the study as a fundamental characteristic of good research.

Six: The research data should be safeguarded in every feasible and reasonable way, and the identification of individual respondents with any portion of the data should be destroyed as soon as possible, consistent with the research objectives.

Seven: The research data obtained for one purpose should not thereafter be used for another without the consent of the individual involved or a clear and responsible assessment that the public interest in the newly proposed use of the data transcends any inherent privacy transgression.'[7]

Admirable in intention though such a code may be, its full application would frequently invalidate the valuable work of the social scientist.[8] Whilst the Gallup interviewer may preserve your anonymity, in other, longer-term, projects it is vital that the original respondents are followed up at intervals for additional information. The capacity to update data over time is fundamental to the detection of changing attitudes, for example. So such research implies that the records are identified, and there you have a dossier which says when you were interviewed, what your responses were – you were once suspiciously sympathetic to the Black Power movement perhaps, and now you think nurses are right to go on strike.

The American Supreme Court Justice Brandeis described privacy as 'the right to be alone – the most comprehensive of rights, and the right most valued by civilized men' – an excellent definition and coda.[9] But it was the sublime Greta Garbo who distilled the idea to a subjective, even existential meaning, by her famous sigh, 'I want to be alone!'[10]

Others have echoed the cry. 'To be left alone' is an inalienable right of privacy according to Judge Cooley (see *Torts*, 2nd ed., 1888). It should have, as we have seen, a positive and negative aspect, and refer to a variety of circumstances – to choose to mix or not to mix. It is the right to be left alone, *but also the state we would like to be in.*[11]

The law does not give us a right of privacy, either in Britain, or in most states of the US.[12] It is ensured *only* in relation to the legal protection of our reputations or properties. One cannot sue for the 'emotional pain brought about by the invasion of one's privacy.'[13]

We do not have an absolute of privacy; we cannot commit murder in conditions of privacy, and use that as a justification for keeping the police from investigating the crime. But unless we are hurting others, that is, our actions are 'self-regarding', we can argue that the law should keep its nose out of the matter. Sexual behaviour is an area where the liberal claims the right of privacy, even if the majority disapprove. Today sexual relations between adults of each, or both sexes, are not interfered with by the law if they involve the *consent* of the participants, and exclude minors, but such a concession is of relatively recent date.

How far is privacy a human right? Article 12 of the *Universal Declaration of Human Rights*, and Article 17 of the *United Nations Covenant on Civil and Political Rights*, provide that 'no one shall be subjected to arbitrary interference with his privacy, family, home or correspondence, nor to attacks upon his honour and reputation', and that 'everyone has the right to the protection of the law against such interference or attacks'. Article 8 of the *European Convention for the Protection of Human Rights and Fundamental Freedoms*, provides that 'everyone has the right to respect for his private and family life, his home and his correspondence'.[14]

In 1967, a conference of international jurists defined the individual's right of privacy as protection against: interference with his private, family, and home life; interference with his physical or mental integrity or his moral or intellectual freedom; attacks on his honour and reputation; being placed in a false light; the disclosure of irrelevant, embarrassing facts relating to his private life; the use of his name, identity, or likeness; spying, prying, watching or besetting; interference with his correspondence; misuse of his private correspondence, written or oral; disclosure of information given or received by him in circumstances of professional confidence.[15]

The individual was to be protected in the following matters: search of the person; entry on and search of premises or other property; medical examinations, psychological and physical tests; untrue or irrelevant embarrassing statements about a person; interception of correspondence; wire or telephone tapping; use of electronic surveillance or other 'bugging' devices; recording, photographing, or filming; importuning by the press, or by agents of other mass media; public disclosure of private facts; disclosure of information given to, or received from, professional advisers, or public authorities bound to observe secrecy; and finally, harassing a person (e.g. watching and besetting him or subjecting him to nuisance calls on the telephone).[16]

Further to our attempts at defining privacy, we might say that it permits one to choose the people, or at least the organization, to whom one reveals anything about oneself. The statutory right of Government already enables it to insist on a wide miscellany of information, and where it does we should be assured that this will not, *under any circumstances* (i.e. without the reservations of Giro, Ch. 1), be revealed to another government agency or outside body. When we surrender information in a way which is effectively voluntary, such as mortgage or insurance or job applications, we ought similarly to expect, as of right, that this fragment of ourselves will be treated with honour and respect.

It is worth noting, in this context, that the forms we fill in are being accepted, even now, by people whom we do not specifically authorize as known individuals to share the history of our life. We place our trust in them as anonymous servants of the company, or of government, and we expect them to treat us equally anonymously. The Fulton Committee on the Civil Service seemed to suggest that a greater degree of humanity, or personal recognition, was a desirable thing.[17] We believe that the reverse can equally be considered true. It is *right* that we should be treated according to the law, according to the rules, on the basis only of the information we disclose. We should *not* be dealt with according to our temperament, and the reaction to it of the clerk. We should be treated impartially, not in a way which implies that something more is known about us than we have revealed.

If we want to write extremely rude letters about the treatment we receive we should be able to do so without any consideration for the feelings of the recipient. To this extent it is *right* to blame 'the bank' and not 'Mr So-and-so at the bank'. In the same way, Mr So-and-so, we are entitled to believe, does not refuse us an overdraft because he lives across the road and is conscious of our extravagance on a new car; he does it on the official information he has on the state of our finances. Impersonal treatment is a safeguard of our liberty.

Privacy permits one to hide one's past, so as not to affect the present or the future. If you have a bad educational record (a 'late developer' naturally!), or violate the law in any way however trivial, or suffer ill-health, or are a little slow in settling your accounts, the facts should be sufficiently private not to affect your employment, your insurance, or your credit-worthiness. These things, having been forgiven, should be forgotten with the passage of time. The impassive, unremitting memory of the computer will prevent society from ever forgetting, unless deliberate steps are taken to erase the derogatory items from the record. They will not be lost by accident and will always be recoverable by the enquirer into your history. The motivation for such enquiry may well have been increased by the thought (supported by some researchers)[18] that the objector on the grounds of privacy may have a good reason for hiding his past. Or it may be felt that lack of 'openness' is a literally unhealthy sign.[19] Although theology teaches that sin may be forgiven without necessarily being forgotten, sociology remains unforgiving for as long as it remembers. Until those misdemeanours and failings are eradicated from the records, the wayward past remains discoverable, and is always likely to affect adversely present relationships and future opportunities.

It has been suggested by Harry Kalven[20] that there are three changes in national culture already visible, apart from the computer's mine of information, that may bring as by-products further dramatic changes in our notions of privacy. These he lists as:

The decline of the family,
The decline of religion,
The decline in the habit of reading.

He argues that with the tendency, noted above, for each home to be an isolated, enclosed unit, so the family has been a citadel of privacy; it has provided an informal institution within which many essentially private things were fully shared, but kept discreetly away from outsiders. The family circle, he says, 'set a boundary point beyond which things were no one else's business. Family-centred life was deeply supportive of the values of privacy; as it declines in importance, there may be a concomitant loss in our appreciation of privacy as a value'.

The decline in the habit of religion, with its characteristic activities of worship and prayer and silence, may mean that man, no longer ever 'alone with his God' has lost the only real chance he ever has to be alone for peaceful and private contemplation of himself and his contemporaries. The application of a religious faith to his life may well drive a man out to participate in great public affairs, but the impetus comes from 'his private moments with his God'. An absence of faith to many is the absence of the most private thing of all.

And similarly, with the decline in reading – which may in fact have passed its nadir and be renascent – men lost the intellectual privacy afforded by deeply immersing themselves in a book, the world shut out for a space.

Kalven wrote: 'We might see the development of new institutions designed to insure some private moments in otherwise unprivate lives. . . . Possibly some analogue to the religious retreat might be developed. . . . It may be a final ironic commentary on how bad things have become when someone will make a fortune merely by providing, on a monthly, weekly, daily, or even hourly basis, a room of one's own.'[21]

Not a bad prediction, perhaps, made in the early part of 1967, for the craze for 'meditation' that ensued in subsequent years!

According to Jacob, four aspects of privacy must be stressed:

(1) *Solitude* where the individual is left with the 'familiar dialogue with the mind or conscience'.

(2) *Intimacy* where the typical units are the family, friendship circle or work group. 'Without intimacy a basic need of human contact would not be met'.

(3) *Anonymity* where the individual is comforted by being able to get lost in a crowd. 'He does not expect to be personally identified and held to the full rules of behaviour and role that would operate if he were known to those observing him'.

(4) *Reserve* 'is the creation of a psychological barrier against

unwanted intrusion'. It is the human counterpart of the social distance phenomena that prevails throughout the animal world.

It is said that 'the enjoyment of these four aspects, together with the equal enjoyment of the right to surrender each of them, make up to a large extent our conception of liberty'.[22]

It has been argued that privacy and liberty do not *necessarily* go together, that the former is neither a necessary, nor a sufficient, condition of the latter. Few would deny that there is a correlation, however. We would argue that any reasonable definition of civil liberty must necessarily include an adequate guarantee of privacy, and in this context privacy can be said to impinge most seriously upon the *negative* aspect of freedom. We refer here to the dichotomy expounded by such writers as Cranston and Berlin.[23] They posit that freedom has been seen on one hand as a faculty that society has to achieve – i.e. *positive* freedom (implying one rational solution, often tyrannically imposed); and, on the other hand, 'the absence of constraint' – *negative* freedom. 'Constraint' is of course allied with the concept of 'consent' referred to earlier, and these abstractions we are considering can never be other than relative. We would argue that interference with privacy is a specific constraint upon liberty. As soon as one's angle of vision is narrowed, and the abstractions made concrete in any specific area of the invasion of privacy – electronic surveillance by telephone tapping, for example – it becomes clearer that a constraint is imposed upon freedom.

In Britain and the United States privacy has been achieved and it is in danger of invasion. As we are defending what we have been reasonably enjoying, we are fighting off 'constraint', and thus the question is, in our view, one of negative freedom. Thus we would like to see a *right* of privacy established, to safeguard what is *de facto* assumed to be part of the political culture.

Privacy and democracy are interlinked.[24] It is one of four major criteria for a functioning liberal democratic society. First, privacy must be secure, that is 'a protected area of life free from political intervention'. Second, equity must be ensured – 'a well-defined sense of equity shared by the public and regularized political procedures existing for periodically revising the definition of equity'. Third, we must have a precondition that coercion will be limited, and hence constitutional. Fourth, we must have public sovereignty, with universal suffrage and periodic elections.[25]

The connection is probably more fundamental. In order for the individual truly to exist, privacy must be guaranteed. Privacy is a boundary, if you like. Without our notion of the individual, there can be no meaningful liberal democracy. Even if we have a notion of democracy which goes beyond formal liberties – based, say, on the theories of the young Marx – we cannot understand the self from which man has been 'alienated' by modern society, unless we define that ego with such limits as privacy rights. This is part of the heritage of western man, although it need not necessarily be true of group-based cultures, such as the Chinese. A western Marxist would understand the need for privacy in his utopia, whereas a Maoist Chinese would not bother. Minimal privacy has been respected in most experiments, like *kibbutzim*, although in this instance, because all develop in a shared setting, human intimacy can be eroded. One view is that *kibbutzim* tend to destroy the inner life. Bettelheim points out that inner experience is regarded as something of a betrayal, a waste of time, or possibly an evasion of the common goal.[26] It is difficult to be categorical on this point, even from a socialist position.

To many, despite Kalven's view cited earlier, family life may even stifle self-development because of the *lack* of privacy, particularly in conditions of bad housing and the attendant over-crowding. To have 'a room of one's own' is to many a necessary condition of a clearly defined free existence – because without this retreat into physical privacy we are shackled by the demands upon our attention and our sympathies that are inevitable whilst we mingle with our fellow-creatures.

We would not like to over-state the argument that human beings become nastier as they are overcrowded in cities. Much of the recent discussion taking analogies from 'social systems' in the animal world is of debatable relevance.[27] But there is some truth in the point such studies make, however, and we cannot dismiss the small-group experiments made with human beings, examining the effect of the deprivation of 'normal' environmental conditions. As we are increasingly starved of physical, psychological, political and social space, we suffer and diminish as human beings, in the opinion of the present writers.

No doubt human beings can adapt, over time, to a changing environment; we have a decided cortex-advantage over animals, and can learn much better than they. We are markedly different, as Arthur Koestler has pointed out.[28] There is also an enormous range of social responses to environmental conditions, as illustrated by the wide range of societies mankind has developed. Some protected privacy, many did not. Yet the relationship between 'man' and special Western, modern, social circumstances is unique. To interfere with this exceptional blend of personality and society would, in our view, be foolish.

Today, we find that there is some ambiguity in the youth sub-cultures which are group-based, where privacy is less emphasized. Indeed some regard this type of phenomenon as ominous, and point to the adaptation of modern man to the scarcity of space in cities before the century is out, as the population increases. We would argue that it is probably *because* of such pressures that we must take up an active campaign to safeguard privacy rights. But if people, like some of the young, do not seem to bother, why worry? If the *majority* did not bother, would it be justified, on the basis of the criteria of democracy outlined above, to campaign actively for preservation of one of the conditions? Here we must make a distinction between that privacy involving interference by authority, and that in which people are less inhibited about some aspects of their personal life. There is obviously some point where the two interact, but we would argue that there is a core-meaning to privacy, and that if one allowed one's notion of private space to be slowly eroded, then eventually this would lead to incursion by public authority. We appreciate the degree to which the youth sub-culture is antinominian, but point out the implications of their group-bases: some political youth-based groups have not been outstanding for their tolerance of opponents' views, and reject the ideas of liberal democracy. Is it far-fetched to suggest that their attitude with regard to private space is closely related to their hostility to traditional notions of democracy?

John Stuart Mill argued that liberty and space were closely related. As he put it: 'howsoever we may succeed in making for ourselves more space within the limits set by the constitution of things, we know that there must be limits. . . . There are ultimate laws which we did not make, which we cannot alter, and to which we can only conform'.[29]

Yet, liberty depended on making sure we safeguarded the amount of the *spatial* dimension we had won, or might increase. Although Mill was referring to physical space, he did not distinguish it from psychological space. He insisted that 'It is not good for man to be kept perforce at all times in the presence of his species. A world from which solitude is extirpated is a very poor ideal. . . .'[30]

Edward Shils suggests that invasions of privacy are bad because they interfere with the individual in his control of what rightly belongs to him. 'The "social space" around an individual, the recollection of his past, his conversation, his body and his image, all *belong* to him. He does not acquire them through purchase or inheritance. . . . They belong to him by virtue of his humanity and civility – his membership in the human species and his membership in his own society. A society which claims to be both humane and civil is committed to their respect. When its practice departs from that respect for what belongs to the private sphere, it also departs to that degree from humanity and civility.'[31] This statement by a distinguished contemporary social scientist sums up the role of the 'space' concept in the liberal tradition.

The theme of scarcity and conflict is of course not new, and Locke, and Bentham had pointed out the tension before Mill, and long before recent 'pop' zoologists. Bentham, for example, saw in all history 'a universal scramble'. But the liberal notion of the State arose to deal with the psychological anxiety rather than physical acquisitiveness.[32] Men were anxious about the contention for what they had achieved. Later, rights were extended to those with little or no property – the Englishman's home became 'his castle' – unless he was a squatter! Privacy rights were *de facto* broadly distributed. The conflict between scarcity and liberty still continues. The State tries to assuage the former with technological means (more efficient government via computers, etc.), but in so doing threatens the previously prescribed limits to the violation of political space. Scarcity *on a world scale* is the major problem of our time, and is probably getting worse as the rich nations get richer and the poor poorer. The conflict between scarcity and freedom, in the global context, is destined to present the challenge of the next decades. The pressures affecting privacy as we enjoy it are not just intra-mural.

Practices relating to privacy differ from country to country.[33] Whereas the US has never had a population register, Sweden has a number of them, including tax and general population information files, which are open to inspection by the public. British Ministries on principle protect confidentiality – for example, with data collected by the Inland Revenue. Quite often, there are special safeguards with respect to aggregation of statistics of firms, so that a figure for less than five firms combined will not be available, and we are not able to have even these if one firm has the bulk of the market. Individual returns may be handled by statisticians within Ministries, but not by Ministers or senior civil servants. Britain had its national register during the war, but gave it up soon afterwards. There is a national resistance to asking too many questions. Some are sanguine about the prospects for the future, like Peter Hall,[34] who advocates the Swedish formula; another view strives for a balance: 'Unfortunately general education on the subject of storing information about citizens lags well behind the technical advances. Somehow or other a right balance must be struck between the preservation of a sensible degree of privacy and the provision of information which could help to improve many aspects of planning, and, therefore, standards of living.'[35]

Hardly anything in our lives remains *totally* unknown to others. To discuss privacy reasonably therefore requires recognition that we are not talking about *total nondisclosure* but *selective disclosure*. The concern is with unauthorized access to private data, and misuse of authorized data. Commenting on the theory of 'implied consent' to publication, one paper says: 'Certainly, public figures, particularly those who appeal to the public for elective office, have implicitly consented to a yielding up of some area of private personality. The comings and goings of a Mayor or Governor, or Hollywood starlet, and a public evaluation and discussion of their strengths and weaknesses in their public roles are proper subjects of news reports, analysis and research.'[36]

No doubt there are limitations to what can be taken as 'implied consent' on the part of the famous, at least in this country. But what can be understood as implied consent on the part of the average citizen? This is a very important, and fundamental political question. Given the tendency of the State to grow in power, and for private as well as public bureaucracies increasingly to interfere with our lives, the time has surely come for limits to be defined. We are required to disclose so much these days, that there is correspondingly much more opportunity for abuse by those seeking unauthorized access. The data-revolution is a political disaster. One would think that university departments would give the matter some consideration, and return to the study of public policy and law as opposed to the present behavioural exercises on which many spend their time; although we are not totally critical of some research of this kind being carried out, we do not think the broader questions should be neglected. Scientists and technologists are equally to be blamed when, having invented the machines that facilitate the collection, storage, and retrieval of the data, they accept no further responsibility.

As a Fellow of the Royal Society recently observed: 'At present we achieve some privacy because Big Brother has trouble scanning all his files at once. But, to the distress of the National Council for Civil Liberties and some computer engineers, there is a risk that computers may now make the bureaucrat's dream a reality and supply a complete dossier at the flick of a switch. There are such obvious medical advantages in this that it is likely to come about unless the public shows unusual vigilance.

'Throughout history there has been a risk that technology, while pursuing one good objective, may do unpremeditated harm in another direction. The hazard is enhanced as technology becomes more powerful. Every innovation must therefore be watched closely so that it can be checked before the harm outweighs the good. But who is to do the watching? . . . Technology will not be controlled until more people take the trouble to master the facts and assess the arguments put forward by unofficial scientists. The interests of the public, the bureaucrats and the businessmen all deserve attention, but they are not always identical.'[37]

Some of the 'norms' of privacy and freedom, whilst respected as for the majority good, are expected to be infringed. Such offences as cheating on expense accounts, violating traffic laws, smoking in prohibited places, are regarded by some as almost 'normal', and at a lesser level – but an important one – a man can do alone things which etiquette forbids in public: he can put his feet up on his desk, and scratch himself where it itches.[38] We also respect, for example, much organizational privacy (business secrets), or the secrecy of ritual in societies such as the Masons. But the 'public face' (or public myth) and the organizational reality may be very different. One recalls the remark of Gandhi: 'We would all be Christians if it were not for the Christians.' The public does not see things as they are – neither the fundamental rationale nor the way of working. There is, on the one hand, the *Organizational Ideal*, where all decisions are rational, discussion fair and free, and representation by leaders loyal to supporters. But there is also the *Organizational Fact*; decisions are often irrational, discussions mingle the harsh with the comic, and personal motivations predominate.

Even the existence of such unpleasant facts does not support an argument for making public all of the decision-making meetings which now take place in private. It is plain that a jury must reach its decision with no intervention, and we would contend (despite the pressures from some quarters) that the Committees in which national security policies are discussed are also right to retain their privacy. There must be places where men can argue *to*, rather than *through*, each other; where they can be honest, unconstrained by the need to adopt a posture for the benefit of Press or public. This is especially important if it is appreciated that men are most averse to retracting some earlier statement, or to being persuaded to depart from some earlier position, when many eyes are watching.

Surveillance in such contexts, then, can be regarded as inhibiting freedom, and liable to distort resultant action.

The same is true of surveillance of the individual. While in some relationships (as in some organizations), some surveillance can be justified as either wholly beneficial or even essential, it never loses its inhibiting and consequential quality. The watch kept by a parent over a child, or by a supervisor over an employee, must certainly be maintained – but *it must not be total.* Even if the child misbehaves when not watched; even if the employee slacks when not watched; they must not be constantly watched, because constant surveillance impacts upon free personality. It does this in three distinguishable ways: First, the very knowledge that one *is* being observed is itself restricting, and ultimately psychologically destructive – as Orwell showed so well. Secondly, the observation of behaviour cannot be objective. The subjective opinion of the observer colours the 'facts', and the result of the surveillance is thus inevitably a distortion. Thirdly, if modern film and sound recording techniques are employed in the surveillance, even more distortion is liable to occur. Primitive man, faced with explorers' cameras, turned away for fear that 'a part of him' was being taken, and might be used to harm him in the future. With the advent of 'data surveillance' – Westin's phrase for the all-pervasive data bank – this primitive concept becomes too close to truth for our comfort.

One of the most-emphasized aspects of an experiment which set out to give workers better working conditions, to discover whether their output went up (the Hawthorne experiment),[39] was the fact that no-one was looking over the workers' shoulders. With less surveillance, the workers felt freer and more fulfilled in their work. Since part of the resentment about industrialism (and factory production, in particular) is blamed upon its dehumanizing tendencies, it is arguable that surveillance is a significant element in the process of 'alienation'. The feeling of being constantly watched, even if it is partly illusory, breeds resentment.

In a free society, the less surveillance the better. The idea of individual responsibility involves the minimum of surveillance, although paternalists might not agree. Today, innovations in the technology of surveillance turn the whole world into a nursery, and citizens find their conversation 'bugged' as electronic ears pick up their noises, just as a baby-sitting device monitors the sleeping infant.[40]

As the then vice-president of the United States, Hubert H. Humphrey, put it in 1967: 'We act differently if we believe we are being observed. If we can never be sure whether or not we are being watched and listened to, our actions will be altered and our very character will change.'[41] An unpleasant catalogue of the ways in which we *are* being 'watched and listened to', if we are in America, was published in 1964.[42] All that has changed since then is the technical skill (*a*) in producing counter-measures to defeat intrusion, and (*b*) producing new devices to beat the counter-measures. That the devices have spread was illustrated during 1968 by a BBC television programme in the 'Europa' series, showing how the craze for 'bugging' has reached Italy.

It is the relative sophistication of our society which has brought a demand – and we hope to have shown, a *necessity* – for each of us to have some area of privacy into which no-one intrudes. In older, more primitive societies, life is the life of the community. Mrs Dorothy Lee, a cultural anthropologist, in her book *Freedom and Culture*,[43] based on her research amongst the Tikopia observes that: 'They find it good to sleep side by side crowding each other, next to other children or their parents or their brothers and sisters, mixing sexes and generations. . . . Work among the Tikopia is also socially conceived and structured; and if a man has to work alone, he will probably try to take a child along. In our culture the private office is a mark of status, an ideal; and a man has really arrived when he can even have a receptionist to guard him from any social intrusion without his private consent.'

It is technical developments of new designs for living, and the political developments which stressed the worth of the individual as a being of some dignity – with the wisdom to use his vote intelligently – which have elevated the concept of private personality to the status it now has. Especially in Britain, perhaps, do we not have the notion of each man's home his castle, each man's newspaper his bastion against conversation? And yet we have to note a growing tendency amongst the more-reported events, for people to act and react more violently, less considerately, with blatant lack of regard for the disturbance caused to others.

But privacy is, whilst essential for sanity in the way of life we have developed, still classifiable as an 'essential luxury', like warmth and clothing. In the view of some, like those thinkers contributing to the projects concerned with developments in society as we move towards the year 2000, privacy is something which will become increasingly scarce in the coming decades. In *Daedalus*,[44] Stephen Graubard wrote that of the two things that have most changed our lives between 1930 and 1965, one 'was the great expansion of the Federal Government and federal power. The extent to which the state now concerns itself with and is an agency for change would have been inconceivable in 1930.' In other words, privacy has already been whittled away. And Martin Shubik added that 'If we wish to preserve even modified democratic values in a multi-billion-person society, then the computer, mass data processing, and communications are absolute necessities. It must be stressed again that they are necessary, but not sufficient . . . [they] provide the refinement – the means to treat individuals as individuals rather than as parts of a large aggregate [but this] will not be an unmixed blessing. Problems concerning the protection of privacy will be large. . . . A computer check of central files could supply the individual with an extensive dossier whenever he needed it [and] supply the dossier to others unless appropriate checks on availability are established.'[45]

Another writer, George A. Miller, in the same publication, mentioned 'the temptation for a government to keep complete dossiers on all its citizens, and *particularly those who are intellectually most active*' as quite real. 'It will be necessary to develop and instil a code of professional ethics among the scientists who use such data, and in some cases legislative safeguards may be required to protect the individuals from the invasion of his privacy that such technology will make possible.'

Our society is increasingly a legislating society. A continuing dilemma of Government is the reconciliation of demands for more controls to benefit the community – road safety, consumer protection – and thus inevitably more government servants to implement the controls, against demands for reductions, or freezes at least, in Government expenditure at all levels. To a large degree, to one observer, increasing legislation is destroying many personal freedoms, and this in itself is a breeding ground for increased civil nuisance, for demonstration and riot.[46] We are in a tight circle (which may well prove to be a spiral) of encroaching legislation breeding a lack of restraint which, in turn, breeds demands for new legislation. *The permissive society is in many ways paradoxically becoming a more restrictive society*, and against this tendency runs a tide of resentment, or lack of concern for other people's rights.[47]

Thus, if most of us become oblivious to the comfort, dignity, liberty, and unwritten rights of others, we shall find inevitably that those we cherished for ourselves have disappeared, together with our freedom.

Notes

1. For the psychologists' interpretations of privacy, see Charles Fried, 'Privacy', *Yale Law Journal*, Vol. 77, 3; January 1968; p. 475p ff. Also Raymond A. Katzell, 'Psychological Investigation and the Right to Privacy', *Virginia Law Weekly*, Vol. 17, 4; October 15, 1964.
2. 'On Liberty', John Stuart Mill.
3. *Hearings*, D, p. 292. See also Erving Goffman, *The Presentation of Self in Everyday Life*, New York, Doubleday, 1959.
4. See also R. M. Guion, 'Personnel Selection'. *Annual Review of Psychology*, 1967, 18, 191–216.
5. *Hearings*, C, p. 214 (Ruebhausen and Brim).
6. See also Amrine, M., 'The 1965 Congressional Inquiry into Testing: A Commentary', *American Psychologist*, 1965, 20, 859–70.
7. *Ibid.*, p. 221. See also Gideon Sjoberg (ed.), *Ethics, Politics and Social Research*, London, Routledge & Kegan Paul, 1969. This collection contains a number of essays on relevant ethical considerations involved in social research, and the right to privacy. The latter may of course clash with that of free speech – 'a value more obviously supportive of social science' according to Richard Colvard (p. 341).
8. But see V. Lovell, 'The Human Use of Personality Tests: A Dissenting View', *American Psychologist*, 1967, 22, 383–93, where similar limitations are accepted.
9. See Brandeis and Warren, 1890.
10. Actually this often took the form of 'I want to be *left* alone', both in her movies and in press interviews.
11. See Donald Madgwick, *op. cit.*, N.C.C.L., pp. 3–4.
12. For a comprehensive review of American Court cases dealing with a 'right to privacy', see William L. Prosser, 'Privacy', *California Law Review*, Vol. 48, 3, August 1960.
13. Donald Madgwick, *op. cit.*, N.C.C.L., p. 6.
14. Cited in Madgwick, *op. cit.*, N.C.C.L., p. 2.
15. *Ibid.*
16. *Ibid.*, pp. 2–3.
17. See *The Times*, August 5, 1968.
18. See M. J. Rosenberg, 'Cognitive Structure and Attitudinal Affect', *J. Abnorm. Soc. Psychol.*, 1956, 53, pp. 367–72 and Bennett, C. B., 'What Price Privacy?' *American Psychologist*, 1967, 22, pp. 371–6.
19. S. Jourard, 'Healthy Personality and Self-disclosure', *Mental Hygiene*, 1958, 56, pp. 91–8.
20. *Daedalus*, *op. cit.*, p. 879.
21. *Ibid.*, p. 881.
22. See J. Jacob *op. cit.*, p. 2, quoting Westin *op. cit.*
23. See summary and critique in R. B. Berki, 'Political Freedom and Hegelian Metaphysics', *Political Studies*, XVI, October 1968, No. 3, pp. 365 ff.
24. See David Apter, *The Politics of Modernization*, Chicago: Chicago University Press, 1965, pp. 450 ff.
25. *Ibid.*
26. Bruno Bettelheim, *The Children of the Dream*, London, Thames & Hudson, 1969. The author did not spend very long in the Kibbutz in question, so his conclusions may not necessarily be valid for the whole system.

27. We refer to the writings of Lorenz, Ardrey, Morris and others.
28. See *Observer*, September 28, 1969.
29. See Sheldon S. Wolin, *op. cit.*, p. 318; see also Edward Shils, *Privacy and Power* in *Hearings*, C, pp. 231 ff. on the idea of social space.
30. See Wolin, *op. cit.*, p. 323.
31. Shils, *op. cit.*, p. 242.
32. See Wolin, *op. cit.*, p. 324.
33. See 'Big Brother's Stick', *The Economist*, September 6, 1969, p. 53.
34. Hall, *op. cit.*
35. *Ibid.*
36. *Hearings*, C, p. 177 (Reubhausen and Brim).
37. N. W. Pirie, 'Gardyloo', *The Listener*, September 11, 1969.
38. See Westin, *Privacy and Freedom*, *op. cit.*, p. 35.
39. See Paul Blumberg, *Industrial Democracy: the Sociology of Participation*, London, Constable 1968, especially Chapters 2 and 3, on the forgotten lessons of the Mayo experiment.
40. See also Edward Shils, *op. cit.*, p. 242, for the arguments on the right of the employer to indulge in television surveillance of his employees.
41. Foreword to Senator Edward V. Long, *The Intruders: The Invasion of Privacy by Government and Industry*, New York, Praeger, 1967, p. viii.
42. Myron Brenton, *The Privacy Invaders*, New York, Coward-McCann, 1964.
43. Published New York, 1959.
44. *Op. cit.*
45. *Op. cit.*
46. See Lord Goodman, 'The Decay of Liberty', *The Spectator*, May 12, 1968.
47. See for example recent letters in *The Times* on the subject of morality and censorship, prompted by the review 'Oh Calcutta!', especially the curious reasoning of Archbishop Fisher of Lambeth—the alleged violation of privacy involved; letter of August 12th, 1970.

Chapter 8

PRIVACY THREATENED

We have attempted to show, in analysing some aspects of privacy, how closely associated it is with modern concepts of freedom and democracy, and also how vital it is for the flourishing of individual personality. What we still possess of privacy must not be destroyed. We turn now to observe some of the threats to our privacy, and particularly those which are the corollary of computer information systems.

Before doing so, we must reiterate that we are not necessarily seeking for new *positive* freedoms which must be hard-won, but are instead making a plea for positive action against further erosion of our existing liberties and protesting against the indifference of those who, by doing nothing, allow the threats to build up. It is no part of our argument that the individual requires a cocoon of absolute isolation; that would be the death of society just as certainly as would absolute transparency. It would also ruin democracy – though perhaps that is already receiving a mortal blow from mass withdrawal. Whilst 'participation' is a new warcry of the socially alert, apathy and self-concern are more predominant than ever. One commentator has called this a 'vicious state of selfishness', and points to the sheer size of everything as largely responsible: Everything is now so large – cities, government departments, businesses, the population itself – that individuals can no longer identify with the community. In an island crammed with 50 million people, every man has become an island on his own.'[1] If a majority feel that 'nothing that *I* do makes much difference' and at the same time that 'it is a question of every man for himself – a question of me against them, "them" consisting principally of business organizations and the Government',[2] then democratic 'participation' has already become a mockery. And if the ancient truth that 'no man is an island' is increasingly denied, there may be an insurgent demand for greater positive privacy, far beyond the scope of the objections we raise to prospective intrusions upon current privacy.

For our lives are, of course, far from completely private now. Most of us could not bear if it they were, for we are naturally gregarious and *communicating* animals, as well as self-regarding creatures. However introspective our nature, such emotions as we experience demand *sharing*, whether they be joys or sorrows, expectations or worries. Yet still we are wary in selecting those with whom we share our confidences. Three categories may be discerned of recipients of our secrets: first, our 'nearest and dearest'; second, the passing stranger in train or public bar (with whom, as pointed out earlier, our 'anonymity' is retained); and third, the Organizational World, which extracts vital information from us either with our implicit consent (e.g. for jobs, for insurance, for our health) or by compulsion (e.g. tax and census returns). We do not always appreciate, perhaps, the full extent of the consent we give. A pertinent example is the form which the Ministry of Social Security requires one to complete after thirteen days' sickness, to establish entitlement to additional earnings-related benefit. The claimant should sign this form, authorizing the Ministry to make '*any* necessary enquiries' to establish the veracity of the declaration of earnings. The privacy-conscious (but how few they are) will no doubt delete or amend this wording and initial the alterations.

We have shown how important it is that the Organizational World must respect our confidences, neither dispersing information to any other recipient, nor using it for purposes other than that for which it was supplied. Yet during our investigations some strange things have become apparent. Even without computer systems, information which may well be thought private, or even thought to fall into the stricter category of 'confidential', does come to light in quite unsuspected places.

Medical information, as has often been said, is generally regarded as the most sacrosanct of all. Only the confrontation of priest and penitent is as private as that between doctor and patient – and in the former situation nothing is put in writing. But if you wish none but the qualified physician to be privy to your ailments and distresses, do not consult the surgeon of a British ship, for his daily surgery report is available for scrutiny both by his Captain and by the Company which operates the ship.

Again, if you value the absolute privacy of your medical record, keep your child out of hospital. For, as Dr J. H. Stiff pointed out,[3] when a child is discharged from hospital a notification is passed automatically to the Local Authority giving details of the case, and this 'may contain details of the mother's past medical history.' Dr Stiff went on to comment: 'I have yet to hear of a single occasion when the parents' permission has been sought or granted . . . it is both unethical and discourteous that this practice should continue . . . in a field where confidentiality has been of paramount importance.'

Professor John Anderson, of King's College Hospital, has commented that 'the existing [medical] records system is vulnerable when deliberately challenged'.[4]

Does the average person, completing his income tax return, stop to consider whether his declaration of Deposit Account Interest in excess of £15 will be checked? Probably, in his innocence, he would imagine that the Tax Inspector only bothers the bank for confirmation of the amount if there is anything at all suspect about his return. Very likely the unsuspecting citizen does not know that *every* bank, for *every* deposit account, sends a statement of the interest earned in each year to the Inland Revenue. The depositor is neither told, nor asked. It just happens.

And whilst we consider the activities of the tax-man (against whom we have no personal animosity), remember that he is *compelled* by his working rules to follow up any report he receives, whether delivered in malice or inadvertance, which suggests that a false return may have been made.

The Department of Employment and Productivity has a form which not many people have seen, yet which concerns a great number. It is known as an E.S.2. It is sent, in bundles of anything from a dozen to a hundred, to a selection of employers of labour, from time to time, and each one bears the name of an employee – again, an apparently random cross-section. (How these names were selected makes for interesting conjecture; presumably from among Inland Revenue files?) Under the Statistics of Trade Act, 1947, the employer receiving these forms is 'required to furnish information' about each of the named employees, over several pages, relating to salary, bonuses, working hours, expenses, etc., etc. This form, when last seen, had all the signs of being a computer input document. A case of, 'More men know Tom Fool than Tom Fool knows'? There have, of course, been attempts in the US to restrict the use by management of this type of personal information, but none has so far met with success.[5]

Mr Kenneth Baker, MP, mentioned earlier as having introduced the first Parliamentary Bill specifically designed to control computer banks, was interviewed on BBC radio in February 1969, in connection with his Bill. He revealed, in the course of the programme, that there are investigative agencies who will undertake, for a suitable fee, to discover anyone's current bank balance accurately to the last penny, within twenty-four hours. No doubt the banks would protest their adequate secrecy, but obviously there are ways in which their restrictions can be beaten.

Anyone who has entered into a hire-purchase transaction, or any form of credit purchase, should nowadays *expect* both the personal data he supplied in his application, and information about his reliability in making the repayments, to be widely available. Most people do not expect this, of course, but it is so. Each application for credit must be checked, and there are now organizations whose entire resources are devoted to providing the checking service. Such agencies receive information from the credit-granting companies and will sell it to anyone. 'Central Register of Defaulters Limited of Cromwell Road, London S.W.7, is a typical firm, advising large retail organizations who want the names of potential customers checked. When an account is overdue for payment, Defaulters writes to the customer, pointing out that prompt payment will "avoid unpleasantness". The unpleasantness is in the final notice: "TAKE NOTICE that failure by you to make a payment direct to this collector within the next seven days may result in your name being registered as a defaulter both locally and nationally. This registration will stop you obtaining any further credit in the future".'[6]

Possibly the 'Defaulters' records are computerized. In the USA, credit-granting is certainly the computer's business. Many bureaux already have instant-retrieval systems, and it is but a short step to set up direct links between them. Highly personal information is being sold, as a unique commodity, without the knowledge or authority of the subject.

The Bank of England has issued a circular to banks which deal in foreign currency, asking for the *names of individuals* who hold deposits of certain currencies of certain size. The legislation which enabled the Bank of England to make approaches to other banks in fact made it a condition that 'no such request shall be made with respect to the affairs of any particular customer of a banker'.[7]

Whilst the debate continues about the future of broadcasting services, the most appropriate method of financing them, and evaders of licence payment, the Post Office has introduced a new form. This document (form No. T1207) is despatched to every householder in selected areas – the distribution no doubt under the control of the postal-coding sequenced computer files we heard of earlier – asking him in a seemingly innocuous way to say whether he has a radio and/or a television set, and also whether he has a licence, 'so that the records can be brought up to date'(!) That is, effectively, a challenge to everyone to say whether they are conforming to the law. Quite clearly there will be a follow-up check on those who (within their rights!) tear up the form. There has been no Parliamentary sanction for this action, and whatever one may think of the relative honesty of licence evaders, it is quite clearly an unauthorized bureaucratic intrusion. It is in fact one of the more serious of cases, since the mere non-return of the form will be the first link in a new chain of information-hypotheses.

Threats to privacy which are not commonly known or recognized as such thus already exist. There is no doubt that the above is a far from exhaustive list: and this is in a largely documentary world. When *all* the records are computerized, and that proverbial 'press of the button' will release them, who can doubt that there will be greater and ever greater leakage and abuse?

Senator Edward V. Long subtitled his book, *The Intruders*, 'The Invasion of Privacy by Government and Industry' (published in 1967)[8] pointing out the threats. This was before the realization of the added menace of computer technology was realized, although he cites one illustration in this area which we have already used (see Ch. 4).

The threat to privacy in the allegedly free societies of the West is serious. Ex-Vice President Humphrey points out the need for safeguards, and states that President Johnson had to tell his Government agencies in 1965, not to use electronic surveillance except in cases affecting national security.[9] The Supreme Court in 1966 tried to define the limits of privacy, and Congressional sub-committees like that of Senator Long highlighted the legislator's concern.

We know that privacy is one of the first values attacked and undermined by totalitarian governments. For example, the Nazis tried to destroy the citizen's sense of individual privacy by wire-tapping and the pre-dawn arrest.[10] A leading Nazi, Dr Ley, boasted 'There is no such thing as privacy for the individual in National Socialist Germany. The only person who still enjoys some privacy in Germany is someone who is asleep.'[11]

So far we have dealt solely with those people who are 'entitled' to receive information – whether such entitlement has been fully explicit at all points when the facts were originally established. We have pointed to some of the leaks that are already visible in the net of data collection, and must now show that the conversion to a computer system makes a considerable further breach in the procedures that safeguard our privacy.

For one thing, the computer technologists will be privy to the data files, with no inhibitions deriving from an inherited respect for traditions of discretion. Those who operate computer systems are not part of the machinery. They are human, and therefore fallible. This aspect must be emphasized, because not only will they display the vulnerability common to mankind, but the effect of their errors and indiscretions will be amplified by the greater *quantum* of material about which they could be potentially aware. It is not possible to produce a general law about this, but one could set out empirically testable propositions to suggest that the greater the amount of data handled, the greater the number of confidential items, and the greater the need for responsibility on behalf of the operators of the system.

The more provincial the system, the greater is the probability that the operator will know the individual involved. One of the present writers inadvertently discovered from a computer file that an acquaintance, to all appearances the possessor of no more than an adequate income, in fact had a considerable interest-earning investment. It is impossible to pretend that such knowledge has no effect upon one's relationship with the individual. If any one of us knows more about a person than that person has specifically revealed to us, that person's privacy has been violated.

A group of Conservative lawyers postulated a comparable situation on a broader scale. 'Suppose a national data bank were created for use by Government and local government officials and agencies. Suppose all the information received by the Inland Revenue, National Health Service, National Insurance Scheme, and other Government Departments, were fed into this single data bank. Considerable economies might result. Frauds on the Revenue might also be reduced. But, without appropriate regulation, the data bank would give even minor officials more or less complete information about the financial situation, illnesses and other private affairs of their acquaintances; one's doctor could know all about one's finances; one's near neighbour, employed in the Inland Revenue and not on speaking terms, could know more about one's recent illness or operation than one did oneself.'[12]

This is a danger which is typical of the computer threat and which, clearly, would not exist without the machinery so to collate and to distribute information. More people, either having access to the computer room, or to its files through the remote terminals of a data bank system, will derive new and private knowledge about their fellow-citizens *which they should not have.*

The above are, in a sense, 'accidental' lapses in the protection of secrecy. There will however also be deliberate intrusions. One can hardly doubt that a whole new range of deviancy will occur, spawned by the opportunities provided by the new technology for blackmail, industrial and commercial espionage and so on. The greater the amount of data processed, the greater the harvest for those with illicit access during any time-sequence. The skilful blackmailer could arrange to be supplied with regular details of the credit-card transactions of the rich. From these he could infer irregularities of conduct from say, visits to night-clubs, seaside hotels, etc., whilst the behaviour pattern of his sample was normally quite different. One moral is: if you are taking your paramour 'on the town,' cash settlement is the optimal strategy.[13]

In certain medical work, it is necessary to establish and place on record the frequency of intercourse between marital partners. In the wrong hands, such an item becomes positively pornographic; to a prospective employer, it could be sufficient to infer the stability of the connubial relationship and thus to formulate a hire/no-hire decision.

A sad fact of life is that we are all more prone to indulge in critical and scandalous gossip than praise. 'Perfidious human nature' demands compliments and thanks, yet is quick to perceive faults in others and to assign blame. Are not the most amicable of conversations often those in which the participants unite in creating an edifice of condemnation upon the shredded reputation of another? Gossip is never disinterestedly objective, but relies on the revelation and dissection of the indiscretions, faults, and nasty habits of the person under review. The human animal does not exhibit, characteristically, that proverbial simian sagacity of withdrawal from the receipt or communication of evil. The computerized dossier supplies an inexhaustible fund of innuendoes for those who would, like Viola in *Twelfth Night*, 'Holla your name to the reverberate hills, And make the babbling gossip of the air Cry out.'

In a paper written for the US President's Crime Commission it was observed that: 'Because of the fallibility of humans, our society has a need to forgive and forget and because of the fallibility of our present information systems we have the capacity to forget and thus forgive the errors of a man. This capacity could be limited by the inhuman use of a national computer system. At the very least the potential existence of such a system forces some attention to the question of what circumstances allow for the forgiveness of what kinds of errors.'[14] And the same writer made some apposite remarks upon the likely intrusions to a computer system by the villainous fringe of society: 'The law enforcement community has known for a long time that organized crime will use its unlimited financial resources to penetrate a system by attempting to corrupt government employees if enough is at stake. The most obvious area in which organized crime would have an interest in penetrating the system is in its attempt to acquire legitimate enterprises. There are some non-criminal organizations that would have an interest in penetrating the system – newspapers, private detectives, and credit agencies.

Con-artists with deep psychological insights using personal information stored in such a system could sell, coerce, or even pose as government officials on the basis of having such information. While these concerns are not related to privacy *per se*, they do raise the spectre of a national system being used to the disadvantage of the public.'[15]

To pass on to a further danger: always more and more information is required by the 'manipulators' of society. Much of this can be obtained from the regular Censuses, now computerized and thus more speedily available. It is common knowledge that the information taken at a population census is strictly confidential. The 1965 Census Regulations included the provision (Regulation 21) that 'A person having the custody, whether on his own behalf or on behalf of any other person, of any forms of return, enumeration books or other documents containing confidential information relating to a census shall keep such forms, books and other documents in such a manner as to prevent any unauthorized person having access thereto.'

A responsibility rests upon enumerators, and all recipients of returns, right up to the Registrar-General in person, to ensure that nothing is divulged. Yet curiously enough the General Register Office operates a fairly profitable line of business in selling census information. What is sold is in the form of statistical summaries, broken down into electoral 'wards' – about 220 houses, on average. Any person, or any organization, can purchase such information which, whilst not containing any specific names and addresses with related personal facts, does give a useful 'Identikit' outline of a relatively small sector of the population.[16] B.I.A. Sales Ltd. – a reputable mail-order firm – bought the summaries for every one of the 39,000 wards and parishes in the 1966 10 per cent sample census. From these they can discover the ages and sex of the population, the ratio of immigrants, the type of housing, the way the people travel to work, their type of work and social class – all very valuable for a sales campaign. 'It is time,' said the *Sunday Mirror* in its best trenchant style, May 18, 1969, 'the census takers, the experts and the politicians started remembering whose business they are supposed to be minding.'

When we come to that time so often forecast in these pages, when for each of us there is a computer dossier – or a set of dossiers – the advertiser will become even more interested. His business is to sell, and the amount now spent on research into the most appropriate market, and the best advertising 'image' and media to be used, is phenomenal. Give him more and better data on the habits of the population and he will have no scruples against using it. So when he finds out one's income and employment; that one has not bought a new car for six years but has expensive electrical kitchen machinery and a colour TV; if he finds that one has a new suit every six months but does not smoke or drink; he puts with this the details of any books or records one has bought or borrowed from a public library, and all in all, he has a picture of one's susceptibilities (further qualified, of course, by examination of the records of the rest of one's family) sufficient to send an 'irresistable' offer.

Thus can we lose freedom of choice along with our privacy, without knowing that we have done so, because the Achilles' Heel of a consumer's habit will be discovered and concentrated upon to a degree which will strain the balanced judgement of even those most relatively resistant to conditioning and sales propaganda. Moreover, if we are not aware of this special effort, we shall be all the more vulnerable.

In an earlier chapter we commented that the use of computer systems in military decision-making does not strictly constitute an intrusion of the civilian's privacy. When, however, massive armed power is attempting to pacify a nation in which its presence is an anomaly and its degree of control negligible – i.e. the American situation in Vietnam – the occupying force becomes inevitably a 'manipulator' of the indigenous population. 'How, after a decade of war,' it has been rhetorically asked, 'can the allegiance of particular people in particular areas be determined?'[17] The attempt at such determination is made, by using computers.

'The demands of the machine for information are inexhaustible.... The most ominous feature of the war in recent years is that the machine has now moved to a phase where the quality of information, as opposed to its quantity, is now virtually irrelevant.

'Hopelessly thwarted in its attempts to improve information *input*, the US Command in Saigon has devoted its most skilled resources to rendering its information *processing* ultra-sophisticated. Then, for the substance of tactical and strategic efficiency it has substituted the appearance. It has invented what is, in effect, a computerized "extermination machine".[18]

'Based upon a "mish-mash" of snippets of field intelligence, some good solid fact but largely speculative guesswork, the computer works out a bombing programme.

'It is all superlatively mathematical, and the fact that each scientifically selected raid gives a calculable but never calculated chance of killing civilians in the process is accepted.

'It was probably inevitable that so tidy a technique would be extended. . . . The High Command in Saigon is now extending the idea of computer selection to individuals – as well as to suspected areas. This year the programme aims to "eliminate" 33,000 individual Vietnamese civilians who – it has been determined by the computer – are Viet Cong sympathizers. The programme, "Project Phoenix", is said to be up to schedule.

'The Viet Cong, of course, do not need computers to identify their enemies, which gives their massacres a less random character – an impressive factor for a peasant debating which side to back.

'If the "machine" of war – particularly that in the air – fails to discriminate effectively between friend and foe, indiscriminate conduct by the troops in face-to-face situations is scarcely surprising.

'The real horror of the American operation in Vietnam is not simply the sum of its oft-remarked faults – inexperienced infantry, bureaucratic rivalry, gross defects of intelligence, unselectivity of its fire-power. It is quite simply that it has evolved a technology of war that, even if it were staffed at every level by paragons of expertise and virtue, cannot be anything but atrocious.'[19]

Within the less phrenetic environment of a nation supposedly at peace with itself and its neighbours, sections of government nevertheless tend to 'manipulate' sections of society. However non-tyrannical its motivation, the planning functions of government – including land usage, economics, industrial development, transportation systems, etc. – require a basis of survey data upon which hypotheses may be constructed. From these hypotheses decisions will be taken that may inconvenience, disrupt, or utterly destroy the lives of hundreds – the Greater London Ring Motorway is a salutary example.[20]

Survey data will derive from two primary sources: observation and classification of physical conditions (buildings, vehicles, etc.); and the response from interviews with individuals such as those conducted by research groups and, of course, the Census data. It has been argued that the aggregation of such data in one 'archive' is a way of reducing fears that individual circumstances might be disclosed – that 'no aggregated data . . . would be traceable to an individual'.[21] But the whole purpose of such data collections is admitted to be the manipulation of society: 'The somewhat disembodied survey findings relating to individuals can be greatly enriched by the use of ecological data relating to that particular environment from which the sample of individuals was drawn, and can thus be of enhanced value to theorists, practitioners and policy makers. . . . [The data can] lead to highly illuminating comparisons between areas, which are useful for a variety of administrative planning decisions as well as for more theoretical purposes.'[22]

Two other points made in this same paper tend to vitiate its own argument about non-identification: (*a*) a consortium at the University of Michigan which is aggregating survey and political data 'makes available . . . voting records in the two Houses of Congress, and *biographical data on Congressmen* [our italics] . . . to institutions and scholars' – the precise recipients are not identified; and (*b*) the 1971 UK census will use, instead of the previous untidy hotch-potch of electoral wards, parishes and districts, the internationally acceptable grid reference system to identify the geographical sub-divisions. This means that the basic unit for computer storage of data might be the convenient grid of 100 metres square – so that an individual whose property is at least this large *would* be identifiable. (In fact, considerable effort is being devoted nationally to the development of an extension to the grid reference system that will enable a *one* metre square to be codified and identified; pinpointing to this degree will vastly increase traceability.) It appears that the results of the 1971 Census – which will presumably be as available for distribution to other government agencies, and for sale to any interested parties, as has been the case with previous censuses – will be of immense value to all manipulators of society.[23]

Where economics are at stake, it is conceivable that the data could be sufficiently *dis*-aggregated, or disinterred, from the archive which Phillipson describes, to the advantage of business rivals – particularly in an economy which has large sections of the market controlled by a small number of firms. As the same writer rightly points out, data may be misused *via* a data archive – 'Even the knowledge that a survey on a particular product or market has been carried out may be of value to a competitor.'[24]

The paper goes on to show that the decision as to what data is acquired, under the direction of a 'National Council for the Data Bank',[25] must depend upon the actual and potential users. These users, in the view of the present writers, would be widespread and multifarious – and could include the unscrupulous. Such a broadly-based co-ordination of aggregate, ecological, and personal data as is proposed could be very little different from the American National Data Centre which was vetoed on the very grounds of inadequate safeguards. We cannot concur with the warning that 'unless the archive is responsive to user needs and interests it will simply turn into a punched card morgue',[26] unless it is intended as a subtle implication of the piquant point that even a cemetery allows identification of the residents.

Much fun has been made of the computer 'dating' services which, for a suitable fee, will attempt to find partners of the opposite sex, whose appearance, background and temperament are likely to be compatible with the enquirer's own. A new battery of satirical shots have also been fired at that constant target of cynicism, astrology, since an enterprising business established a service of 'personalized and computerised' astrological assessments and predictions.[27] Neither of the present authors has found it necessary to test the efficiency of these services, but we assume that the client must offer a meticulously detailed self-analysis in order to gain the maximum benefit – and away go some more personal facts into yet another computer file. One would hope that these enterprises never become sufficiently popular to tempt a Government to nationalization, though far-sighted sister agencies of greater repute may well see the advantages of acquiring lists of this sort through merger (indeed, it might be in the *short-term* interests of the client if they were, of course, to make more complete the otherwise entirely subjective portrait that he offers of himself).

Tyrannical, totalitarian government could so easily move from *suggesting* whom we meet and marry, and what activities we should indulge in, to *arranging* that these things be so. In recent memory, after all, the Nazis had their human stud-farms where S.S. 'volunteers' could produce, with suitable Aryan Isoldes, the racially pure additions to the 'master-race'. We have already referred (in Ch. 4) to the efforts of equine experts to produce sure-fire winners, by the computerized identification of performance patterns through several generations, and the isolation of hereditary features. By controlled and selective breeding, regulated as carefully as the experimental mutations contrived by an expert grower of roses, a 'perfect' horse may one day emerge. The scientists in theoretical biochemistry are beginning to understand much more about the fundamental structure of genes, and although they are years away from (and indeed may never reach) the ability to change personality or inherited health patterns chemically, the mere fact of identification and classification is enough to permit experimental cross-fertilization of any species. And once a thing *can* be done, the burden always seems to rest upon a few tortured consciences to convince the rest that it should *not* be done. When a biologist can proclaim that 'Reproduction, although a private act, has widespread social consequences and is not a private affair',[28] it is clear that the last word on population manipulation has not yet been spoken.

We conclude these comments on some of the threats to privacy by a brief recapitulation: that whether the data is true or false; whether or not the computers are programmed and operated faultlessly at all times; in all circumstances the information emerging from computer files will tend to be relied upon as a portrait of the 'real' person whatever contradictory evidence there may be.

For example, recent work in criminology which purports to correlate driving offences with general delinquency, will tend to persuade decision-makers to make inferences from minor offences. The more unsophisticated the person concerned is in his statistical approach, the cruder the inference. This is a clear illustration of the adage that a little sociological knowledge is a very dangerous thing.

This point can be further illustrated in another small area of that computer activity now commonly called M.I.S. – management information systems. Management needs statistical information and summaries of activity. The good manager will not necessarily accept the reports he receives as irrefutable, let alone the conclusions they appear to justify. With computer reports, it becomes much more difficult to question either the substance or the detail of a tabulation. When one knows that figures have been collected, thoroughly analysed, and presented in a clear consistent way, it is hard to remember that they originated from a foreman's docket in the busy context of a shop floor, or a grime-besmirched time-sheet filled in with a stub of pencil and a tongue in cheek. The greater the reliance of management systems on computers, the greater the tendency for information to be unquestioned as it emerges from computer systems.

Each of us is, both to himself and to others, a very complex network of inter-related feelings, reactions, knowledge, habits and principles. But information systems will make it possible to annotate our responses, our 'actions, reactions and transactions', and build up a picture of our character that is well-delineated and predictable. There will be no confusion or contradiction about it; it will be a solid, incontrovertible block of facts, delivered instantly on demand.

As a leading British writer on cybernetics put it: 'My electronic image in the machine may be more real than I am. It is rounded; it is complete; it is retrievable; it is predictable in statistical terms. . . . There is no ambiguity, no loss of history, no rationalization. I am a mess; and I don't know what to do. The machine knows better – in statistical terms. Thus is my reality less real than my mirror image in the store. That fact diminishes me.'[29]

Notes

1. Duff Hart-Davis, 'Permissive Britain', *Sunday Telegraph*, November 23, 1969.
2. *Ibid.*
3. *The Times*, February 22, 1969.
4. *Computer Weekly*, August 21, 1969.
5. See, for instance, P. Ask, 'Discrimination in Hiring and Placement', *Personnel*, 1967, 44, pp. 9–26.
6. *The Sunday Times*, March 2, 1969.
7. *Daily Telegraph*, October 17, 1969.
8. Long, *op. cit.*
9. See Foreword to Long, *op. cit.*, p. viii.
10. See Long, *op. cit.*, pp. 21 ff.
11. Cited in *ibid.*, p. 22.
12. *Computers and Freedom*, Conservative Research Dept., 1968. The Society of Labour Lawyers has also been working on a report on privacy – part of which was published in modified form in J. Jacob, 'Seven Dangers of Computers', *New Society*, December 11, 1969.
13. A salutary computer analysis of one man's day is included in the Appendix, 'Data Surveillance Sheet 1987'.
14. *Hearings*, C, p. 223 (S. Rothman).
15. *Ibid.*
16. Lance Hoffman has shown how even a 'statistical' file can be used to reveal information on a single individual – see his paper CGTM 67, April 1969 (Stanford University, California).
17. *The Sunday Times*, April 23, 1969.
18. *Ibid.*
19. *Ibid.*
20. See David Wiggins, 'London: Arithmetic of Devastation', *The Spectator*, October 4, 1969, pp. 435–6.
21. Michael Phillipson, *Making Better Use of Survey Data*, London, P.E.P. Publications 1967, p. 64.
22. *Ibid.*, p. 59.
23. For American fears on the uses of their 1970 Census data, see Arlen J. Large, 'A Curious Business', in *Wall Street Journal*, March 31, 1969; also Joshua Lederburg, 'The Mysterious Computer will not Abet Witchhunts', in *Washington Post*, July 26, 1969. See the following for background: Hall, *op. cit.*
    R. E. Barraclough, *Finding Documents by Geographic Areas*, author, 1965 (mimeo), and earlier papers.
    V. Engwall, and E. Larsson, *Methods for Determining Co-ordinates for Community Planning*, Report 104, The National Swedish Council for Building Research, 1964.
    E. M. Horwood, *Using Computer Graphics in Community Renewal*, H.U.D., Washington D.C., 1963.
    L. S. Jay, *The Development of an Integrated Data System*, T.P.I., London, October 1966.
    H. Wallner, 'The Information System of Community Development: The Real Estate Register Reform, The National Land Survey Board', Stockholm, 1966.
24. Phillipson, *op. cit.*, p. 64.

25. It is not clear whether this is an already extant body, or merely a proposal.
26. *Op. cit.*, p. 65.
27. In New York City, there is a service offering an 'Astroflash Horoscope by I.B.M. Computer' – an I.B.M. 360 machine is stored with 15 million astrological inputs.
28. N. J. Berrill, *The Person in the Womb*, London, Angus and Robertson, 1969; quoted in *Daily Telegraph*, November 27, 1969.
29. Stafford Beer, *Computer Weekly*, August 21, 1969.

Chapter 9

FURTHER ILLUSTRATIONS: CREDIT, HEALTH AND LOCAL GOVERNMENT

Having looked at the technology, the threats, and those aspects of privacy which computers have begun to invade, we now focus attention on some specific areas in a little more detail, so that the implications of an electronic superstructure to society may be made cleaner.

The three areas we have chosen are of great importance to the average citizen. They affect his pocket, his health, and the provision of municipal services, respectively. We should like to make it clear that these are by no means the only areas in which the computer is carrying an increasing proportion of the burden, but are those which impinge most closely on our everyday lives. We merely wish to discuss recent developments in these areas, and observe some of the potential dangers to individual freedom. Again, we draw on some of the insights of American commentators on the new trends, but much of the evidence is drawn from British examples.

We place these extended illustrations at this point in the discussion because we feel that a sufficient awareness has been developed, after considering questions basic to the nature of privacy and its possible abuse (in the last two chapters), to aid appreciation of the dangers inherent in the computerization of our daily lives, unless adequate checks restrict possible abuses. We have inclined to understate the dangers, but practical experience of the more immediate intrusions will doubtless point up our argument.

COMPUTERS AND MONEY

Internationally, banks (State and commercial) and money-changers are becoming computerized. The sectors of this vast, gnomic, complex we wish to consider are credit-rating agencies, and personal bank accounts.

The credit bureau,[1] or agency, is part of a relatively new but flourishing industry. It has sprung, of course, from the very profitable business of selling goods without the exchange of cash – on hire-purchase agreements, instalment plans, by credit cards, and the variations of 'credit sales'. Everyone seems to benefit; the consumer who gets his goods without having to save up the hard cash; the retailer who has made a sale; the financing body, taking its fixed-rate or interest-compounded cut. There is one proviso in this sequence of delight. If the consumer has not the funds to cover the credit, or defaults on his instalment repayments, everyone loses.

Consequently, to support a society that demands to be able to 'Buy Now, Pay Later', the person who approves an application for credit must reduce his risks, and compare the loan-risk he is taking with the chance of refund. Naturally, he wants to find out what he can about the borrower's probity, reliability, and financial resources. The credit men seem to reduce this to a matter of the three Cs': Capital, Capacity, and Character.

A whole new series of procedures for investigating the background of the applicant for credit came into existence, and the larger retailers started to compile their own 'black lists' of defaulting and fraudulent customers – which they shared with other organizations to mutual advantage. There was a ripe opportunity here for someone to do the job more thoroughly for them; hence the credit bureau. Over 2,000 such bureaux now exist in the USA.[2] As clerically-based organizations, they got along by 'collecting information relating to the financial standing, credit, character, responsibility, and general reputation of persons, firms, and corporations engaged in business and furnishing this information to subscribers for a consideration. The purpose of such a service is to provide a standard of trustworthiness which will permit the subscriber to safely conduct business with the stranger or distant customer.'[3]

However, where there are voluminous documentary records, clerical methods are simply not good enough. The 'subscriber', applying for information about a prospective customer, wants an immediate rating; the bureau rapidly runs out of space to file and retrieve all the data. So the computers are brought in. With their aid, the bureau can augment and keep up to date its compilation of relevant data on the purchasers of the nation, adding to the files from time to time all new agreements; all applications for credit whether accepted or rejected; any unsatisfactory payment history, and such publicly available records as bankruptcies, divorces, criminal proceedings. Anything that has a bearing on the 'three Cs', in fact.

'A typical credit file contains a person's name and adress, family status, place of employment, approximate salary, credit income, charge accounts, payment income and even, in the case of insurance company files, medical and hospital records and "moral hazards" –

extra-marital affairs, homosexuality, heavy drinking or other social observations which could affect the risk.'[4] In fact it is not only insurance companies who go into such depth; circumstantial detail, serious or trivial, fact or hearsay, is all grist to the credit-assessing business.

How does it work? In Los Angeles, two hundred girls are available all day to receive telephone calls. They answer queries from subscribers to Credit Data Corporation, who want to know about any of the eleven million people in the files. 'About 100,000 inquiries a day are for checks on credit-worthiness, typically from retailers who want to know whether to let a new customer open an account. The girl who answers taps out the customer's name and address on her keyboard, and the IBM 360/65 computer searches through its huge memory for the appropriate record and flashes the details up on the girl's TV screen to be read back to the subscriber.'[5] Another 200,000 queries a day deal with the authorization service backing up several bank and oil company credit cards. 'Whenever a customer wants to charge more than a certain amount against a card – typically $25 – the shopkeeper or garageman has to call CDC for a computer check.'[6] A similar though not nearly so advanced system is used in this country with the Barclaycard. The normal limit of credit with this is £25, though some cards have a special indicator showing a higher limit, and some traders dealing only in expensive goods – furs, for example – have a regular authorization to charge larger amounts. For deals over the limit, the tradesman phones the computer centre in Northampton for clearance. There are no real-time enquiry facilities at present, though they will be introduced soon; clearance or rejection of the credit is given by reference to a regular print-out of the computer's master files – right or wrong!

Although a good deal of fuss has been made in the USA about the credit bureau, it is always the abuses that hit the headlines. The bureaux are not irresponsible dirt-mongers; their continuing in business and their reputation depends upon the accuracy of their reporting. If a society wants to live on credit it must accept that there will be checks to prevent losses. For the most part, data in the files will be factual, and enquiries will not be frivolous or malicious. It is in the interests of the great majority of consumers that their credit worthiness should be established quickly.

Nevertheless there are, appropriately enough, some black sides to this 'black list' business. Given the prospect, only too realistic, of a network of credit files covering the country, there is a readily detectable danger 'in the possibility that the wrong information may get fed into the credit-rating system; that Mr X may find it impossible to buy a car on HP because he once refused to pay for an unwanted magazine'[7] that was pushed through his letter-box unsolicited, and followed by letters demanding payment (but this should be taken care of by the recent *Inertia Selling Bill*). Some of the information will be 'sensitive' and should not be seen by those who are not genuinely entitled to it. Yet no doubt government would find excellent reasons for getting into these files occasionally – and in the USA, they do. It is a proud boast of the Associated Credit Bureau of America, on behalf of its member bureaux, that FBI agents are constantly checking the records for information in connection with their investigations, and the *Wall Street Journal* has reported that Government investigators get some 20,000 records each year from the New York Credit Bureau alone.

Professor Westin told the Congressional Subcommittee: 'I decided to try an experiment myself to see just how easy or difficult it would be to get information from credit bureau. On the afternoon of February 20, 1968, I asked a member of my staff at Columbia [University] to . . . ask for a report on the character of a female research assistant. He indicated in the letter that she was being considered for promotion. . . . We have no credit purpose. We offered no credit basis for the inquiry. Columbia is not a credit-grantor or client of the Greater New York Credit Bureau. The letter must have arrived at the credit bureau in the morning mail of the 21st. At 10 a.m. on that same day the executive manager of the credit bureau telephoned and read us a full "previous residence report" . . . containing information about her residence, employment, and credit history in another city before she came to work in New York, and similar information since her arrival in New York. The report included entries for questions about her character, habits, and morals, how she was regarded by her employer, whether there was any indication of illegal practices, past or present, any suits, judgements, or bankruptcies, her estimated monthly income, other income from rentals, investments, *et cetera*, and a considerable list of other items.'[8] He went on to say that no call had been received from the Bureau attempting to verify whether the author of the letter or the woman in question did in fact work at Columbia; neither was any effort made to see whether the woman wished the information to be revealed.

Following the telephone call, a full written report was supplied, and is reproduced in the Hearings (pp. 8, 9). Westin comments: 'It seems to me it was an outrageous disclosure of personal information and a breach of this woman's privacy.'

As a direct result of the exposure in the Subcommittee of the practices of the Bureau, legislation was introduced into Congress that would restrict the release of credit information by both the agencies and by banks. Yet even whilst that was being discussed, the Inland Revenue brought a law suit against a bureau for refusing to allow it to examine an individual's file.[9]

A British commentator on electronic and legal matters has repeated a common criticism of this type of file in his suggestion that we 'suppose, for example, John Doe buys goods from a trader and those goods fail to conform to the implied conditions of quality under Sale of Goods Act, 1893, Section 14, and suppose further that John Doe refuses to pay for those goods. Surely he deserves some protection from being registered as a bad debtor in a credit agency's records. Yet the chances are that he will be so registered because the *agency will not ask him why he has not paid* [our italics].'[10] That is the great difficulty of computer records. They do not explain *why*. Documentary records can always accommodate more than the 'bare facts', by marginal notes or additional bits of paper. Machine systems are very rarely sufficiently flexible to permit the addition of trivial memoranda. 'The computer said so' – but it did not say why.[11]

To the outside observer, it appears that what were formerly the 'Big Five' Banks – or is it 'Four', or 'Three', now? – have gone quite mad over computers. The value of the hardware they have, either installed or on order, runs into millions of pounds. Basically, they are used for the bulk 'bread-and-butter' work of cheque handling, standing order payments, and credit transfers. In their advertisements, the banks vie with each other to maintain that despite complaints of inadequate and inaccurate computer-produced statements, they will still regard you as a special customer and give personal treatment. Their machine centres are increasingly complex installations of inter-communicating computers, whose tentacles are gradually extending to every branch in every town and village as all accounts are centralized. So profitable is this for the manufacturers – so profligate are the banks in their expenditure – that they have designed specialized terminals for the banking service, which combine all the features of a powerful accounting machine with the capability of retrieving and updating clients' accounts remotely at the computer centre. If, as has been suggested, the use of cash will gradually diminish to be replaced by credit transactions, it may also be that the kind of credit bureaux we have been discussing will disappear, for 'Tomorrow's consumer will have one cash/credit account with one financial institution. When he buys a suit, the salesman will insert the customer's cash/credit card in a slot in a telephone, dial the appropriate numbers to represent the amount of the sale, and wait for an approving signal from the bank's computer. The customer's bank account will be reduced – or his loan account charged.'[12]

Change in banking methods on this scale would, of course, make a radical difference to our shopping habits, and also to banking practice in this country. As one side-effect of such instant accounting, notice that at present you can write a cheque for £1,000 at 9 a.m.; should it be presented at the bank for special clearance at 10 a.m. but your balance be inadequate to meet it, the cheque will not be 'bounced' at once. You have until the close of the business on that day to cover the cheque. An instantaneous transfer world might not be so considerate.

How would a fully computer-run bank work? The client would present his plastic card to the cashier, who would have a similar card identifying him to the central file *via* a touch-tone telephone with two special slots. Both cards in the phone, a few taps, and the computer checks a projected withdrawal against the balance then, through an audio-response unit, gives a verbal authorization or refusal. Instant information on the state of the customer's balance would always be available to the bank, and this 'service' might even be possible direct from the comfort of the client's home, if he could use his card through the telephone system – not a fantasy given the probable communications advances of the late '70s.

According to one Chicago bank President already using a system such as this, the problem of safeguarding confidentiality is not too difficult: 'Unauthorized access to information is prevented by limiting the data that can be obtained by individual banks, by individual people (senior officials can obtain more information than the cashiers), and by changing the appropriate code immediately a customer reports that his card has been mislaid. The customer's signature continues to be the primary security check. The computer is not on-line in the sense that it actually effects the transaction; it merely shows the available balance, the actual balance being changed that night when the cheque goes through.'[13]

Using special touch-tone telephones, with an overlay placed on it to assist the operator, calculations can be made when using the computer apparatus, provided first identification is indeed satisfactory. Thomas Markle, the bank President cited, sees that direct communication with computers through ordinary telephones will greatly expand. 'Most banks have not grasped the value of communications', he maintains,[14] anticipating that every person with a telephone will be a potential customer of an efficient bank. Simply by dialling the computer, with coded-card slots in the instrument, bills will be paid and other transactions completed instantaneously.

There is a French bookseller who would probably welcome greater immediacy, provided it is concomitant with greater accuracy.

Just before departing on holiday, he noticed an over-credit of six million francs in his account. He notified his bank, received assurance that the error would be corrected, and went happily on his holiday. On his return, he discovered a mound of dishonoured cheques awaiting him. Knowing full well that his account was not in the red (though certainly not six million in the black!) he made his protestations – and discovered that the computer had got completely mixed up whilst attempting to correct the original large credit. It now showed a 23,000 franc overdraft. The bank would allow no redress until the next quarterly balance; meanwhile, under French law, he was liable to severe penalties for issuing bad cheques. Eventually, a commercial tribunal forced the bank to give way and honour the cheques.[15]

So, when this banking revolution has fully come (and in our view it is not a question of 'if', but simply 'when'), our financial dealings and the secrecy with which we expect them to be handled will be subject to the proven fallibility of the computer, the proven fallibility of computer programs, the proven and familiar fallibility of the telephone system, and the certainty of attempted infiltration by public and private investigators.

We can offer neither solution nor consolation for those who wish to retain their privacy. Their only alternative will be to eschew the system completely and return to keeping hard cash in a tin box under the bed. This independence of spirit will require an invincible resolution and will-power, for the customer proffering cash will be regarded with suspicion: 'What's up with you? Isn't your credit good enough?'

COMPUTERS AND HEALTH

Nobody quite knows what to do to get the National Health Services better organized. The Government's 1969 Green Paper, presenting some proposals, was welcomed by no one, and the Minister promised to have some more discussions and try again later. With 700 different health authorities – local Councils, Hospital Boards, Executive Councils, etc. – representing entirely different types of administration; with two different sources of public income – rates and taxes – and some private-patient income; with the sturdy independence of some of the leading hospitals which are renowned for their specialist expertise in certain branches of medicine; with the professional pride of the local doctor in knowing and caring for his patients being submerged by overflowing waiting rooms; with complaints from all sides of wasted money, wasted time, wasted hospital beds, overworked and underpaid nursing staff; all this presents a dilemma indeed.

So many of those who devote their lives to medical science – one of the few remaining professions which the layman would call a 'vocation' – are far too busy dealing with the problems of today to be able to give time to constructive thought about tomorrow. It is this lack of opportunity for reflection and planning, rather than any innate resistance to change, which is hampering the introduction of computers into medicine. There is a widespread recognition in the profession that there must be change, and that computers are potentially valuable tools, but the pressure is rarely off for long enough to see how and where they fit in. A recent report of the BMA[16] is critical of the Health Department for failing to enunciate a computer policy that would encourage and stimulate their intelligent and discriminating use in the war against disease.

But there are some who have found the time to experiment, and indeed to prove that a better service can be given, whilst freeing expensively-trained, skilled staff from the vast burden of mundane clerical tasks to allow them to do their *real* work.

The four points at which a computer can share the load may be distinguished as prevention, diagnosis, treatment, and sheer administration. The last of these need not be expanded upon here; it covers in general those same processes of payroll, personnel, financial control, statistics, etc., common to any organization, though it has been shown that within a hospital environment these tasks may conveniently be integrated with the scheduling of appointments both for out-patients and admissions.[17]

Prevention is primarily the job of Local Authority Medical Officers, through their clinics and the schools, in co-operation with GPs. All MOHs have a responsibility to encourage parents to agree that their children shall receive the course of immunization against those diseases for which there is a satisfactory antigen. With conventional administration of such a prevention programme, 'a child's ability to resist certain infections is dependent either upon the persuasive powers of its mother's medical advisors or upon the abilities of the mother to remember to what place she should take her child at what time on what day. This is not good enough.'[18] Hence, following the lead of West Sussex, several local authorities now use a computer system to schedule all appointments automatically as they become due (under guidance as to vaccines, time-scales, etc., issued by the Ministry). Parents are notified by postcard of the time and place to take their child; the clinic or the GP receives a list of the children to expect and the treatment to be given. This list is simply ticked in an appropriate column and returned to the computer centre to update the file. All would claim that substantially higher protection indices have resulted from such schemes.[19]

Another aspect of protection lies in the early detection of those conditions which become serious if neglected. The Regional Hospital Boards operate the familiar mobile Mass X-Ray Units which, merely by local advertisements giving notice of their visits, attract a satisfactory proportion of the public to undergo regular chest examination. (An odd pronouncement at the end of 1969 threatened to extinguish this service.) It is not so easy to persuade women to undergo the simple and painless test for detection of cancer of the cervix, despite the public pressure for the provision of such facilities and the use of newspaper and poster publicity. Again, as with the children, it has been shown that a direct personal invitation to a specific time and place for an appointment significantly improves the response.[20] 'But the clerical work and the tasks of visiting the women in their homes and talking about cervical cytology in the surgery were found to be more time-consuming and laborious than the clinical effort involved.'[21] Again, a computer solves the problem, as the paper just cited shows. A relatively simple file, a relatively simple computer system, and the health of the community is improved. In response to invitations by letter, '72·5 per cent of women . . . consented to have routine cervical cytology and breast examinations'.[22]

In diagnostic work, the computer may seem to have a much smaller role to play, accepting the contention of the BMA that 'Automatic diagnosis is one of the most persistent of popular images of computer applications in medicine, yet it is still a remote and possibly impracticable dream.'[23] Whether a patient arrives for consultation with his GP, or at a hospital, there are so many intangibles in his appearance, his attitudes, his responses, which enable the skilled doctor to go beyond the obviously detectable or describable symptoms. No one really expects that we shall ever get patients diagnosing themselves, by indicating their troubles through an on-line terminal to a computer. Nevertheless, if an information store, representing the accumulated knowledge of all illnesses – major symptoms, side-effects, and treatment – is available to the physician it could be of enormous value in supplementing his own knowledge and experience. One commentator suggests we consider 'a greatly simplified [*sic*!] case. A middle-aged patient complains of pain in the lower thoracic spine, loss of weight and loss of appetite. He has a low temperature and no history of previous injury. This data can be taken by an assistant, and fed into a previously programmed computer. The computer searches its stored data and finds that possible conditions associated with the symptoms are myelomatosis, a secondary deposit to a primary malignant growth, or bacterial infection. It therefore recommends a blood count, a serum calcium test and phosphorous test, a Bence Jones protein test and an X-ray of the spine and abdomen. These tests eliminate the first two conditions and suggest that the bacterial infection may be tuberculosis, staphylococcal, brucellosis or typhoid. The computer then recommends an antistaphylococcal titre and blood culture . . .'.[24] And so the example goes on, illustrating if nothing more the vast gulf of reconciliation between the vocabularies of the medical, as against the computer, scientist.

Perhaps we should leave this maze, to consider the completed diagnosis and the hospital treatment. As we have shown (Ch. 4), nursing staff can be relieved of some of the pressures associated with the constant monitoring of intensive care patients, by the intervention of a computer to detect potentially critical changes in their condition. A simple computer can in fact monitor the body temperature, blood pressure, heart action and respiration of a number of patients at once, so that only one nurse is needed to watch over it. Sometimes the same system provides immediate corrective measures: for example, if there is cardiac disturbance, the heart monitoring circuit can incorporate a cardiac pacemaker. The mortality rates of patients who are admitted after heart attack have been cut in half since the systems were introduced.[25]

In Europe, Sweden currently leads the field in hospital computerization, and there are those who maintain that whatever the costs and whatever the difficulties Britain must learn quickly from this pioneering work, or our own hospitals will simply be overwhelmed and unable to maintain even the present standards of care and attention – which are themselves not all they might be.[26] As one example, Danderyd Hospital, near Stockholm, has a file of 1½ million personal records; the system allows for the retrieval and the updating of a record directly from a terminal, and during 1969 it was demonstrated by linking a visual display unit in Montreal, Canada, to the computer. 'Using a Univac 494 computer system, data is stored on each person's medical history, allergies, blood group, etc. These are coded according to the identity number which each Swedish citizen is allotted at birth, and by keying in this number a doctor or nurse can have a full report on the patient displayed almost instantaneously on the terminal screen. Information is held on three levels, with safeguards against access to certain types of information by unauthorized persons. An example of the data allotted restricted access is maternity or psychiatric history.

'Provision has been made for a total of 60 information levels, allowing the system to handle highly detailed information on, for example, chronic cases. As more levels are used, doctors hope to build up complete medical profiles which will not only serve as an aid to treatment, but can also be used for diagnostic and preventive medicine.'[27]

In another Swedish hospital, Karolinska, a '£500,000-a-year project – aiming to develop nothing less than a complete information system suitable for a wide range of large and medium-sized hospitals – is now nearing the end of its first phase. . . . [it has] entailed a complete reorganization of the way doctors and nurses handle information about patients'.[28] This report emphasizes the disorganization of records which is the unfortunate 'normal' state of things in the majority of hospitals, and a frequently-heard complaint of medical men with better organization in mind. The appended diagram demonstrates how, ideally, a patient's hospital record is subject to progressive but ordered expansion. Typically, today, this record is in fact a heterogeneous collection of all shapes, sizes, colours, and designs of documents, with perhaps X-ray plates as well. It may take hours to unravel the relevant data from an old file when a patient is readmitted.

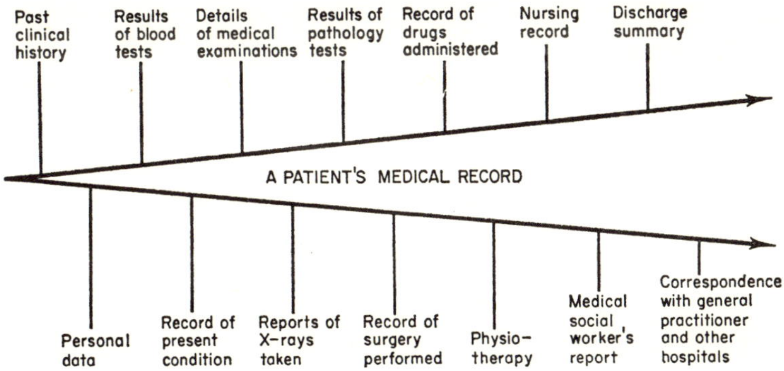

When it is appreciated that the hospital needs information from the GP, and vice-versa; and that documents also pass between both of these and the local authority; and that within the health authority there exists a further multiplicity of documents deriving from the various medical incidents in life; and that these documents are not standardized across administrative area boundaries;[29] the conclusion reached by many people that every citizen should have a single, central, continuous record, representing every contact he has with the health service right from the midwife's report of his delivery (or even the ante-natal clinic progress reports) is not surprising. And we must not leave the impression that the hospitals and medical specialists in this country are idle, for that is far from true. Their efforts are largely independent, but on the whole well-documented so that each may profit by the research of others. Notable work was done by a team under E. D. Acheson, at Oxford, in the analysis of methods of linking together the records affecting medical care which originate from widely-varied sources.[30] The Ministry of Health, whatever its shortcomings in the eyes of the BMA, is devoting considerable time and manpower to research into the most useful projects and methods for computers. In the newly developing area of Thamesmead, the full integration of staff in new health centres has provided an opportunity to start almost 'from scratch' and a new approach to medical records is being tried with a computer system.[31]

A working party established by the Society of MOHs is endeavouring to reach a standard design of record card applicable to all children from birth, which can be annotated by, and of common use to, local authority health departments, clinics and hospitals. This card is not specifically intended for a computer project, but the study includes people with the expertise to advise on the suitability of the suggestions for ultimate computerization. Meanwhile, another team under the direction of the National Computing Centre, LAMSAC,[32] and the Ministry of Health, is to work on the development of standard computer systems for all the current responsibilities of local health departments, taking account of the requirements for interchange of basic and statistical information with other bodies.

We consider much of the progress in modernizing medicine to be praiseworthy, providing that it continues to be concerned with *people*, and not merely with numbers and experimentation. We are also anxious that traditions of privacy and confidentiality be continued. There are also questions of computer errors which, in this area, could cost lives.

In our view, there is no *intrinsic* objection to the rationalization, and computerization, of the health service, *provided that* there are soundly based restrictions in the system to prevent the large number of workers who would need access to the records from recovering those parts which they need not, and should not, know.[33] We can place considerable trust in the high tradition of doctors and health workers for confidentiality. There are those who suggest that in this, as in other cases, computer filing achieves *more* security than a paper-based system; one response to this is the argument previously advanced – that the effort and skill required to extract data illegally might be greater, but the information coming out of the system, being the accumulation of what is now in several dozen different places, would make the benefits of abuse or corruption, from a single act of intrusion, far greater. The issue is, therefore, not clear cut.

Notice, too, that one suggested legal protection for an individual against misuse of 'his' file – i.e. that he should have the right to demand a print-out of it – would probably be highly inappropriate in this instance. Not every patient ought to be 'told the worst' about his condition; nor is it always true that his relatives and friends should know every comment of the medical advisers. One severe critic, quoted earlier, is of the opinion that 'psychiatric, medical, evaluative material . . . [does] not belong in the computer files of any governmental agency, if there is any risk that the information will receive any degree of exposure'.[34]

Which proviso must surely mean that those who would show an increasing interest in the availability of such material – prospective employers, for example, particularly in such demanding tasks as air traffic control – must be legally (and irrevocably?) barred from obtaining the data *in any way whatsoever*.

Finally, it is pertinent to observe that within such central files the association of records common to one family would prove a vital adjunct to the prevention of, and the understanding of, many illnesses. Yet any man has the right to change his name, and to disassociate himself entirely from his relations. This is his private concern. Will this computer file be allowed to 'forget' who he previously was, and break down the chain of relationships? Probably not, for the sake of the common good; that man's freedom is then violated.

It is probable that the invasion of privacy in this area is of a slightly different nature from the other sectors we have examined, but it shares some common characteristics of the dilemma, for we find that there are implications from the development of data banks which may be either unanticipated, or only half thought through in relation to their consequences for certain values we would like to preserve. One of these is the confidentiality of medical records.

COMPUTERS AND LOCAL GOVERNMENT

The current projects, and the plans, of *central* Government Departments have already been exemplified in some detail. The date when functionally separate computers of such Departments will be first linked together is not possible to forecast. One can hazard a reasonable guess that it will occur under the auspices of the National Data Processing Service, who already have control over both Giro and

Save As You Earn, where there exists a substantial argument for the automatic transfer of money. We have suggested other potential areas of information sharing. We have also postulated that, in *Local* Government, 'mini-dossiers are inescapable' (Ch. 6). This section shows why this is so.

'It is a characteristic of local authority transactions that their records accumulate, for the larger a concern is, the more ramifications there are to its affairs and the more important becomes the retention of records in a tidy and easily retrievable form. And local authority business is . . . government business, the biggest concern of them all.'[35]

Most of the major local authorities have not been slow in recognizing the benefits available from a computer installation. The 'first' is probably claimed by Norwich City, who plunged into the deep end in the late 1950s, but most other authorities – Counties, County Boroughs, and some Urban and Rural Districts – have subsequently come into the swim, either directly with a computer of their own or indirectly through the use of a nearby installation on a 'service' basis.

The trend of use has followed the typical pattern of office computers: first the payroll, then extension to other financial work, then a gradual appreciation of the machine capability for many other clerical tasks, then increasingly experimental and esoteric projects. The other notable claim to a 'first', in the present context, must be that of West Sussex County Council which (under the direction of Mr C. W. Mallinson, County Treasurer, also currently Deputy Chairman of the National Computing Centre) inaugurated a real-time service in January 1968.

Summarizing the achievements of this authority, Mallinson has written: 'Nine [remote terminals] are now installed, in various departments of the council, the Sussex Police Authority – whose headquarters is some 40 miles away from the computer centre, and three county district councils . . . the facility of obtaining full information [from a single record] or any part, is extended to all files held in the random access storage device. In all cases, there are security procedures to prevent information being obtained by persons who have no authority to have it, and this is under the operational control of the chief officers concerned – not the computer staff.'[36] A further use made of the direct links to the district council offices is that for payments of rates, 'Information obtained automatically from paper-tape-producing receipting machines and from other sources punched into paper tape, updates the [hereditament] record via the data transmission part of the terminal.'

To further illustrate the point that, given a computer program capable of handling the transmission of data, distance is no obstacle, one may cite a news report of a congress in Vienna of the International Union of Local Authorities: 'The session which had most to offer in the way of entertainment was one conducted by Mr C. W. Mallinson . . . [who] introduced a "live" link-up between a computer in County Hall, Chichester, and a typewriter terminal in Vienna. The idea was to show how "information retrieval" works and how it can save time and labour. No one who watched this demonstration could doubt the soundness of Mr Mallinson's belief that in the next ten years or so the development of the use of computers in local government generally which we have witnessed up to now will be dramatically exceeded.'[37]

The demonstration was 'entertainment'; the background is deadly serious. Although at this time, two years since West Sussex went 'real-time', no other council has yet done the same, there are many who are slowly feeling their way towards similar – and indeed even more sophisticated – systems. Although the West Sussex system has its security checks on release of information, its designer (Stone) would wish these to be even more stringent – but this would have made the programming even more complex and costly (see Ch. 11), and unless there is legislation of the kind already once rejected by both Lords and Commons there can be no guarantee that the councils now planning terminal-linked computer projects will implement even minimal safeguards.

But why should they be needed? If, as a large number of people would fondly imagine, local government is nothing but 'rates, rents, roads, and refuse', why should the individual ratepayer be concerned – except on grounds of cost – if the council instals a large and modern computer system? An excellent publication provides a salutary corrective to such a view, and demands extensive review here, for it describes as no other publicly available document does the wide range of *personal* affairs dealt with by a local authority, their inter-relationship, and the prospects of integrated computerization. It is certain to be taken by many councils as 'the shape of things to come' and used as the basis of their own plans – irrespective of whether the proposals of the Maud Commission for 'unitary' authorities, and a new substructure, are put into effect.

The report[38] represents ten man-years' worth of intensive, and extensive, study of all departments of Haringey council – and it concludes that five or six councils ought to form a consortium to share one large computer. Haringey council itself has a total staff of 9,600, for a population of 254,000. Excluding 2,800 teachers, what do the rest of the staff do?

The keynote of the report is 'the diversity and complexity of the authority's responsibilities. These responsibilities can be stated in general terms as being the welfare of the population, the maintenance and improvement of the environment, and the provision of certain essential community services and amenities'. The principal services and responsibilities are listed (pp. 9, 10), a total of over 50 items; some typical volumes of activity for a year[39] (pp. 71 ff.) are:

Public Health Inspectorate inspections	35,504
Children, vaccination and immunization	19,643
Clinics (ante-natal, infant, dental, etc.)	98,534 attendances
Health visiting and home nursing	149,133 visits
School health, inspections and treatment	80,304
Meals-on-wheels	34,000
Children, in care, under supervision, court cases	1,214
Repair and maintenance council housing	30,000 items
Footways, trenches, gully works	36,528
School pupils	34,400
College and adult student	17,400
and, of course,	
Rates –	85,000 heredita- ments
Roads –	1,350

The reader of the report is left in no possible doubt that there is hardly a single operation performed by the council's work force which does not involve information about some person or persons. It would be fair to conclude that everybody on a council's staff knows something about somebody. Yet there are major inefficiencies. 'The weaknesses in the present arrangements are the natural consequence of primarily manual methods of record-keeping in scattered offices where pressure of work is often considerable. In general there is little circulation of information between departments and even in some cases between sections of a department.... The consequences in terms of the duplication of records are obvious on investigation, and, moreover, these records are not in fact perfect duplicates – there are inconsistencies in terms of completeness, currency and hence accuracy' (p. 8). Exemplifying this, the study found (p. 11) that eight separate departments or sections maintain independent records of commercial premises – and 'Significant discrepancies have been found between most of these records, some of which contain information which is seriously out-of-date, or are otherwise incomplete'.

Even more significantly, 'Information regarding personal movements revealed every day to the Rating section, and annually to the Electoral Registration Officer, is not acquired by other sections to enable them to amend their files . . . the records kept of any household may be out-of-step in different departments, or even in different sections of the same department. Consequently fruitless appointments are arranged and abortive visits and inspections are made. Such errors invariably waste time and money and reveal inefficiency to the public; occasionally they cause further distress to bereaved persons' (p. 12).

It would be entirely wrong to interpret these criticisms as an indictment of the methods of the one authority, Haringey. The same situation would be found in almost every local authority in the country, resulting from the independence which each enjoys to conduct its own affairs under the direction of its own local Councillors (within certain constraints imposed from Westminster), and the high degree of autonomy which each Departmental chief officer has, with responsibility directly to a sub-committee of the Council rather than a conventional 'pyramid' managerial structure. Inevitably, separate filing systems, separate record structures, disparate identification and retrieval methods, have grown up, designed each for its own particular objective. No one department can tell how much its interest in a particular property, or a particular person, overlap those of another department. Without completely centralized and integrated filing, there will always be 'significant discrepancies'. Without computerization, there will never be centralized and integrated filing.

But, given 'a large computer equipped with mass storage devices and linked to all major departments by telecommunications', there can be a central policy for the handling of information. 'The borough will store on the computer any information needed to fulfil this centralizing function – basically the common items of information relevant to the work of more than one department, and cross-references to more extensive files of information' (p. 13). Each department can then put in what it knows, and take out what it needs, with the assurance that the information is always the latest (and therefore the best) that anyone knows.[40]

Despite the work of LAMSAC and its predecessors,[41] in the encouragement of authorities to get computers, to use them intelligently, and to save systems and programming costs by common development projects, the sharing of machines and programs has been minimal. The one claim that may be made is that information and expertise have been freely interchanged, with a harmonious relationship between the DP staffs of autonomous authorities.

Now there seems to be movement towards a greater co-operative effort, as suggested in the Haringey Study. For example, 'a comprehensive investigation has been started into the most economic and practical method of bringing modern data processing facilities within the reach of every local authority in Wales'.[42] The rest of the world has forged ahead; Britain lags behind. Besides the USA, Israel, Austria, Germany, Holland, Italy and Japan are well advanced in

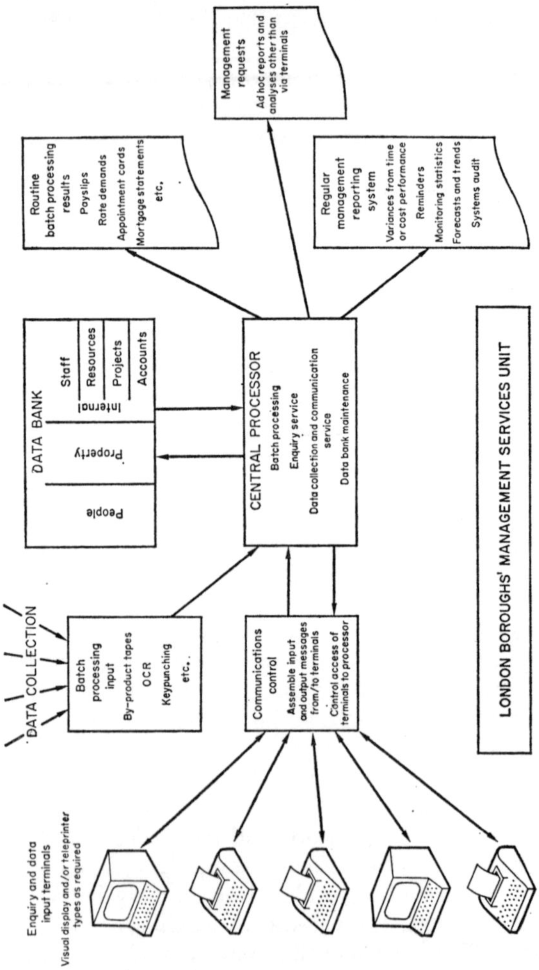

centralizing municipal computer power. Just seven regional centres serve the data processing needs of both central and local government in Denmark; in Sweden 100 authorities share a machine.

The entire concept of a local authority data bank is both unchallengeable, and potentially catastrophic. Against the postulation that this is the *only way* that services to the community can function adequately and relatively economically, there is no argument. Yet in its potential for the abuse of information, for the abuse of power, it is frightening. The Haringey Report, by the very fact that it ignores completely any mention of *un*favourable consequences, reveals what Cicero called 'The arrogance of officialdom'. It is an illustration of another kind of 'law' of bureaucracy: that men of good-will, serving the community in their appointed place, to the best of their ability, eager to perform their proper function as efficiently as possible, simply fail to take into account the adverse effect of their actions upon those affected.

Let us take a simple example of a relatively minor abuse that is unlikely to arise in the absence of a data bank. There are a number of people who quite deliberately do not pay their rates until they receive a final demand, on the (anti-social?) grounds that they, instead of the council, should have the benefit of an extra two or three months' interest on the money. There is no intention on their part of evading payment; they are acting within their rights.

Suppose one such person is a self-employed builder, who does a small repair job on one of the council's properties and submits a bill for the work. Bills are paid weekly, through the computer; this one is omitted due to a card punching error. The clerk investigating the 'rejects' should prepare a hand-written cheque to clear the account, but whilst obtaining the particulars from the data bank he discovers that the man's rates are overdue. So, why bother? Throw it into the 'LBW' tray – 'Let the Blighter Wait'. This is, nevertheless, an abuse of information and of authority.

Another interesting speculation may be made upon a specimen case given in the Haringey Report – which again fails to suggest the undesirable possibilities of the case. 'Let it be supposed that the Council are concerned with a site and properties which have been represented as unfit by the MOH [Medical Officer]. The site is one of appreciable area and there are alternative uses to which it might be put and these involve different time-scales for redevelopment. . . . It appears that if developed for housing there might be considerations of school needs, transport and shopping facilities, whilst development for business or commercial purposes might give rise to a need for a road improvement scheme.

'There will be a considerable amount of basic data contributing to the factual background which can be produced to assist in such a case. . . .

'(*a*) An analysis of the property . . .
(*b*) A list of occupiers
(*c*) A list of known owners
(*d*) Details of businesses carried on . . .

(*f*) Details of households for which information is held for any Council purpose . . .

(*h*) A synopsis of any pertinent questionnaires or surveys recorded in the historical data bank for town planning, relating, for example, to employment, traffic or leisure activities.'[43]

The policy decision to be made — difficult enough, in any circumstance – *ought* to be made on the basis of the most desirable prospect for the environment and the community as a whole. But let us see who those occupiers are . . . the data bank may show that some of them are awkward characters, persistent pesterers of the welfare office and 'non-co-operative' to official visitors. They will not easily be got out; that will affect our time-scale and our legal costs. And the owner of those three middle houses – his address looks familiar; let us try another sort of enquiry. Ah yes, he lives next door to a prospective Parliamentary Labour Party candidate; we had better be careful there or we shall have a big public fuss. And then there was that (*f*) in the list: '. . . *any* Council purpose . . .'. That sounds dangerously similar to the credit rating files considered earlier; the file might be full of all kinds of misleading fact and dangerous fiction. Given a data bank, factors become available to influence decisions, that may turn out to be not only an infringement on the privacy and the freedom of the individuals directly involved, but also *not* in the best interests of the community as a whole.

The people who work in our Town and County Halls have more and more to do, as their services and the demand for their services grows and grows. It was said in the early days of the Welfare State: 'A net of security, woven by all the arts of statesmanship so as to be proof against human folly, is being stretched under the anxious passage of our lives.'[44] But at the same time, 'The England in which we live is a land of diminishing freedom. That is inevitable; you cannot have it both ways. If the public purse is to underwrite for us the adventure of living, then our lives, at every turn, must be open to the public scrutiny. We shall have inspectors calling at unwelcome hours to satisfy themselves that the law's requirements are being observed; we shall have to fill in forms, answer elaborate questionnaires which seem to us to be of no importance; we shall queue up at the doors of public offices, and suffer, now from the brusqueness, now from the leisureliness, of public officials.'[45] Today this anti-bureaucratic attitude is probably shared by people of all political camps, particularly the young. The officials are fallible, even if they are backed up by the resources of a computer, and holes will appear in the 'net of security'. But we must set a limit to the 'public scrutiny' that we can accept. If local government is to have its data banks, and it seems that it must, we can only guard such freedom as remains to us by insisting that the separate files are *not* integrated, and *not* cross-referenced, so that *data collected for one purpose is never used for any other.*[46]

This *caveat* must, of course, include a complete inhibition upon opening the files of a local authority to the investigations of a central government agency. Let the Inland Revenue, and the Social Security, make their own contacts with the citizen, not delve into the dossiers compiled for other purposes. 'There is no question that a large-scale centralized data system which had no inhibitions on the information which it collected and no restraint on what it made public or how it made information available to other parts of the Government might indeed constitute a serious threat to privacy and liberty.'[47] But such integration and centralization is seen by the seeker after efficiency and economy as nothing but a pleasant prospect, greatly to be desired and swiftly to be devised.[48]

CONCLUSIONS

This more detailed examination of just three areas will have shown both sides of the coin; the clear and shining face of progress, liberation from drudgery, techniques from which the general public is the beneficiary; and the darker reverse, upon which the image of the free citizen is irreparably scarred. Perhaps we exaggerate; but the balance of advantage *lies*. It is false to assume that every argument favours computer methods. Can we admit that every electronic prospect 'pleases, but recall that man is vile?' (as an afterthought). We could well have added other examples, and developed each in greater depth, but must leave this for others – hopefully, those closely concerned with the specific projects – to work out in detail.

It is not enough to play the Cassandra role and then stand aside. The next two chapters will, therefore, deal with what can be done to protect the individual from the harm that men and their machines may do. We suggest some legal, and technical, safeguards to combat the threat to freedom which computers pose. After this, we shall try to draw some broad lessons about the way society should face the more general consequences of technological change, most of which will arise, we anticipate, from the increased widespread use of computers for 'problem-solving' and 'person-indexing'.

If we wish to preserve the benefits of the new machines without paying an unduly high price in the loss of values – some traditional, others less so – we must have adequate legal and technological safeguards. To find out what these are, and how well they might work, is no easy predictive task. The problem is a complex one, but it is not insuperable in terms of problem-solving. If we cannot come to substantive grips with it now, the next decade may be too late.

Notes

1. One whole volume of the *Hearings* to which we repeatedly refer is devoted to Commercial Credit Bureaux, and an alarming experience, retailed by Westin, will be summarized below. For the reader with particular interest in this topic, *Hearings*, B, is essential reading. For others, it is necessary to explain the background.
2. The N.C.C.L. has shown that the Tracing Services Group in the UK has records on 4 million people, increasing by 30,000 weekly (*Monthly Bulletin*, August–September 1969).
3. *Hearings*, B, p. 159 (Thomas E. Harman).
4. R. I. Miller, 'Computers and the Law of Privacy', *Datamation*, September 1968.
5. *The Sunday Times*, June 15, 1969.
6. *Ibid.*
7. *Observer*, June 8, 1969.
8. *Hearings*, B, pp. 6–7.
9. See *Data Systems*, March 1969, pp. 20 ff. Also US Newspapers, November 7, 1969, the Senate having passed the credit-file Bill on the previous day.
10. Jacob, *op. cit., supra* (N.C.C.L.), p. 5.
11. For a discussion of a strong law on credit-reporting, adopted by Massachusetts, see J. Hanlon in *Computer World*, October 8, 22, and 29; 1969. Also Dale Gibson and John Sharp, *Privacy and Commercial Reporting Agencies*, Legal Research Institute of Manitoba Unit, Canada, October 1968.
12. *Hearings*, C, p. 198 (Karst).
13. *The Times*, June 12, 1968.
14. *Ibid.*
15. See *Computer Weekly*, November 20, 1969, p. 12.
16. See *The Times*, November 4, 1969.
    See also *The Times*, December 9, 1969 – at the Bank of Montreal 'almost everything we do will be converted to computer operation. We will literally wipe our desks and counters clean of all the manual book-keeping and routine chores'.

17. See *Computer Weekly*, October 9, 1969, p. 6.
18. T. Mc. L. Galloway (C.M.O.H., West Sussex), 'Management of Vaccination and Immunization Procedures by Electronic Computer', *The Medical Officer*, April 19, 1963.
19. See e.g. the Annual Reports 'The Health of West Sussex', 1963–8.
20. See R. W. Newmark, *J. Coll. Gen. Practit.*, 12, 1966, p. 86.
21. J. Saunders and A. H. Snaith (W.S.C.C.), 'Cervical Cytology', *The Medical Officer*, June 2, 1967, pp. 299–303.
22. Saunders and Snaith, 'Cervical Cytology Consent Rate', *The Lancet*, July 26, 1969, p. 207.
23. *The Times*, *op. cit.*, November 4, 1969. But other reports of 'computer psychiatry' seem more blindly optimistic.
24. *The Times*, August 14, 1969.
25. *Ibid.*
26. See *Public Service*, November 1969, p. 4.
27. *The Financial Times*, September 18, 1969.
28. *The Sunday Times*, May 25, 1969.
29. For fuller discussion, see M. E. Abrams *et al.*, 'A Computer-based General Practice and Health Centre Information System', *J. Roy. Coll. Gen. Practit.*, 16, 1968, p. 415.
30. See E. D. Acheson, *Medical Record Linkage*, O.U.P., 1967; also *Record Linkage in Medicine* (ed. Acheson), London, E. & S. Livingstone, 1968.
31. R. Smith, *et al.*, in *Lancet*, 1, 1966, p. 650.
32. Local Authorities Management Services and Computer Committee.
33. Some actual 'horror' stories of leaks are told by Paul Baran, 'Remarks on the Question of Privacy raised by the Automation of Mental Health Records', Rand. Corp. Paper P-3523, April 1967.
34. *Hearings*, C, p. 71 (Miller).
35. *Local Government Chronicle*, October 25, 1969, p. 2028.
36. C. W. Mallinson, 'Computer Development in West Sussex', *Local Government Chronicle*, August 23, 1969, p. 1581.
37. *Local Government Chronicle*, July 5, 1969, p. 1240.
38. *London Borough of Haringey Long Term Computer Project, Initial Study*, London Boroughs' Management Services Unit, 1969.
39. Every authority produces copious annual statistics, for Ministries, Councillors and residents. For a further list of typical services, see also W. P. Davey, 'Local Government Computer Development in Wales', *Computer Bulletin*, December 1969:
    'A typical local authority [provides] such widely varying services as education, housing, health, welface, children, highways, refuse collection, baths, markets, abattoir, parks, cemeteries, planning, administration of justice, libraries, police, fire, ambulance, transport and water supply – to name but a few!' (p. 415).
40. Appendix 2 of the Report is reproduced here, by courtesy of the L.B.M.S.U., to whom we are grateful for permission to quote so extensively. The diagram shows the proposed scheme in concept.
41. The Local Authorities Management Services and Computer Committee developed from groups of computer experts formed by the Society of County Treasurers, and the Institute of Municipal Treasurers and Accountants – an indication of the broadening of interest from purely financial applications to all spheres of council activity.
42. Davey, *op. cit.*, p. 416.

43. *Haringey, op. cit.*, p. 28.
44. Ronald A. Knox (1949), *Occasional Sermons*, London, Burns & Oates, 1960, p. 278.
45. *Ibid.*
46. See A. Mindlin, 'Confidentiality and Local Information Systems', *Public Administration Review*, Vol. 28, November–December 1968.
47. *Hearings*, C, p. 4 (Carl Kaysen).
48. See for example the papers of the 'International Symposium on Urban Data-Management Systems', held at University College, London on April 6–9, 1970; the only dissenting paper was offered by one of the present writers.

Chapter 10

ADEQUATE SAFEGUARDS?

Thus far, we have considered the threats to privacy from a new technology. What safeguards exist at present to stem the tide of instrusions? What improvements, legal or otherwise, must be introduced to deal with the problem? Should the individual be given 'novel rights', as a recent pamphlet put it?[1]

The desire of the public authorities for information, ever-increasing as it is, reflects an appetite for more knowledge, not just about physical phenomena, but also about particular individuals – in order to dominate the environment. This information explosion is a pre-condition of action by the public authorities to increase the efficiency of their already growing responsibility for the parameters of the good life – social, economic, etc. As Edward Shils points out, 'The night-watchman state is now only a dim trace of the past'.[2] The desire of authority for information is unsatisfied, however. Its own powers are limited, both in the physical practicability of seeking it out, as well as the legal barriers which stand between the State and the citizen. Officialdom cannot always oblige the public involuntarily to divulge what officialdom would like to know.[3]

There is, of course, a relationship between these two factors, for legality is itself bounded in part by practical considerations. We are spared the full Kafka-esque unpleasantness by the sheer complexity of the social fabric. The eye and hand of the bureaucrat reach as far as the frontiers of the obvious and the convenient, but even totalitarian régimes have found (to their cost) that omniscience and omnicompetence are impossible goals. Under the Nazis, even in the nation's capital, Berlin, there flourished both a political Resistance movement and a literary Underground.

In liberal societies, there is much the public authorities *do* not know, even when they *should*: the old and sick often starve or freeze to death in their own homes, as there are not enough welfare workers to keep track of potential personal disasters of this kind. The point to be made here does not need over-stressing. Given the tradition of government, and the scarcity of resources for surveillance, privacy remains relatively protected. There are physical ('natural') and economic limits to what rulers can do in a society; there is a law of diminishing returns in information-utilization, at any given state of technology.

The law offers a contrapuntal protection in this context. The individual is protected by his existing rights, and by the constraints placed upon the executive branch of government and other public and private organizations. But the present law is not sufficient to deal with the collection of data and its unauthorized use.[4] The disclosure of private information may be a breach of contract, but it is difficult to define the legal position of information passed on by a credit rating organization. There is also legal difficulty when the information fed into the computer is inaccurate, or when the inferences drawn from it are wrong. English law does not go far enough in questions of protecting privacy compared with, say, Switzerland.

What is the legal position at present? There are a number of parts of the law which deal with, or help to protect us against, invasions of privacy. First, we shall see how these operate in the particular area of privacy-infringement with which we are basically concerned, and second, we shall try to look at the way in which safeguards could be established to deal with existing inadequacies of protection. The question, in general, has been outstanding for a long time in English law, but the oncoming of the computerized data bank has raised it recently, and suggested the need for changes.

It is simpler, as the group of Conservative lawyers found, to point out the defects in existing law than to define either the protection available under existing law or practicable as future legislation. They consider that there is no remedy available against the input, storage and delivery of erroneous information; that the misuse, or deliberate extraction followed by misuse, of data is subject only to relatively weak civil remedies; and that 'existing law ought to be supplemented so as to establish well-defined civil and criminal remedies suppressing unnecessary vexatious invasion' of privacy by the collection and dissemination of data bank information.[5]

The specific legal position, as it applies to computerized data banks, is spelt out by a recent authority:

'There seem to be three possible remedies against the misuse of data banks – defamation, negligence, confidence. A statement is defamatory if it is untrue and is published by one person to another. However, although the burden of proof to show the statement is true is on the defence, and although the law has recognized that a statement literally true may carry an untrue innuendo, this remedy may be limited (for our purposes) by two defects. First, the scope of the innuendo is unclear. Thus it is not at all clear that in the example of John Doe and his defective goods, the credit agency would be liable for telling another trader that he had failed to pay a previous debt. Secondly, if the information were kept not by a credit agency but by a trade association, the defence of qualified privilege would probably protect the association unless Mr Doe could prove there was malice.'[6]

The position here is clearly complicated, and some simplification is in order.

The remaining two categories, negligence and confidence, are of considerable importance, but there are innumerable difficulties to be faced as the law is not very precise. The law of negligence covers a mis-statement about a plaintiff's credit, but only so far as this was made without proper care. 'Proper care' is not easy to define. It would seem that credit agencies, for example, can rely on statements given to them by another, alleging a bad debt. In addition, the law of confidence may be useful to prevent the misuse of data banks, but as an authority points out: 'This action has for one reason or another escaped the attention of most lawyers, but over the years there have been a steady trickle of cases involving it.'[7] A 'steady trickle' is not adequate to formulate a thorough doctrine through case-law. It is very difficult for the citizen to know where he stands in the present legal context. The legal principles relating to privacy need spelling out more clearly.

No doubt, cases may be forthcoming to force clarification in judgements; but a basic statement of principle in a broad privacy bill would enable juries to interpret this over the years as it related to specific requirements, in line with changes in social norms.[8]

Criminal law too, is unclear. We can object to Section 2 of the Post Office (Data Processing) Act 1967, as it allows disclosure 'where required by law'. Secrecy in that Act is propped up by the Official Secrets Act 1911, which allows disclosure whenever this is in 'the interests of the State'. As the Post Office is now a public corporation, we still do not know if disclosure will be required or prevented by law. The Income Tax Act 1952, and the Income Tax Management Act 1964, permit disclosure where this is required by law, but give no definition of such requirements. The Theft Act 1968 too, while not intended to safeguard information, may do so. As one view suggests, 'If this is so, then valuable restraints have been imposed on private data banks'.[9]

The Inland Revenue is very strict, and will not for example 'inform' on someone who tries to put down bribery expenses as being tax-deductible. When some magistrates were found to be cheating on their income tax returns, the I. R. Board refused to disclose their identities to an inquisitive Lord Chancellor.[10]

But some of the safeguards belong to the realm of *departmental practice*, rather than being defined by law. Take, for example, the question of the confidentiality of medical records, which is clearly an important traditional and humane practice to be protected, bound up as it is with the preservation of the autonomy of the medical profession. It is essential to safeguard it in order to prevent breaking the trust which exists between doctor and patient *vis-à-vis* our most precious, often intimate, value – our health:

'[Consideration] of the general practitioner's records of his NHS patients, which belong to the Minister of Health, anticipates what has to be said about the records of Government Departments. The broad principle to be deduced from S. 2 of the Official Secrets Act, 1911, is that disclosure to persons not themselves government employees is not itself unlawful, but becomes so only when the document is handed to a civil servant 'in confidence' and whether or not the document is treated as confidential is, therefore, not a matter of law, but of departmental practice. That such legal consequences as are provided by the Official Secrets Acts should follow from a decision as to departmental practice may seem surprising, but this is probably the only feasible legislative technique. Whether, therefore, the records of Ministers of Health and Social Security are made available . . . is purely a matter for the Minister's discretion . . . there appears . . . to be only one exception: records of patients attending VD clinics. These are specially protected by a Statutory Instrument (NHS(VD) Regs 1948 S. I. 1948 No. 2517, Reg. 3) . . . providing that they shall be treated as confidential.'[11]

This is clearly unsatisfactory, and should be looked into by a Select Committee. This would be a corollary of the citizen's dependence on a public health scheme in a free society. Unless it could be *proved* that benefits would outweigh the disadvantages, we see no reason why records should not be confidential in a *legally* watertight fashion.

If disclosure comes within the ambit of that treacherous area, 'the public interest', information about the individual is not protected. A priest or doctor *must* give confidential information to a Court if this is thought desirable by that body, although this obligation does not apply to a lawyer.[12] Again, there is the need for parity here: either all should be protected, or none of them. An individual's relationship with his priest and/or doctor may be at least as important as that with his legal representative.

The practices of government reflect the state of trust which exists between the government and the people, and upon this our freedoms to a large extent depend. 'A civil society . . .,' writes Edward Shils, 'requires mutual trust between rulers and ruled.'[13] But the balance has begun to shift in recent times, and public distrust has grown as the 'anonymous, information-gathering privacy-infringing bureaucracy'[14] has developed. Westin went even further, suggesting that 'All the government agencies concerned with a problem, such as health, employment, education, etc., whatever their level of government, will be part of an integrated information system and will co-ordinate their information to make decisions. These clusters will also be linked closely to private decision makers, such as employers, educational institutions, insurers, and hospitals. What controls over information collection and circulation will we have ready for these new public agencies? . . . We are now in a last-minute position . . . law and ethical restraints must be the final safeguards in the new information system.'[15]

Before we discuss the possibility of legal protection, let us briefly recapitulate the four areas in which personal information is most sensitive to misuse, though the computer system is most valuable.

A computer system providing all-embracing account-handling would incorporate everything about your income, savings, and expenditure. Another critic cast a worried eye at the possible – and, he thought, likely – disappearance of a last bastion of privacy.[16] The computer system would assess your suitability for further credit on demand, and generate warnings if you appeared improvident. Anyone with access to the system could find out your financial viability. Linked with the State's computer complex, your tax, rates, and welfare benefits would be effortlessly calculated and transferred. So the system 'Will assure everyone that you are living your life reasonably and are in no danger of exercising that peculiar, disruptive and private right you had in the past, namely to have a private bank account which enabled you to have an occasional spree, a privately mortgaged home, a right to decide which creditor to pay when, and otherwise regulate your affairs with a minimum of outside assistance.'

One factor in the spread of new universities since the war has been the increasing demand by employers for paper qualifications. This whole concept of 'assessment by examination performance' is one of the targets of current student bellicosity. How reliable a guide to a person's character are his educational attainments, and who should be able to investigate them? For how long should a man's educational record remain in an instantly available file (to mark him for life as an 11-plus failure?), whether or not in association with other personal information? A computer file could never forget, unless programmed to forget.[17]

The doctor's surgery is the modern confessional for many, and the notes of GPs and specialist should remain confidential. This data would make a most interesting dossier for an over-inquisitive eye. The medical profession has an extremely high standard in its tradition of secrecy, and has its own fears that computerized systems, with all their advantages, are potentially far less secure from unqualified and unscrupulous intrusion than the documentary systems of the present.

As has been mentioned, police forces in America are already benefiting by the introduction of computer methods for filing criminal records. Thus, the whole community benefits, by better detection methods and more skilful crime prevention. But what a danger exists in creating a monster file of all offenders, down to the last parking-ticket and juvenile orchard-pilferer, and thus branding indelibly, for life, every law-breaker. The danger is in failing to sift the minor peccadilloes of the normally law-abiding from the vital data on the crimes of the unrepentant – but who shall say what information is useless to the detective in his search for solutions? As every televiewer knows, a great deal of detective work consists of sifting through masses of information, mostly irrelevant and concerning entirely guiltless people. The computer is the ideal tool – given that it has large and comprehensive personal dossiers; in some investigations anybody is suspect until proved otherwise.

With a plethora of detail, much of it (quite unknown to the individual) tucked away safely in computer storage, one suggestion has been made to attempt to solve the problem of incorrect facts. It involves the implication that at all times when asked to complete official documents a person should have the right to say whether or not the information being supplied may be released to other persons or not; then, from time to time, everyone should be sent a copy of his current dossier together with notes of the levels of restriction placed on each item of data, so that there is an opportunity for each of us to dispute the record. Such a provision was included in the unsuccessful Data Surveillance Bill (see Appendix).[18]

This philosophy has, in part, been adopted by the Association of Credit Bureaux of America, who after stringent Congressional Committee grilling, produced in December 1968 some recommended standards regarding the privacy of their data. One of these is that individuals should have complete and free access, on demand, to any information recorded about them. This represents a definite departure from past procedures, which were to gather everything likely to reflect on credit status, and never to reveal to any private person that he was on file at all.

The new standard is to be welcomed; yet it is not enough. A change in the law could give every citizen the right to examine the data filed about him in any Government or Company file, and to challenge any part of it. This MIGHT readily be done by requiring him to be sent a printed copy every year (with his tax return, perhaps). *But there are too many snags.* It would be very expensive to do; it would bring up thousands of complaints by those wishing to question the data; and, most significant of all, it would be treated by a large proportion of the population as just another bit of waste paper – especially if it emanates from government. It is also highly probable that more information, and more derogatory information, will be recorded about those people in the lower income categories; it is exactly these who will be either incapable of comprehending, or ineffectual in *challenging*, their annual report – and therefore the most vulnerable in all ways. In any case, one may question whether it is always right for a person to see *every* part of his own record – health records, and assessments of performance, come to mind here.

In all these areas listed, and in others too, we are likely to be bedevilled for many years by the aura of mystique that will continue to surround the computer. Despite its well-known fallibility – nearly always human errors in programs rather than machine malfunctions – which has produced cheques for 1d, and threatening final notices of unpaid bills when in fact a refund is due, there is every indication that the facts stored in an information-processing computer will be treated with greater sancitity than Holy Writ. The computer professional already knows that 'the computer said so' is a statement implying neither accuracy nor proof. Many more people have to be trained to think the same way, because wrong facts *will* get stored, and wrong answers *will* come out, and there is no reason whatsoever why not only the facts as produced, but the programs which manipulate them and the decisions taken based upon them, should not be challenged.

One critic noted that: 'There is a legitimate fear of the over-centralization of individualized information and the proliferation of people having the capacity to inflict damage through negligence, sloppiness, thoughtlessness, and sheer stupidity. These people are as capable of damaging others by unintentionally rendering a record inaccurate, or losing it, or disseminating its contents to unauthorized persons as are people acting out of malice.'[19]

The danger is that the technological trend must lead to more centralization, and increase the influence of organizations. On both counts the individual is at a disadvantage. (Time-sharing devices may reduce the centralized form of the organization on the other hand, but one must not be too optimistic here.)

The creation of an ombudsman has been a significant feature of the recent tension between governing and governed, and it is most likely that his powers will be increased. Already there is a movement to supplement the service by a local government obudsman. It may well prove possible to set up a kind of 'technological ombudsman' who, by having experts at hand, can keep a check on the activities of data bank computers, examine the programming used, insist on re-runs of the data, or even postulate the errors and generate his own tests of the systems.[20]

The National Council of Civil Liberties[21] has suggested the following:

'1. That a Data Bank Tribunal be established, with jurisdiction over both public and private data banks.

2. That the data bank should supply each individual with a print-out containing:
(*a*) the purposes for which that information is being used and has been used since the last print-out,
(*b*) the names, addresses and organizations to whom the information has been supplied since the last print-out.

3. Such a print-out should be issued
(*a*) when the subject first goes into the data bank,
(*b*) at periodic intervals,
(*c*) at any time on his request.

4. The Data Bank Tribunal should have jurisdiction
(*a*) to order erasure or correction for inaccuracy or irrelevance of the information,
(*b*) to order limited use of the information,
(*c*) where a correction is ordered to compel the data bank to inform all those persons to whom the incorrect information has been given,
(*d*) to sit in camera.

5. The print-out information should omit that which it is clearly undesirable to tell the subject, e.g. if he is a criminal, the details of his

modus operandi. A 'confidential report' for the purposes of employment does not fall into this class.

6. A failure to challenge the print-out should not be evidence of an admission of its truth.

7. Where the data bank contains pooled information provision must be made for information to be released only for the performance of the duties of the recipient.

8. The tribunal ought to have the assistance of an officer who can check on the compliance with these arrangements and the accuracy of information under 5 above.

9. An individual wronged by misuse of information about him ought to have the remedy of damages and rectification of the bank. The measure of damages should be double damages with a statutory minimum so as to ensure compliance. An extension of the criminal law is probably unnecessary.

10. These provisions should apply to public and private computer data banks and also to conventional data banks, so as to avoid any tendency not to computerize because of the complications these reforms would make.

11. A licensing scheme, or the establishment of a new profession of data-bank operators should be introduced. The law rightly governs the organization of the solicitors' profession, because persons holding themselves out as solicitors must have not merely a high standard of competence but also of integrity. So also, persons with the kind of sensitive information about the individual that is stored in data banks require an equally high level of integrity'.

We would go further. There may be the need for a change in the criminal law to cover cases of a very specialized nature, involving erroneous facts, mishandling of data, abuse of confidentiality, and so on. It may also be necessary to have a higher (Appeal) Court procedure through which such cases of computer disputation could be taken, and which could even decide that certain questions should not be asked in questionnaires, or at least not in the ways intended at that time. It is known that representatives of Local Authorities, in discussion with Ministry of Technology staff, have considered invoking a High Court Judge to advise on legal standards of data protection.

Some of the technical safeguards that it is possible to provide in the computer system will be described in the next chapter. Computer programs can be written to give a great deal of protection to the data, and arrange for multi-layered checks before anything is released.

One thing remains – to achieve a plateau of awareness at all levels of computer usage of the potential dangers, and the practicable solutions. A very strong professional code should probably be set up for practitioners in the computer-data-processing world, like the doctors' Hippocratic Oath. It is encouraging news that the British Computer Society, to which some 20,000 computer people belong, is hopeful of producing a code of ethics for the profession;[22] and that it has also set up a special group to consider all aspects of the computer and privacy.

To achieve any degree of security, top echelons of administration must be convinced of its necessity. Any scheme which allows for regular, or at least 'on demand' inspection of his file by an individual clearly puts up costs, and for computer systems and programming people to design security procedures into their data-handling jobs may well add 20 per cent or more to the development costs. Not all management may be sufficiently enlightened to appreciate a moral responsibility to offset some of the benefits by expenditure on protection.

A further safeguard that only management can determine is the practicability of placing *a time-limit* on the storage of data – of some specified kinds, perhaps – so that, like that Biblical seven-yearly purging of debt, it is erased after a certain period had elapsed. Computers can be *made* to forget, and data in agreed categories should not be allowed to be placed on ineradicable tape.[23]

The resourceful, ambitious, or even public-spirited (dangerous phrase!) chief will always be eager to make the best use of the best information available, and it may not always be right that he should have it. A news report mentioned an approach to the Ministry of Social Security by a Local Authorities Association, for help from Ministry records in tracking down bad payers of rent and rates who have moved house.[24] The Ministry refused, claiming confidentiality for its data, which is a cheering sign. But the public interest, and in the case cited the loss of public money, are powerful arguments for sharing information. The future demands for inter-departmental exchanges, at all levels, are quite unforeseeable; all that can safely be said is that when they do occur they are most likely to be to the detriment of the individual's freedom.

As examples, one can see that a road designer might be very interested to see a dossier on all the people whose houses lie in the way of his ideal route, to get some idea how costly legal objections might be; any organization considering an application for credit, or insurance, or mortgage, would be interested in a computer file showing the person's history as a good or bad ratepayer.

In order to deal with the new technological challenge we must have a clear idea of what we want to protect. Those who handle the 'hardware' must be given both general and specific guidelines. What is private, of course, varies from generation to generation, from culture to culture, and so on.[25] For example, information about incomes is private in Britain, but in the US you can go into a tax-office and find out the detail of anyone's tax return.

Again, there may be invasions of privacy which we do not know about, and even if there are breaches of contract (as when a credit agency gives wrong information about us to another firm) we may never hear about it, yet find we have been refused an account. American thinking on the subject is that data banks are permissible for credit purposes, but safeguards must be established. The suggestion that we should have the *right* to a print-out of all information stored about us in data banks seems very wise, with the one reservation mentioned earlier.

The greater the amount of information to be treated in the citizen's favour, as private and confidential, the better. There are too many forces operating in the opposite direction for us to encourage them, as we disapprove of many of their consequences, intended and otherwise. Where print-outs exist as a right, the State or organization concerned would not be able to conceal what it knows or has said is 'confidential' against the citizen's interest. If material is used for a 'confidential report', concerning, for instance, his promotion in a firm, he should have a right to see if it is accurate, and he should be able to challenge it if it is false. But this is a problem not confined to computer systems.

As an American lawyer recently wrote: 'If the observation of totalitarian societies, hospital or prison life, has taught us anything, it should be that an individual's life ought not to be an open book – unless he chooses to make it so. Society has a right to demand that the pages be exposed from time to time, but anyone who wants to compile the book by collating the pages and publish the contents without the permission of the author must accept responsibility for its accuracy and proper application. Nathaniel Hawthorne and the Concord transcendentalists observed in the nineteenth century that it was a most serious crime to probe the secret heart. If we fail to protect ourselves against the reach of our own technology, there may well be no secret hearts to probe.'[26]

The fact that the threat from the computer has raised the problem of privacy should enable us to deal with it by attempting some general legislative guide-lines, and at the same time come to grips with the special area of data banks and the rights of the individual. It has already been mentioned that several attempts have been made by our Parliamentarians, both Lords and Commoners, to introduce Bills defining new rights of privacy suitable for an electronically-monitoring age.

The Privacy Bill, introduced to the House of Commons by Mr Brian Walden, MP, was the result of two years' work by a study group of lawyers, and attempted to provide civil remedies for all kinds of intrusion and dissemination of information. The publication of the Bill provoked an immediate and highly predictable attack by the Press Council, reiterating the usual presumptuous claim of the press that it must be free to enquire and investigate. If something is true, said the Council in effect, it is right that it should be known. We have already shown that this is a dangerous philosophy. The very fact that such a proposition can even be implied is evidence enough for a reassessment of private rights.

Unfortunately, the statement of the Press Council, and the self-righteous editorializing of many papers, achieved their probable intention of clouding the debate on the Second Reading of the Bill.[27] The general intention of the Bill, and the principles of human rights, were almost submerged by attack and defence of the press. Most of the Members who spoke were lawyers, accustomed to prolixity, and despite the exhortations of Mr Speaker the debate ground a slow way to inconclusiveness.

Only three features are notable to our purpose: (1) Mr Eric Lubbock charged the Government with being as much a violator of privacy as any other agency – a charge which no one developed, and only the Home Secretary attempted to rebuff; (2) a Commission, under Mr Kenneth Younger, is to study and report to the Government as to *whether* (an unsuccessful attempt was made to change this wording to 'what') legislation is desirable for the protection of individual privacy; and (3) at the end of the debate, less than three dozen Members remained interested, to hear a supporter of the Bill (Mr Niall MacDermot) suggest that computer data banks need separate, and speedy, legislation – a view which we share.[28]

Critics of the Parliamentary system, insistent upon abolition of the House of Lords, might usefully compare this debate with that in the Lords on December 3, 1969, concerning computers and privacy. It is the latter which demonstrates an understanding of people's feelings, a deep concern for the true liberties, a cogency in conveying genuine hopes and fears, and a *freedom* to indulge in genuine debate without adopting specific postures to satisfy the electorate. On the other hand, the (elected) US Senate's discussion in this area was of a very high standard. Mr Alexander Lyon, MP, already once unsuccessful, is still active[29], as is the Parliamentary Committee for civil liberties. One may be assured that some new legislation will eventually become statutory, though whether it will cover both human rights and data banks is open to conjecture. There is no reason why we should not take action on both fronts. But for choice, the data bank situation deserves priority, because it is more of a contingent danger to freedom, because it can be tackled more swiftly than the general point, and lastly because we have survived without a general privacy law, and probably could continue to do so.

It would of course be the most satisfactory solution if we were able to advance on a number of fronts, given the interest which has been raised by the recent debates on both general and specific aspects of privacy. In the next chapter we turn to the technical safeguards which might improve the individual's protection against the invasion of privacy, and unauthorized access to confidential data held in computer storage.

Notes

1. *Computers and Freedom, op. cit.*, p. 3.
2. Edward Shils, 'Privacy and Power' in *Hearings*, C.
3. But in 1966 over 10,000 officials had a right to 'Lawful trespass' upon property – excluding the staff of Gas and Electricity Boards.
4. As was pointed out in a talk by Sir John Foster, QC, 'The Legal Implications of Surveillance', B.C.S. Privacy Group meeting, L.S.E., November 11, 1969.
5. *Computers and Freedom, op. cit.*, pp. 10–11.
6. J. Jacob, *op. cit.*, N.C.C.L., p. 9.
7. *Ibid.*, pp. 9–10.
8. The problem of protecting privacy was first faced in a substantive legal context in America ,in the *Harvard Law Review* in 1890, by Brandeis. and Warren
9. See Jacob, pp. 10–11.
10. According to Sir John Foster, talk, November 11, 1969, *op. cit.*
11. P. R. Glazebrook, 'Medical Confidences, Research and the Law', in (ed. E. D. Acheson) *op. cit.*, 1968.
12. See Jacob, p. 10.
13. Shils, *op. cit.*, p. 247.
14. *Ibid.*
15. *Hearings*, D, p. 300 (Westin).
16. Stephen P. Sims, *Data Processing Magazine*, USA, July 1966.

17. Dangers relating to even old-fashioned political files in universities are discussed in *The Times*, February 21, 1970. See also E. P. Thompson, 'The Business University', *New Society*, February 19, 1970.
18. Also in Bills before the Californian State Assembly, and the Canadian Parliament.
19. *Hearings*, C, p. 76 (Miller).
20. This has also been suggested in the USA, see *Computer World*, August 20, 1969, p. 8.
21. Jacob, *op. cit.*, final recommendations. They are based to some degree on *Computers and Freedom*, *op. cit.*
22. For a report of a B.C.S. discussion, see *Data Systems*, November 1969, p. 33. The Code accepted by the comparable US body, the A.C.M., is reproduced in the Appendix.
23. The vehicle licensing computer at Swansea will deliberately *not* forget anyone; it will be the responsibility of a person selling or 'laying-up' a car to delicence it, otherwise he will still be charged.
24. *Daily Telegraph*, June 2, 1968.
25. People today are less likely to worry about the stigma of being known to have been divorced, or illegitimate, although we think they should have the *right* to keep these facts private if they so choose.
26. R. I. Miller, 'Computers and the Law of Privacy', *Datamation*, September 1968.
27. Hansard, H. C., January 23, 1970.
28. The Younger Committee's terms of reference do not, however, allow it to deal with invasions of privacy by Government departments.
29. See *The Times*, November 8, 1969.

Chapter 11

FURTHER TECHNICAL PROTECTION

'No computer system can be safe against error and abuse.' It was in these words that a legal expert familiar with computers, summed up the evidence offered to the Congressional and Senate Hearings.[1]

These words must form a haunting refrain to a consideration of the action computer designers, systems analysts, and programmers can take to safeguard information. Whatever is done, however much time and money and ingenuity is spent, errors will creep into the data and lurk there undetected and unsuspected; important private facts will leak out, through inadvertence and malpractice, to those who should not see them.

The basic question must be *whether computer files will be as safe as conventional ones*. There is a vocal school of thought maintaining that the files will be even better protected; such a view is generally to be adduced to a lack of technological appreciation, whereby the bemusing fact that the machine stores all its data in 'binary digits' (or 'bits') makes it seem an obvious barrier against casual intrusion. This overlooks two objections: first, that the object of many of the computer programs will be precisely to make the data readable, at local and remote points; second, that the 'bits' are only coded representations of characters, falling within no more than half a dozen standard codes. They cannot be 'read' with the naked eye, but can be readily interpreted by anyone with a little knowledge.

One writer has said: 'The list of incidents is endless, and the tragedy is that until your own computer becomes involved, the chances of adequate precautions being taken are very remote. Why is this? The obvious answer is that managements are unaware of the risks undergone. Why are they unaware? Among the many reasons are, first, *a false sense of security* generated by the apparent technical complexity of computer systems: and second, top managements who are often sadly lacking in any real understanding of computers. A one-week introduction-to-computers course, a quick conducted tour of an installation, and a demonstration of the machine's capabilities (often no more than a ludicrously rigged print-out) are generally considered sufficient for what they need.

'In fact, this "instant pre-packed computer knowledge" does more harm than good. It adds to the misguided impression that computer systems, especially software, are so complex that they defy understanding by outsiders and must therefore be secure from misuse. Perhaps in the very early days of machine language programs, there was a degree of justification for this belief. But today, with high-level programming languages and the extensive use of manufacturers' common packages, the security-through-complexity claim loses any validity it might have had.'[2]

The ways of protecting information – against destruction, corruption, or intrusion – can be conveniently set out in two sections, defining first those features which the computer manufacturer must provide, built into the basic design of the 'hardware' and its accompanying operating 'software', and those things which the user must undertake to implement.

(*a*) *The manufacturer's responsibility*[3]

These are some of the features which will have to be arranged before the machine reaches the user. They are not listed in order of importance; some are already normal practice whereas others do not exist – but should.

1. Any computer that is supplied for multi-programming – that is, serving several users simultaneously – must have absolute protection within its central processor so that no job can be inadvertently corrupted by any other that is running at the same time. Each separate program, or each user's task in a full 'multi-access' system, must be allotted its own separate section of memory by the control program, and a system must then operate to ensure that the limits of this section are never violated. Thus no program, by accident or design, is able to interfere with the information handled by another. Only the control program itself, which organizes the rest of the tasks in the machine, has uninhibited access to all parts of memory – and part of the control must naturally be that no-one and nothing is allowed to interfere with *that* program!

2. All input and output instructions should be rigidly controlled, to the extent that the computer must simply treat them as illegal unless they occur in a special protected environment, or protected control program. All user programs must, effectively, issue a 'request' to this special screening device for a record to move from its storage on the file into the main memory of the machine. This request

must also be accompanied by a separate set of limiting instructions, which normally the manufacturer's software itself should arrange to set up. The importance of this deliberate complexity is readily seen if it is recognized that in earlier computers it was normally possible for anyone with a little knowledge to use the operator's console, and recover a record from its file, and print it out. This must be made impossible. There is always the chance that engineers and operators may learn ways of 'beating the system' and bypassing this protection, but the problem then becomes one of their integrity. The hardware must apply the constraint of complexity; the software should reduce all genuine program input and output to simplicity.

3. With mass storage devices, facilities should be available which allow the user to prevent all operations which would put new data in selected sections, so that the vital data held there *cannot* be destroyed. One might even go further to provide conditions under which access of the read/write heads to a particular section would be inhibited in all normal operational conditions, so that the data in that store would remain completely protected, unless released by the most senior staff of the computer division under their personal supervision.

4. Every storage device which is capable of being disconnected from the computer, and operated under 'manual control' (for the benefit of engineers, who in this way can perform essential maintenance or repairs without requiring the whole computer) should have a special lock to control manual or automatic operation. Thus, no outsider could gain access to files through the manual controls.

5. Every storage device, and every terminal, should have an independent switch for its main power supply, and that switch should be lockable. A method similar to that of an ignition switch and starter on a car might be suitable; though it might be more convenient if the key could be removed from the machine once power was on, and need not be reinserted to turn it off. The important thing is that only the authorized user is able to switch on.

6. All data, as we have described, is 'coded'. Whenever it is sent over public communications circuits, it should be further transformed by some 'scrambling' or 'ciphering' process, to make life difficult for the wire-tapping eavesdropper. The manufacturer must therefore supply terminals which can perform scrambling transformations. The organization using the computer should be able to define any cipher-

ing system, and ideally be able to change this at will under its own control.

7. Since, as we shall see below, 'password' identification will form an important feature of all systems – the terminal user being required to type a private code which the computer will recognize – all those terminals which produce a printed copy of messages sent and received must be fitted with a 'print suppress' switch, so that such a password can be transmitted without being printed.

8. Many of the connections between computers and their networks of terminals, between computers and faster input/output units working at distant locations, and between computers and computers, will be established when needed over the public telephone network. Either the user will dial the computer, or the computer will send out signals that are effectively 'dialling-up' the subscriber. When this occurs, there must be a built-in assurance that the connection is correct. At the present time, the Post Office will not in fact allow the generation of dialling pulses by automatic equipment such as computers; it is somewhat over-cautious about the efficiency of its own telephone exchange equipment. The facility is, however, readily available under the American private-enterprise telephone system, and will be demanded here. All the computer hardware must therefore have a built-in code which identifies and authenticates it, and which is automatically double-checked whenever a connection is established. Such a code should be in part fixed, and in part variable by the user.

But manufacturer's safeguards are not enough. There are still dangers to be faced. The question of whether a computer can be rigged in spite of these protective checks was recently raised in a critical examination of computerized ballot-counting.[4] The election involved was the contest for mayor of Los Angeles in the summer of 1969 when the voters in this four-fifths white city nearly elected a black candidate Mr Thomas Bradley, against the veteran incumbent, Mayor Sam Yorty.

Researchers from Systems Research Inc. included Dr James Farmer, its chief. He observed that: 'You might suppose that a cheat must have physical access to the computer centre while the count's in progress. Not necessarily. He could as easily rig it given access a day or two earlier, when no one's around.'[5]

The team found that one would not need a great knowledge of computers to rig the supervisory program, which would be all that would be necessary to switch every tenth vote to a rival, for instance.

There would be sufficient of a crowd in the computer room on election night for an outsider to slip in with a new program. The report thought that 'Someone could easily modify this program. "It wouldn't be too hard to find someone willing to do the brainwork," says Farmer, "and, considering what students have done in the past, that's where I'd look for an accomplice. Once he'd fixed the supervisory program, the computer would do the rest. Someone would have to be bribed to slip a few extra cards – perhaps as few as two or three – into the deck." '[6]

The team were not of the opinion that the election was fraudulently carried out, but intended to show the dangers from the application of the new technology. The city administration has set up a committee to look at the election, and there may have to be a recount.

There are those who are ready to attack IBM, who run the $10 million contract for counting votes in Los Angeles County, and fight 'corporate control of the US voting process' by a Congressional inquiry. 'It's easy for technologists to smother the layman's protest,' says computer expert Phyllis Huggins, *Newsline's* editor, 'but in the end society won't tolerate it. In our zeal to computerize everything in sight, we're forgetting to consider whether the rights of society are being damaged. Computerdom is due for a black eye.'[7]

It would seem to be reasonable *not* to take manufacturers' safeguards for granted, although pressure must be kept up for these to become as water-tight as possible. No less important are user precautions, to which we now turn.

(*b*) *User Precautions*

An extremely valuable summary of the threats to information privacy and the measures which can be adopted to arrive at safeguards is provided in a recent paper[8] and the following points have been derived from this with adaptations to clarify technicalities. Its comprehensiveness obviates the need to seek further for problems and solutions, and enables us to concentrate on the effectiveness of the counter-measures available.

The four main classes of protective measure will be described first, and each then set against the types of identifiable threat, to explain its value. It is assumed throughout that the protection required is that which is appropriate to a multi-access computer system, with remote links – i.e. that protection in an entirely 'in-house' installation (and against 'in-house' intrusion in a larger system) is a matter of the integrity of and control over the local staff.

PROTECTIVE MEASURES

1. Processing restrictions. These are largely covered by those items listed as the manufacturer's responsibility, but there are other things the user may decide to do. He may wish the computer control program to restrict access to certain files, so that they are only available to any one user program at any one time – though such an inhibition would in practice limit the advantages of a multi-access system. More probable would be a constraint such that only one program could change or update information in a file at any one time, and that while it was doing so no other program could gain access. Thus while several simultaneous 'read only' programs could run, the dangers (attributable in the main to accidental factors such as program or hardware faults) of information corruption by simultaneous 'writing' of further information are obviated.

It is also possible to arrange for both program and data to remain in memory for only the briefest time, while they are actually required and operative. Immediately the information is finished with, or the program has completed its task, the memory can be erased. If the program becomes inactive (as when waiting for a terminal operator to respond), it can be temporarily removed to a fast auxiliary storage device and the memory erased, to be recalled and restored when the operator's response materializes.

It could also be arranged for certain files to be held on dismountable devices, which can be removed entirely from the computer except for certain authorized activities, although this again detracts from the advantages of a fully real-time, on-line, multi-access system. In such cases the software would request the computer operator to place the file on the machine, and also to signify approval of the request, whenever a remote user indicated through his terminal that the data was required.

2. Cyphering. This approach is also called 'transformation'. As pointed out above, all transmissions whether of speech, music, pictures, or data, are in a sense 'coded' for they all require that the original 'input' be transformed into a series of impulses. The right equipment is necessary at the receiving end to re-convert these serial signals. Similarly, of course, all data actually stored within a computer is coded into electrical and magnetic signals, and has to be decoded for display by printers or cathode screens.

Although it is one of the anomalies of the computer world that several different coding structures are called 'standard', the fact that there is no single standard is no great obstacle to the intruder. If he knows the type of computer, he knows its internal code. If he knows the type of terminal, he knows its fixed code. If he does not know either, the range of possibilities is relatively so small that a little experimentation will readily reveal which is used.

Only genuine cryptographic methods can make computer codes, and transmission codes, incomprehensible. Certainly all confidential data should be given the protection of at least a minimal form of transformation in all remote transmission. It is desirable that all data in files should also be ciphered so that it no longer conforms simply to the internal coding structure of the computer. Ideally – and a computer is the ideal tool to handle this – ciphering should be performed according to randomly selected patterns which change from day to day, or from file to file, or even from enquiry to enquiry, so that the cipher is virtually impossible to break. But one cannot, unfortunately, ignore the high cost of implementation nor the 'unproductive' processing time which the maximum protection will involve. Since 'no computer system can be safe against error and abuse', and *absolute* accuracy and secrecy cannot be guaranteed however sophisticated the transformation techniques, there must be a balance between the degree of sensitivity of the data and the penalties of cryptography. Nevertheless, Baran has maintained[9] that even minimal privacy transformations in both storage and transmission of data are a valuable deterrent against eavesdroppers, and are therefore essential. Hoffman has shown that the cost in terms of computer resources for the operations of coding and de-coding, is ·007 seconds[10] – which is a lot of time in computer terms!

3. Intrusion monitoring. A protection is afforded by the inclusion of programs to detect illegal attempts to extract information. This may be arranged to give immediate warning, or to provide an 'audit trail' for subsequent analysis. By analogy with the car, this protection can be like an automatic warning device which sets off the horn and lights if there is any attempt to interfere with the car, or like the police attempting to identify a thief by his fingerprints after a stolen car has been recovered. Obviously the former is more effective – but it is also more expensive for the owner; the same is true of data protection.

Petersen and Turn give a good description of what they call 'threat monitoring': 'Threat monitoring concerns detection of attempted or actual penetrations of the system or files, either to provide a real-time response (e.g. invoking job cancellation, or starting tracing procedures) or to permit *post facto* analysis. Threat monitoring may include recording of all rejected attempts to enter the system or specific files, use of illegal access procedures, unusual activity involving a certain file, attempts to write into protected files, attempts to perform restricted operations such as copying files, excessively long periods of use, etc. Periodic reports to users on file activity may reveal possible misuse or tampering, and prompt stepped-up auditing along with a possible real-time response.'[11]

In simple terms: Stop them if you can; try to catch them if you can't.

The Data Surveillance Bill (see Appendix) would have required that 'The operator of each data bank . . . shall maintain a written (!) record in which shall be recorded the date of each extraction of data therefrom, the identity of the person requesting the data, the nature of the data supplied and the purpose for which it was required.' The drafters chose, therefore, the cheapest of methods – to record *all* extractions of data and allow a visual scrutiny of this record to suggest which may have been illegal. *Who shall watch the watchdogs*? And who is going to pay for the computer filing space that will be needed to hold this audit record before it is 'written' at the end of the day – perhaps 500,000 or more enquiries – and give 'absolute' protection against tampering with *this* file? These points are mentioned to emphasize again that any protection is costly, and that no protection is perfect.

4. Password control. All access control must depend upon this strategy, in one form or another. If the computer is to scrutinize, authorize, inhibit, or record all remote entries into its files, there must be a method by which it can establish the identity of the terminal user and verify that he has authority to proceed. So far, this has most often been accomplished by allotting to each authorized enquirer a private 'password', which the computer uses to 'recognize' him, and to establish the extent to which he may have access to the files. It may, for example, allow him to retrieve from some files but not others; it may allow him to alter some files but not others; it may restrict him to obtaining only certain items out of the files.

However, simple unvarying passwords alone are not adequate to protect sensitive files. They are too easy to find out. Indeed, experiments with a fairly simple system have shown that people who knew nothing about it at all could break the security after about five hours' work. That is a very small outlay in terms of the information-benefit to be won from a centralized and concentrated computer filing system. Some form of password which is 'instantly disposable' like paper tissues, seems to be needed. If both terminal user and computer could take the next in a list of random numbers, each number would be the right password for one and only one transaction.

A novel idea based on a similar principle – the use of random, or apparently random, numbers – has been suggested.[12] Under this system, each time a caller established contact with the computer, a pseudo-random number would be printed out on his terminal. He would perform some very simple (mental) calculation on this number, perhaps in a process unique to himself, and send the result to the computer. The computer, having made the same calculation on the original number, decides whether his reply is correct and viable to permit him further penetration into the system. Even if no 'transformation' of data is used, the wire-tapper or other eavesdropper does not learn much from such a communication, for he only sees two apparently unrelated numbers, and even quite a simple calculation can be very hard to break – especially if it incorporates the time of day, and is therefore different for each transaction.

It should go without saying, but unfortunately is unlikely to be true in all real-time installations, that any legal 'owner' of a file which is protected by a password key should be able to change the password at any time, through his terminal, without the central computer staff knowing anything about it. The file is his, and the control over it must be made fully his.

Extensions of the password principle look possible in the future, to provide other and better ways for the computer to 'recognize' a user. It may be possible to fit to the terminal a small reading device into which a personal identity card, like a credit card, must be placed before any transaction is accepted from the keyboard. Relatively cheap equipment may develop from the current research into electronic coding of finger-print patterns, which will be able to 'read' the print of a finger placed on it, and give a positive identification of the individual. At some more distant date, recognition may be accomplished by the 'voice print' of a person making contact with the computer over a telephone line.

Another necessity in one view is that there should be electronic data processing security specialists, just as there are security experts in other walks of life. 'A satisfactory EDP control system cannot be maintained in any company of reasonable size without a group of skilled computer-security specialists, independent of the EDP line management, to design, implement, and monitor the various control procedures. Such a group would check for failure and sabotage, would plan for emergency back-up in the event of a computer system failure, and would conduct periodic tests of duplicate files and other control procedures to determine the ability of the EDP operations to recover according to schedule. And, finally, it would monitor the security system constantly to ensure that new procedures were developed as necessary and that the old ones were removed when outdated.

'Management probably will not find such control experts readily available in the labour market; it may have to develop its own corps. Again, management must weigh its risks and then act accordingly.'[13]

Also, let us add, management must recognize that this elite becomes another stratum beyond the main EDP stream who will have the power to *break* security, and whose integrity and legality must be impeccable. It has been said elsewhere that 'by relying entirely upon their own staffs, managements run the grave risk of more than defeating the desired objective. Their own staffs are themselves a permanent, changing and major security hazard. By participating in a security exercise, they could well be introduced to previously unthought-of possibilities. Also, too detailed involvement of the people against whom security precautions are directed is not far short of handing out keys to the safe. There is therefore an obvious requirement for independent experts. This could mean calling in reputable or management consultants, and/or using the advisory services of firms specializing in security. Whatever approach is adopted, managements should tread cautiously, for there is only a handful of people in the UK with real experience of the technical, operational and managerial aspects of computers as well as the peculiar security problems inherent in their use'.[14]

The problem is further complicated by the proliferation of remote terminals. As another report points out: 'Today, setting up a security programme is complicated by the growing use of remote terminals. It is not uncommon for a company to have its computer in one center, data transmission points in several different cities or states, and assembly of final reports in still another location. When employees hundreds of miles away are in direct contact with the computer files, there must be controls to ensure that the files are not changed from remote locations without authorization, and that classified or sensitive data are available only to authorized personnel in those locations. For instance:

'The number of remote terminals through which computer files can be changed should be limited.

'Identification codes for each terminal and authorization codes should be used for the limited number of employees who are authorized to operate remote equipment. The computer should be programed to check the validity of the codes before it accepts or gives information. Since personnel turnover is high, identification codes should be changed frequently.

'The adequacy of controls themselves should be checked. One way is to have supervisors try to gain access to a remote terminal without authorization. If they can use the terminal without being challenged, so can others.'[15]

SOME SPECIFIC ILLUSTRATIONS

The above, then, are some of the strategies that may – and in one form or another *should* – be adopted to minimize intrusion into computerised filing systems. To see how effective these protections may be, we must now consider some *specific* cases which can be envisaged as jeopardizing the security and secrecy of the information, and point to those *general* counter-measures which are most appropriate against each of the threats.

First, what are the defences against a person who gets his hands on a terminal? He may be an authorized user tempted to 'browse' through other files to see if there is anything of interest, or any person endeavouring to convince the computer that he is an acceptable enquirer. In neither case are processing restrictions or ciphering likely to stop him; provided, however, that there is a good password system in operation his attempts will almost certainly be unsuccessful – and the monitoring of all calls can either alert the computer staff immediately to an irregularity or at least provide *post facto* knowledge of attempts to break in. Whether the intruder is only casually interested, or deliberately endeavouring to tamper with the files, passwords provide good protection.

But then there are those ingenious investigators to whom, as we have shown earlier, information is money, who will bring the electronic gadgetry of 'snooping' into the computer's orbit. They may put their bugging devices in the computer room, or indulge in conventional wire-tapping.[16] Against these data-thieves only complete ciphering of all information can provide a defence. The pulses which they pick up must be incomprehensible without the key. Unfortunately, a greater sophistication is likely to be employed than mere 'tapping' of lines; these intruders may connect their own (identical) terminals on to a legitimate user's line so that they ride along with all his activity, receiving all his input and output; perhaps they may even initiate transactions themselves which the computer will think come from a valid terminal. Petersen and Turn call this a 'piggy-back' entry, and apart from 'limiting the infiltrator to the same potential as the user whose line he shares' see little defence against him. There is in fact a possible counter-ploy, but it is expensive. It uses ciphering, but instead of retaining the same cipher at all times, with terminal hardware performing the transformation, it requires that the terminal have some form of locally programmable memory. The pattern of transformation is then changed from time to time, *not* under the control of a signal originated either by the terminal or the computer (for if it were, the 'piggy-back rider' would pick up the change as well), but under a rigidly controlled time-cycle that keeps the terminal and the computer in harmony. Very expensive!

Against computer personnel there can be no absolute protection. Anyone who understands the programming of the machine, many who understand the operating of the machine, and most of those who understand how to maintain and mend the machine, can safely bypass all the electronic barriers.

'Unfortunately there are those in EDP, just as there are in every other area, who do act from questionable motives. For example:

'A programmer in a bank managed to steal a large amount of money simply by programming the computer to bypass his account number when reporting on overdrafts. He was then free to overdraw his checking account by any amount he pleased.

'On a somewhat larger scale, a group of enterprising individuals in an investment firm raided the customer accounts and then informed the customers that there has been a computer error in the service agency that processed their accounts. Because the public is usually ready to believe a cry of "Computer error!" it was some time before the raid was discovered.'[17]

If we accept that there is no way of supplying absolute security against technical staff, then *all* the suggested safeguards are still worth while – because they make it more difficult for even the experts to intrude. Indeed, it is conceivable for protection to be applied so thoroughly that the amount of work necessary to penetrate the screen becomes an almost adequate deterrent. All information, like gold, has its price. If it costs £2,000 of effort to get £500–worth of information, the data is safe; and if commercial considerations were the only thing making security necessary, expenditure on security up to the potential value of the loss would be economic sense. Yet if the information store is potentially as priceless as Fort Knox, and if with the best safeguards it costs only £10,000 to effect a break-in, that data is *not* safe.

There is one other class of deliberate infiltration – the simple physical acquisition of removable files, on tapes or discs. It is not far-fetched to envisage a crude raid upon a computer centre, in which the 'swag' is a pile of magnetic tapes. The haul would be stowed at the thief's own computer installation where he could examine the files at leisure. And the moral of this story is: keep the computer room secure, and cipher all data in all the files.

There is also the need to keep a check on strangers:

'There is every reason to keep unauthorized personnel and visitors out of the computer room. Yet many companies view their computer installations as showplaces, welcoming visitors with relatively little supervision and failing to provide even minimum security precautions. These companies apparently have not considered the possible losses from damaged files or lost programs and the consequences of having equipment out of service.'[18]

And an anecdote reinforces the point about controlled access. The story is a true one:

'A large insurance company in an East Coast city recently gave a ladies' garden club a tour of its EDP facilities. The spinning tapes and blinking lights impressed one visitor so much that she felt she had to have a souvenir of the occasion. She later said, "I hope I didn't do anything wrong. There were all those boxes of cards on the table, and I just reached into the middle of a box and took one." Perhaps this lady only caused a program to be rerun. A more serious possibility is that the card may not have been missed at all, and the center is still trying to correct the resulting confusion.'[19]

Lastly we must envisage the accidental errors, either by people or machines, which open up files that should be locked. It is always possible for a user accidentally – e.g. by mistyping – to set off a train of events that are neither intended nor desirable. The computer programs will always have some errors left in them, perhaps lurking unsuspected for months or even years, which one day will cause a leak in security. One enquiry program known to the present authors suddenly started transmitting perfectly correct and valid replies to the wrong enquirer – in fact reversing simultaneous answers. An unhappy coincidence had – not surprisingly – been inadequately catered for in the program.

The hardware itself will develop faults from time to time, and these may result in mis-handling of data. This is in fact extremely unlikely, since such is the sophistication of computer design today that almost any error will instantly halt the computer for engineering attention. Nonetheless, 'When management does think of computer control systems, it tends to focus mainly on fraud, and there have been some widely publicized cases of this. But the real problem for most companies is not fraud but ordinary human error, which can cost a company millions of dollars without criminal intent on anyone's part. Computer security thus involves a review of every possible source of control breakdown – a highly demanding but not impossible job.'[20]

In relation to accidental or intentional release of confidential data, we ought to envisage the computer control system as a 'control maze', to use Wasserman's term. Breakdowns in one part could be corrected by controls in another area. Interlocking controls would be the optimal solution, and control responsibility must be placed in the hands of groups throughout the hierarchy, rather than one group or individual

Security does not come at bargain prices. A recent estimate shows the costs involved:

'For simplicity's sake, the purchase price of computer hardware is used as the estimating factor – this reasonably reflects the volume and type of work handled, the complexity of systems, and the overall size of the installation. An investigation covering the three "obligatory" areas mentioned above could (and if done thoroughly, should) amount to about 5 per cent of the hardware costs. A figure very much less than this could be false economy.

'The cost of designing and implementing a security system depends largely upon how much software needs to be written or amended. In the unlikely event of no software work being required, the extra cost should not amount to much more than 3½ per cent of the hardware cost; with software work, an average installation could expect extra costs of approximately 7½ per cent, while extreme situations could easily add 20 per cent. The subsequent, and necessary, monitoring of the system, which includes amendments to cover increases in hardware and production work, could cost 3½ per cent per annum of the hardware value.'[21]

One American firm only brings in its master files and programs from independent storage half an hour before production starts, and they are then independently audited, and constantly reaudited. They estimate they spent as much as $80,000 in a recent year on computer security alone.[22] Such a process is naturally quite inappropriate to the modern installation which requires the major files to be continuously 'on-line' for remote enquiry and up-date processes. The extra problem faced by the DP manager here is that of ensuring that any file which is inadvertently corrupted can be quickly re-created from a copy held in a fire-proof, theft-proof environment together with copies of all changes since the last master copy was made. Fundamental decisions are needed here, to maximize the insurance and minimize the cost. The frequency of 'dumping' (i.e. copying out) the current file will be a factor of the anticipated change-activity on the file and the time necessary for its re-creation in the event of destruction.

This is a slightly different angle on data security – the *physical* protection of the files. It may be concluded from the lurid advertisements by the makers of fire-proof safes that many companies' documentary files are inadequately safeguarded. It is also true in electronic data processing.

This discussion has shown that the threats are various, and the counter-measures few – but all immensely desirable and effective over a wide range.[23] Every restriction and every safeguard that is built into the computer system will inflate the costs above those of a system with no protection, but it should be clear that economic reasoning alone is not the arbiter. For the social, political and psychological health of the community, privacy in the conduct of the individual's affairs is vital.

Notes

1. J. Jacob, *The Times*, April 30, 1969.
2. G. F. Parker, 'Keeping Computers Safe', *Management Today*, p. 29, September 1969.
3. Thomas J. Watson, Jnr, US Chairman of I.B.M., has stated flatly that no manufacturer can safeguard a data bank against 'human corruption' (*San Francisco Chronicle*, April 6, 1968.
4. See Charles Foley, 'Can Vote-counting Computers be Rigged?' *Observer*, November 1, 1969.
5. *Supra.*
6. *Supra.*
7. *Supra.*
8. H. E. Petersen and R. Turn, 'System Implications of Information Privacy' in Vol. 30 of the *Proceedings of the A.F.I.P.S.*, Thompson Books, Washington, 1967. A tabular summary therein is reproduced, in part, in Lance J. Hoffman, *Computer and Privacy; A Survey*, Stanford Linear Accelerator Center, California (PUB-479; 1968). See also David K. Hsaio, 'A File System for a Problem-solving Facility', University of Pennsylvania, 1968.
9. *Hearings*, A.
10. Lance J. Hoffman, Paper CGTM 76, Stanford University. He says elsewhere (statement to California Assembly Committee, September 22, 1969) that 'The computer industry has the knowledge to implement reasonable privacy safeguards, but it has not done so because buyers of computers have not found it worthwhile to pay for these safeguards.'
11. Cited in Hoffman, *supra*, p. 20.
12. Hoffman, *op. cit.*
13. Brandt Allen, 'Danger Ahead! Safeguard Your Computer', *Harvard Business Review*, November–December 1968, p. 101.
14. G. F. Parker, *op. cit.*
15. Joseph Wasserman, 'Plugging the Leaks in Computer Security', *Harvard Business Review*, September–November 1969, p. 124.

16. Two bills in the California State legislature which would have legalized 'official' electronic eavesdropping were rejected: see Paul N. Halvonik, 'Right of Privacy Upheld in State Legislature', *American Civil Liberties Union News*, Vol. XXXII, August 8, 1968.
17. Allen, *op. cit.*, p. 99.
18. Wasserman, *op. cit.*, p. 125.
19. Allen, *op. cit.*, p. 100.
20. Wasserman, *op. cit.*, p. 120.
21. G. F. Parker, *op. cit.*, p. 36.
22. *Ibid.*, p. 37.
23. See W. Schweisheimer, 'Embezzlement by Computer', *The Bankers Magazine*, July, 1970.

Chapter 12

SUMMARY AND CONCLUSIONS

We will now draw together the threads of our argument, and offer some conclusions. In the attempt at prophecy, we may be felt to have overdramatized at certain points, but as we declared at the beginning, we are not alone as 'provisional catastrophists'. In this matter as in many others, all that is necessary for evil to triumph is that good men should do nothing. We hope to arouse good men to action, for there is provision to avert the 'catastrophe'. We also hope that the medieval scholars were wrong when they wrote 'A strong imagination brings on the event'.[1]

Computers are going to change the lives of men in unprecedented ways. More than the steam engine, electrical power, nuclear energy, or any other revolutionary invention of industrialization; more than any prior change in techniques, small or great;[2] society will be changed more perhaps than men will be able to bear. Much of this change will be for the betterment of our lives, individually or collectively; potentially there could be many changes for the worse. At the very least, those who know and care must strive to come to terms with the new power and ameliorate its effects.

Men will say there has always been change, and that mankind has always had to cope, to learn anew, to modify habits and attitudes. So far as it goes, such an argument is unquestionable, but it does not go far enough to offer hope for this decade. It does not take account of the increasing *momentum* of change, the change to a new order. If society continues to behave as though there were only gradual mutation, on the assumption that men *will* cope, *will* have time to adapt as before, then the 'catastrophe' is inevitable. We have to learn to adapt to a new freedom and a new potential for power, because the accelerating pace of technological invention and application has brought us to a new level of advance. The computer is just one of the results of this greater activity in research; yet in itself this machine adds a new dimension to the acceleration, for its power brings an increased ability to obtain knowledge to anyone who requires it, and permits the evaluation of those hypotheses which hitherto (because of the sheer impossibility of producing results with manpower alone) remained unverifiable.

The case for using the computer is simple and impregnable. It is the tool for experimentation beyond the wildest dreams of yesterday's scientists and researchers; it is the tool for efficiency in the modern office. Should the sceptic enquire 'efficiency for what?', the answer is 'efficient for public service and the improvement of our civilization'. Whether it be the services paid for directly by a client to a business, or the services paid for by the various revenues of Her Majesty's Government, they will be more effective with computer power for information.

The case for individual privacy, for freedom of thought, word, and deed, is neither tangible nor irrefrigable, since the issues involved are based deep in human motivation and reaction. At the psychological level, it is generally insufferable for the individual to lose control over the direction and ordering of his own affairs. Where religious or philosophical beliefs are involved, this aspect can assume an overriding importance as an issue of 'free choice'. At the organizational level, it is dangerous to attempt to control by mechanical means those who react according to quite other than mechanical forces. Modern society abounds with examples of the disruption that results from such attempts. At the social level, it is impossible to conduct normal interpersonal relationships in a situation where one's actions may be subject to scrutiny and where trust is completely absent.

The two arguments, for the computer and for freedom, come into conflict in our time. Therefore, one or the other must be tempered.

Our privacy is threatened by the computer because it may, if used to its full power, both hold and spread abroad all the incidents of our life from beginning to end. Our freedom is threatened by the computer because its information-power demands that it be given more information, on the evidence of which conclusions may be drawn, plans made, for directing us (corporately and singly).

Modern notions of privacy and freedom threaten to inhibit the full capabilities of the computer. If they are to be retained, computer power must be strictly channelled. Its information must not be exchanged with other computers. Its files must be given costly protection against inadvertent or deliberate infiltration, and against corruption of facts. There are some records which, since absolute security is impossible, cannot be put on computers at all.

Our conclusion must be that the new powers should be kept in check. Human dignity is more important than human efficiency – even when that efficiency is justified by a theory of improved society. No owners or users of data banks, alone or in joint integrations, can be allowed to heap indiscretion upon interference, tyranny upon our vulnerability.

We have endeavoured to remain objective in our assessments, for there are many who distrust and ridicule any apologetic which betrays emotion. In the last resort, though, we would maintain that this *is* a matter of emotion. A threat to our freedom is something that all would *feel* to be wrong, and the *feelings* of a multitude are of more significance than the statements of many committees. There are times – and this we believe to be one of them – when the warm blood of emotion might conceivably be more significant than the cold-water assessments of logic. Or at least, we must find a balance between the Appollonian and Dionysian reactions to the problems of survival. Faced with the consequences of 'scientific progress', and his role in the process, Einstein declared that he wished he had been a simple plumber! The only sane approach is that of the Italian radical Gramsci, 'pessimism of the intelligence, optimism of the heart'.

As has been said earlier, society, and its organizations, seem to have a propensity to encroach upon privacy. It constantly challenges the individual who has painstakingly set up barriers against it. One aspect of this effort on the individual's behalf is his attempt to keep society at a distance in certain spheres of his behaviour – which may be thoroughly repectable and law-abiding, not even eccentric, yet to him are important and private. But society, even in its least organized form of the village gossip, cannot stand *not* knowing what is going on. Society, in its attempt to control its members – often in principle for mutual benefit – needs information, and considerations of privacy deny much of this. While privacy remains, society cannot see the whole man; and *total control* requires *total information*. Even for a less comprehensive surveillance, relative privacy is an obstruction that must be continually assailed.

Privacy can never be absolute, but it must be preserved in at least its present form in a free society. The battle to establish the rights of the individual was a long struggle. In many countries the fight continues to establish even the most basic human rights. But the irony is that in the countries where democracy is most advanced, where the essential rights are largely accepted, other aspects of technological progress threaten the benefits. These contradictions of the system are accelerating at a frightening pace, and may negate the *material* advances which the hardware promises. The value of privacy and freedom far outweigh the loss of a small amount of technical efficiency which safeguards would entail, particularly at the high level of Gross National Product *per capita* enjoyed in advanced societies.

We have described the Congressional hearings in the US extensively. As far as Britain is concerned the prospect is not entirely black. Among other bodies, the British Computer Society is looking at its professional responsibility; some MPs are beginning to challenge publicly the computer plans of Government Departments; the National Council for Civil Liberties launched a campaign to preserve privacy as part of its contribution to International Human Rights Year. The Society of Conservative Lawyers produced a paper on *Computers and Freedom*, showing an awareness of the dangers. There is even an organization, sounding a little flat-earthish, called the International Society for the Abolition of Data Processing Machines, which, if having small hope of achieving its implied aim, does at least provide a useful (and worldwide) challenge to the possible tyranny of technology. Parliamentary Bills have been introduced; editors of national newspapers and magazines have pricked some consciences. And so on. But all this is insufficient, and we have suggested further legal and technical safeguards, believing that both legislators and the 'datacrats'[3] have their responsibilities.

Given the dangers, a far more radical solution might be suggested. It would be deliberately to reverse the trend to more and more 'monolithic' bodies; it would limit very strictly, and eventually attempt to diminish, the power of large State *and* private organizations at the same time. This may not be so impossible. Many people hope that it is still possible for citizens to band together to do something worthwhile on their own initiative, without having the bureaucratic disadvantages which size brings. A striking demonstration is certainly needed for a major shift in attitude. There have been minor victories by enterprising groups over State authority, but to take one widely evident example, it is still the planner's dream for us to have 'tidy' living conditions – homes here, shops here, children out of the way over there, green space here, traffic at full speed this way. All intellectual integrity insists that this 'tidiness' destroys our cities, destroys our natural gregariousness, deprives us of the 'little shop round the corner' (so that we *have* to use our cars to go shopping, thus worsening the traffic problem), encapsulates us and sterilizes us against casual encounters with old friends on the High Street. Of course, town planners use computers too. . . .

If these tendencies are de-humanizing in the existing state of organizational society, and data-technology offers the possibility of fact-farmers making our lives no freer than a broiler-hen, a certain retrenchment might well be in order. Either this, or we face an increase in nihilistic responses; a well-known Labour peer observed that 'The consciousness that we are living in a society where liberty of individual action is constantly diminishing, is having a marked effect on younger people. The unrest and *malaise*, the unsatisfactory relationship between the young and the mature may, in part at least, be due to an increasing sense of social claustrophobia that the young feel, with ample and increasing justification.'[4] Will Traditionalists and Utopians yet join hands to prevent a Technological Armageddon?

The very nature of Government, we have shown, has undergone considerable change. While supporting the value of social security in the modern Welfare State, we might draw a parallel between modern notions of 'ruling' and the feudal concepts of communities in which the master cares for the tenants while the people serve their lord's need. Governments believe that their obligation and the demands of the citizen coincide in a requirement to enhance both economic strength and physical well-being. As Edward Shils points out, 'Doing or trying to do so much they think that they must increase their knowledge proportionately . . . they must draw on the increased and deepened stock of knowledge in the performance of their tasks of governing as governing is now understood.'[5] The paternalistic state is a problem for politicians both left and right.

Inevitably, this demand reaches further into privacy. The intrusive perception, interception, recording, examination, extrapolation, and dissemination of both corporate and personal affairs faces us as a real possibility, and because it stems to a large degree from apparent benevolence and goodwill it is all the harder to criticize. So, in returning to a near-feudal system on a national (or even international) scale, we face its same perils, no longer localized. In what Tocqueville called 'feudal liberty', the local grouping remained private *vis-à-vis* central authority. 'This was not accompanied by protection of the private sphere within localities. Inferiors – apprentices, children, serfs – had no rights to privacy from masters, parents, bailiffs; there was also little privacy among approximate equals who lived their lives in contiguity and who shared the same spaces and institutions.'[6]

A 'night-watchman' State has as its goal no more serious intent than the protection of collision within, and from invaders without, its territory. Even the most admirable Welfare State digs deeper into every life, needing to know more and ever more, to ensure that none shall suffer material unease. It is unrealistic to deny we pay *some* price for the *undoubted* benefits.

Against the 'pessimistic' outlook of most prophets (in fiction or serious dissertation), we might contrast Michael Frayn's novel *A Very Private Life*[7] in which the élite, far from establishing an authoritarian and personality-destructive rule above the rest of civilized humanity, have withdrawn into the most impregnable privacy. All communication is through the 'holovision', a TV-phone of three-dimensional capability, on which no one can be called unless they wish it. All sensations are artificially induced by drugs, and all necessities are piped into the doorless, windowless homes. It is all a cosy, sterilized, Nirvana – but still it is underpinned by a poor, dirty and ignorant culture of workers. The élite do not care about them, or take any notice of them, and certainly do not control them. Effective authority over these latter-day 'serfs' is exercised by the middle-range of intelligence, who perform Gestapolike functions of control.

The Nazi State is part of the demonology of the futurist, for he sees how the conditions prevailing in the Germany of the thirties could not only be repeated, but carried to even worse excess. It has been observed that 'Germany was a country of philosophers and of famous industries. But when thirty years ago the real material power of industry joined forces with the real daemonic power of evil, the man-made values and ideals went like straw in the wind. . . . If we fear the future more than we hope for it, then we do so because the power of technological invention has more often been at the service of apathy, of selfishness, of evil, than it has been enlisted for positive purposes. There is no reason why this power should not be used to create a future with far wider prospects for the individual than now exist – with a greater liberty for him to lead a fuller life as a whole man.'[8]

We would wish to observe, as a gloss upon this text, that the concluding optimism can only prevail if there is a general *will* to use technological power only for good, a will of sufficient strength and determination to insist that the ambitions of the computer user are held in check. There is a terrible cliché of the politicians which currently maintains that Britain must, technologically, 'be dragged, kicking and screaming, into the second half of the twentieth century'. We are among those who dig our toes firmly in the sub-strata of present culture, and insist that it shall not be disturbed *without sound reflection upon and provision against the possible sequel.*

Another view sees a society, increasingly acquiring mechanical slaves, as eventually causing humans to degenerate.[9] With computers, we no longer have to add up figures, let alone think in more complex ways. Only an 'Eloi' elite of programmers will be left cerebrally advanced, in this view, and it should be encouraged to breed faster than the 'Morlocks' (following H. G. Wells' terminology).

But we do not need to look too far into the future. One biologist expressed an extreme view of present society as merely programmed for soulless efficiency: 'The individual is losing his voice and is becoming irretrievably immersed in the complex system of increasingly intelligent artefacts around him. Although the technology to support a biomim civilization does not yet exist, there is little doubt that it will and that we are totally unprepared for its impact. What is happening now is that most aspects of our activities are considered in statistical blocks, programmed for efficiency. Are the diurnal inhabitants of multi-storey office blocks really considered as individuals? Their lives and personalities are computerized, their output is compared to a 'norm', even the time they spend in the lavatory is measured and allowed for. Each day they flock to empty cubicles, take their places, produce their required function, eat identical luncheon meat in their sandwiches, and talk about almost identical subjects – the Cup Final, knitting or last night's TV. Battery buildings for battery people.'[10]

This tendency to dehumanize must be fought with all the strength we can muster. Yet, on the other hand, we have to rely on technology to help deal with our social problems. Stirred up by the wake of a fast-moving economy and technology, some nasty sights, sounds and smells have come to the surface to confront us so pungently that they cannot be ignored. Urban decay, and those made (not 'officially', but just as miserably) homeless; air pollution, water pollution and food pollution; destruction of natural resources, beauties, and functions; road safety; noise. And still we cannot remove the old long-standing problems of crime, ignorance, chronic unemployment and poverty, despite our advances and our increased sense of responsibility for the national welfare.

When problems are as vast as these, one natural reaction is to feel powerless to solve them, and rather to hope that they will go away of their own accord. But people do feel differently about them now. There is a belief that they *ought* to be capable of solution. When our civilization has accomplished so much, how can we fail to get over these trivial difficulties? Our standard of living is constantly on the rise, and we cannot so easily accept that there should be dirt and ugliness, suffering and crime. As the president of the Ford Company in America said: 'As our vision of the future expands, we find it difficult to reconcile ourselves to the fact that as many as one-sixth of our fellow citizens are not sharing adequately – or, in some cases, at all – in our progress to date.'[11]

We do have the resources, now, to come to grips with some of these problems and to find ways in which they may be solved. The computer is a vital tool in this task, as the only means by which all the relevant data may be adequately summated, studied, and extrapolated; it is the only equipment adequate to accept hypotheses of various solutions, and to evaluate these rapidly enough for viable action to be taken.

Computers certainly can collate an extraordinary range of pieces of information. We have cited earlier the latest military application in Vietnam.[12] It seems there is no limit to the uses to which the new machines can be put, whether in the Mekong Delta or by the Local Electricity Board. This is a good example to show that we should not accept the further extension of the role of the computer on the postulation that it makes the (national) State more efficient. As Bertrand Russell has observed: 'No other organization rouses anything like the loyalty aroused by the national State. And the chief activity of the State is preparation for large scale homicide.'[13] The computer system in the Vietnam situation mentioned, is a microcosm of the broader point Russell makes, though many minds both young and old have passed beyond a narrow loyalty to their nation. The present-day movements and hankerings for a wider, surer peace; for a juster distribution of resources; for a fuller acceptance by all races of all other races; these transcend national boundaries. It is no longer to be taken for granted that even the threat of war would now command uncritical wholehearted assent to the proposition that a nation must be defended in *all* and *any* circumstances. Certainly any appeal to latent nationalism to fight against computer tyranny is pointless. Most of the young, and many of the mature, would no longer maintain with Wordsworth that:

'We must be free or die, who speak the tongue
That Shakespeare spoke; the faith and morals hold
Which Milton held.'

The case for freedom is not jingoistic; it rests on *individual* susceptibility; and it is international in its scope.

However, to thinking people, who find that much of even the apparently simple apparatus of their lives is being influenced by the manifold uses of computers, the wonder has faded (though the mystique remains) and resentment has set in. As it has been said:

'It is only natural for people to fall into a line of reasoning like this:

1. There is something wrong with things (there *always* something wrong with things).

2. Computers are new, and moreover we don't understand them. My department store bill was wrong for the second month in a row.

3. There are twice as many computers as there used to be and things are twice as wrong as last time I looked.

4. Therefore, computers must be the source of all our troubles, and their effect is obviously doubling.'[14]

While we do not take up a neo-Luddite position, we feel that society must not be compelled to accept cold efficiency with or without computerization as the main criterion of the public good. Means and ends must not become confused. We must take account of the individual and his ability to be the judge of what is in his best interests. As John Stuart Mill noted: 'The sole end for which mankind are warranted in interfering with the liberty of action of any of their number, is self-protection. His own good, either physical or moral, is not a sufficient warrant. He cannot rightly be compelled to do or forbear because it will be better for him to do so, because it will make him happier, because, in the opinion of others, to do so would be wise or even right. Over himself, over his own body and mind, the individual is sovereign.' (On Liberty). Of course, there may be conflicts of interest. Although the State has an 'umpire' role, and today even more of a positive role, we must preserve the countervailing power of citizen's rights. But will we?

The futurist tends, as already noted, to be pessimistic, for he who would look to the future must always be a critical student of the past, and will see that man rarely has derived unmitigated benefit from his discoveries and inventions. And we see, too, that man is never able to visualize all the side-issues of any new discovery. Who, for example, predicted the chaos of Heathrow and the debilitating impact of continuous reverberating noise when man first made a machine to fly? It was, in a past decade, relatively easy for futurists to predict the invention of radio and television, but who could have predicted the advent of the mind-dulling soap-opera which for the most part swamps the receivers of America?

The more we warn about the future, the more men will recognize that there are opportunities for choice, even if it is impossible to foresee whether the total effects will be disastrous or serendipitous. Civilized man must realize that he has to stop muddling through, and decide what he wants. Social science may give the wrong impression that individual free will, or even social *choice*, has permanently flown out of the window. As a recent critique pointed out:

'Comte's famous dictum in early Republican France, reminiscent of Francis Bacon in a similar period of social confidence in England, was *savoir pour prévoir*. It is for social scientists to know, and for governments to bend the future accordingly. But is there not a fundamental and irreconcilable difference between the social scientists, with their deterministic universe, and governments, ostensibly and hopefully concerned with the maintenance of human freedoms? Is there not a danger of social scientists advising governments that they must act in such-and-such a way if they are to achieve a particular end; *and proceeding to argue that there is no choice over the end since this itself is dependent on yet further causal factors*? [our italics]. Is there not the danger that citizens are to be slaughtered on the altar of some general theory? The short answer is no, since there is no general theory. The idea of the systems theorists is still a dream.'[15]

Edmund Leach pointed out in his Reith lectures that 'men have become like gods, but instead of rejoicing we feel deeply afraid'. We know how far we are trapped in a more or less vicious, circular process: 'Science affects technics and technics in their turn affect the social structure. The resulting development assumes the proportions of an avalanche engulfing mankind. Science and technology further the rise of the machine; machinery makes industries possible; industrialism creates mass populations. Mass populations necessitate scientific management and organization. These in their turn will employ more science, more machinery, etc., etc.'[16]

In a later comment upon Utopian fiction, Professor E. M. Blaiklock has discerned a hidden satire in the title of Huxley's *Brave New World*.[17] This tag, he says, must be looked at in its context in *The Tempest*, for it is the sight of the storm-tattered Neapolitans – ordinary folk indeed! – which evokes from Miranda, who has only known the sight of Prospero and Caliban all her life, the exclamation, 'O brave new world, that has such people in't!' Says Blaiklock, 'We are the Neapolitans, apt to prove on close scrutiny, man's ancient breed.' Human nature changes very little.

Herman Kahn tells the story of a Mexican lying in the sun. The inevitable government busybody comes around to find out why he is not working and 'contributing to society': 'Why don't you get up' 'Why?' 'So that you could go and do some work.' 'Why?' 'In order to earn some money.' 'Why?' 'So that you could buy yourself a house and a garden.' 'Why?' 'So that you could lie out in the sun.' 'I *am* lying out in the sun.' Perhaps we might stop to ponder over some of our goals, and critically see whether or not we are really being 'rational' in much of our so-called purposeful activity; whether we are not on the one hand making a fetish out of technology (treating the machine as an end in itself), or on the other hand acting in ways which are essentially self-defeating (producing so many machines that there will not be space to use them, as in the case of the motor-car).[18]

It is surely the case that the increasing use of the computer for the processing of government information may defeat the end for which it was designed – that is, to increase public welfare. Are we to become the slaves of technology rather than its masters? Are we to be swamped by the new information-systems?

For twenty years and more the plea has been heard that science and politics together should work to improve our lot. It may be they should walk hand in hand – but not hand in glove. Since no one can doubt that the State is encroaching more and more into the life of the citizen, the constant debate of our time is how far it should go. The computer is 'one small step for man, but a giant leap for mankind'[19] in the process of encroachment. The argument as to how much the freedom of the individual ought to be sacrificed for the greater good of society (either now, or for our progeny) would rage without electronics. But when the men of science support and even encourage the all-pervasive State, a peculiarly ominous situation arises. Orwell was not the only man to see that such a relationship between scientists and politicians may readily breed a tyrannical control, leading to experimentation, selectivity, conditioning, and the apotheosis of indignity, constant surveillance.

A leading Labour politician has admitted that there are dangers, amounting even to tyranny, stemming from an all-knowing data bank.[20] Perhaps, he has suggested, it could be made a basic human right for the individual to have on demand a print-out of all the data banked about him, a point referred to earlier in the discussion. He points out that only in a world of total information could we take off the fig-leaf which Adam and Eve were compelled to don when they ate of the tree of knowledge, and forgot the fact that people need not hide things about themselves. Against this view, we feel that the citizen *should* have the option of concealing or revealing personal affairs, whether to others, or the State; and would consider a world of *total* information probably impossible to achieve anyway or, if possible to achieve, a nightmare. Even total self-knowledge need not necessarily be a good thing. Self-deception is often functional, and Man has evolved many psychological protections against knowing himself too well. It is a question of degree, we would suggest, in the case of both the individual and society.

It should not be thought that in defending certain traditional ideas that we are either conservative or reactionary; far from it. We are not against improvements in social engineering. Indeed, in considering the whole question of the implications of computer technology we are advocating advance protections where certain prospective outcomes clash with specific known values. We start from a humanistic viewpoint (and note that even Marx was a traditionalist in this respect). We believe that whether the subject is approached with a religious or a humanitarian philosophy, it is necessary to take a stand on the issue we have outlined. 'What a work of art is man!' sing the young,[21] adopting *Hamlet's* wonder in preference to Malraux's dictum that man is dead. Even the Bultmannesque 'new theology', declaring that God is dead, retains a respect for man as an individual destined for some high purpose. We must not stray too far from that conception of 'self' which can link past and present culture with future technology. The machine must be used to enrich existence – to expand personal freedom, not restrict it.

But 'if religion was formerly the opiate of the masses,' suggests a recent critic, 'then surely technology is the opiate of the educated public today, or at least of its favourite authors.'[22] *Laisser innover* (the new 'conservative' ideology) has taken over from an earlier school. The 'negative externalities' of technology have more recently been denounced by Paul Jacobs, the social critic, in the US; and by Sir Peter Medawar, FRS, in Britain; among a large number of other voices. There seems to be a special Gresham's Law at work – bad technology proliferates, driving out the good.

There is, however, no absolute momentum of which technological progress has a monopoly. As Camus comments: '*The very forces of matter, in their blind advance, impose their own limits* [italics added]. That is why it is useless to want to reverse the advance of technology. The age of the spinning wheel is over and the dream of a civilization of artisans is vain. The machine is bad only in the way it is now employed.'[23] It is a pity we cannot be 'scientific' about the ends to which we turn the machines, but this is an age-old problem. In the Platonic dialogue *Meno*, Socrates does not answer the question of whether virtue is knowledge with a clear 'yes' or 'no'.[24]

We can, by and large, endorse the view that the machine's danger is not from the machine itself but from what men make of it, underlining the view of Samuel Butler in *Erewhon* which saw machines, themselves unable to act, overcoming man by use of them as subordinate organs.[25] To use Norbert Weiner's terms, modern man has a lot of 'know-how', but little 'know-what'.[26]

Indeed, the futurist *par excellence*, Kahn, senses that there will be widespread philosophic questioning in the coming decades, of the issues on which we have attempted a modest contribution in these pages. He relates that: 'It is my personal conjecture, and one which personally always depresses me as well, that by the end of the century, if not by 1980, the experts will have concluded that the computer can transcend human beings in every practical aspect. I do not know what this means in terms of philosophy, religion (particularly cultist worship or hatred of the computer) and even the democratic way of life (shall we have movements for computer civil rights, for computer representation, or even computer domination of certain kinds of issues and processes in which we no longer can trust uncontrolled human beings?). None of the above are likely to be central questions by 1980, but they are all likely to be raised with substantially greater intensity than they have been to date and with a correspondingly greater philosophic and religious impact.'[27]

We are reassured that this eminent futurist can get depressed at times; we often have found it hard to suppress the suspicion that he himself was a computer at the Hudson Institute.

But, this on one side, we feel that we can endorse his emphasis of the need to understand the emergence of the post-industrial culture.

Kahn prognosticates in his conclusion to these recent observations that: 'the most important aspect of the seventies is less likely to be the actual technological developments of the next decade than an increased understanding of what the emergence of the coming technology and the post-industrial culture is likely to mean. Many of us think of this last – the change from an industrial to a post-industrial culture – as being as important in its way as the agricultural revolution of some 10,000 years ago, or the industrial revolution of some 200 years ago. We are also going to see an increasing emphasis on the year 2000 as a millennial turning point. As a result one can expect that one major activity of the seventies is going to be, as I suggested at the beginning, studying, watching, speculating, believing, and otherwise being concerned with the future in a way that would seem to our ancestors to be almost a maniacal obsession'.[28]

We hope that the description of the developments in the field we have considered, and the implications for individual freedom and privacy will, in some way, stimulate a greater awareness of the important issues at stake.

We hope that our discussion of the potential threat to freedom and privacy will impel the concerned citizen to support public action on the matter. If we have concentrated on the dangers, it is because, as Hume suggested long ago 'A man, brought to the brink of a precipice, cannot look downwithout trembling; and the sentiment of *imaginary* danger actuates him, in opposition to the opinion and belief of real safety.'[29]

The greatest danger of all is that the apathetic will consider our thesis entirely 'imaginary', in the sense that it is not, nor will be, a reflection of any 'real' circumstance. We urge the falsity of such a conclusion. The threats are *imagined*, for they have not yet become substantive; but society is on 'the brink of a precipice'.

Notes

1. Noted by Montaigne.
2. See W. E. G. Salter, *Productivity and Technical Change*, Cambridge, C.U.P. 1960, p. 5.
3. See *The Sunday Times*, December 14, 1969.
4. Lord Goodman, *op. cit.*
5. *Hearings*, C, pp. 231–2.
6. *Ibid.*
7. London: Collins, 1968.
8. W. S. Robertson, in an unpublished speech.
9. Garrett Hardin, 'An Evolutionist looks at Computers', *Datamation*, May 1969, pp. 99–103.
10. Kit Pedlar, 'Deus ex Machina', *The Listener*, August 10, 1969. *N.B.* 'biomims' are robot ancillaries.
11. *Hearings*, D, p. 364 (R. J. Miller).
12. *Op. cit.*, *The Sunday Times*, November 23, 1969 (see Ch, 8).
13. Bertrand Russell, *Power: A New Social Analysis*, London, George Allen & Unwin, 1960, p. 144.
14. F. Gruenberger, 'Speaking of Predictions', *Datamation*, October 1969, p. 141.
15. Geoffrey Hawthorn, 'The Scientific Pretensions of Sociology', *The Listener*, October 16, 1969.
16. R. Gerber, *Utopian Fantasy*, London, Routledge & Kegan Paul, 1955.
17. See E. M. Blaiklock, *Layman's Answer*, London, Hodder & Stoughton, 1968, p. 18.
18. Or even data to use them: Art Buchwald has suggested (*International Herald Tribune*, December 27–8, 1969), in typical satiric vein, that 'a crash program to produce enough data to get our computers through the seventies' is needed. 'If our figures are correct, every last bit of data in the world will have been fed into a machine by January 2, 1976, and an information famine will follow.'
19. Astronaut Armstrong's words, as the first man on the moon.
20. Anthony Wedgwood Benn, 'Maintaining Human Supremacy', *New Scientist*, August 7, 1969.
21. Acknowledgments to the musical show 'Hair'.
22. John McDermott, 'Technology: the Opiate of the Intellectuals', *New York Review of Books*, July 31, 1969, p. 25.
23. Albert Camus, *The Rebel*, Vintage Books, New York, 1956, p. 295.
24. See Hans Reichenbach, *The Rise of Scientific Philosophy*, Berkeley, University of California, 1958, p. 50.
25. See Norbert Weiner, *The Human Use of Human Beings: Cybernetics and Society*, New York, Anchor Books, 1954, pp. 182–3.
26. *Op. cit.*, p. 184.
27. *The Times*, October 9, 1969, *op. cit.*
28. *Ibid.* See also Daniel Bell, 'Notes on the Post-Industrial Society', *The Public Interest*, Nos 6 and 7, Winter and Spring, 1967.
29. David Hume, 'An Inquiry Concerning the Principles of Morals', in *Essential Works of David Hume*, New York, Bantam Books, 1965, p. 215.

Appendix I

A BILL

to prevent the invasion of privacy through the misuse of computer information

Be it enacted by the Queen's most Excellent Majesty, by and with the advice and consent of the Lords Spiritual and Temporal, and Commons, in this present Parliament assembled, and by the authority of the same, as follows: AD 1969

Register of data banks.

1. (1) A register shall be kept by the Registrar of Restrictive Trading Agreements (hereinafter in this Act referred to as 'the Registrar') of all data banks as hereinafter defined which are operated by or on behalf of any of the following:

(*a*) any agency of central or local government;
(*b*) any public corporation;
(*c*) any person exercising public authority;
(*d*) any person offering to supply information about any other person's credit-worthiness, whether to members of a particular trade or otherwise and irrespective of whether payment is made therefor;
(*e*) any private detective agency or other person undertaking to carry out investigations into any other person's character, abilities or conduct on behalf of third parties;
(*f*) any person who offers for sale information stored in such data bank, whether to the general public or otherwise.

(2) The register referred to in the foregoing subsection shall contain the following information concerning each data bank:

(*a*) the name and address of the owner of the data bank;
(*b*) the name and address of the person responsible for its operation;
(*c*) the location of the data bank;
(*d*) such technical specifications relating to the data bank as may be required by the Registrar;
(*e*) the nature of the data stored or to be stored therein;
(*f*) the purpose for which data is stored therein;
(*g*) the class of persons authorised to extract data therefrom.

(3) The owner of the data bank shall be required to register the information referred to in paragraphs (*a*) to (*c*) of the foregoing subsection. The person responsible for the operation of the data bank shall be required to register the information referred to in paragraphs (*a*) to (*g*) of the foregoing subsection.

(4) Any person responsible for registering information under this section shall be required to inform the Registrar of any alterations of, additions to or deletions from the said information within four weeks of such alteration taking effect, subject to the provisions of subsection (6) below.

(5) If at any time the Registrar is of the opinion that in the circumstances the information given or sought to be given under paragraphs (*f*) or (*g*) of subsection (2) above might result in the infliction of undue hardship upon any person or persons or be not in the interest of the public generally, he may order such entry to be expunged from or not entered in the register. In reaching a decision under this or the next following subsection, the Registrar shall be guided by the principle that only data relevant to the purposes for which the data bank is operated should be stored therein, and that such data should only be disclosed for those same purposes.

(6) An alteration to the register in respect of paragraph (*f*) or (*g*) of subsection (2) above shall be made by application to the Registrar who shall, not earlier than four weeks after receipt of such application, grant or reject the application giving his reasons in writing.

(7) The register together with applications submitted in accordance with the last foregoing subsection shall be open to inspection by the public, including the press, during normal office hours:

Provided that entries relating to data banks operated by the police, the security services and the armed forces shall be kept in a separate part of the register which shall not be open to inspection by the public.

Records to be maintained by operators of certain data banks.

2. (1) This section shall apply to all data banks which are required to be registered under section 1 above except for the following:

(*a*) data banks which do not contain personal information relating to identifiable persons;
(*b*) data banks operated by the police;
(*c*) data banks operated by the security services;
(*d*) data banks operated by the armed forces of the Crown.

(2) The operator of each data bank to which this section applies shall maintain a written record in which shall be recorded the date of each extraction of data therefrom, the identity of the person requesting the data, the nature of the data supplied and the purpose for which it was required.

3. (1) The Registrar shall submit annually to Parliament a report covering the previous calendar year in which he shall state the number of data banks entered on the register, the number of such data banks which fall within the terms of section 2(1)(*a*) and of section 2(1)(*b*) to (*d*) respectively and the number of instances in which he ordered entries to be amended under section 1(5) or refused an application to alter an entry under section 1(6). Annual report.

(2) The Registrar's report may contain such additional information, statistical and otherwise, as the Registrar may think fit.

4. (1) Any person about whom information is stored in a data bank to which section 2 above applies shall receive from the operator, not later than two months after his name is first programmed into the data bank, a print-out of all the data contained therein which relates to him. Thereafter, he shall be entitled to demand such a print-out at any time upon payment of a fee the amount of which shall be determined by the Registrar from time to time; and the operator shall supply such print-out within three weeks of such demand. Information to be supplied by operators of certain data banks.

(2) Every print-out supplied in accordance with this section shall be accompanied by a statement giving the following information:

(*a*) The purpose for which the data contained in the print-out is to be used, as entered on the register referred to in section 1 above;

(*b*) The purposes for which the said data has in fact been used since the last print-out supplied in accordance with this section;

(*c*) The names and addresses of all recipients of all or part of the said data since the last print-out supplied in accordance with this section.

5. (1) Any person who has received a print-out in accordance with Section 4 above may, after having notified the operator of the data bank of his objection, apply to the Registrar for an order that any or all of the data contained therein be amended or expunged on the ground that it is incorrect, unfair or out of date in the light of the purposes for which it is stored in the data bank. Application for amendment or expunging of data.

(2) The Registrar may, if he grants an order under the foregoing subsection, issue an ancillary order that all or any of the recipients of the said data be notified of the terms of the order.

Offences.

6. (1) It shall be an offence, punishable on summary conviction by a fine of not more than £500, or on conviction on indictment by a fine of not more than £1,000 or imprisonment for not more than five years or both, for the owner or operator of a data bank to which this Act applies to fail to register it in accordance with this Act.

(2) If the operator of a data bank to which section 2 above applies:

(*a*) fails or refuses to send a print-out when under a duty so to do; or

(*b*) permits data stored in the data bank to be used for purposes other than those stated on the register; or

(*c*) allows access to the said data to persons other than those entered on the register as having authorised access; or

(*d*) fails or refuses to comply with a decision of the Registrar,

he shall be liable in damages to the person whose personal data is involved and, where such acts or omissions are wilful, shall be liable on summary conviction to a fine of not more than £500 and on conviction on indictment to a fine of not more than £1,000 or imprisonment for not more than five years or both.

(3) A person who aids, abets, counsels or procures the commission of an offence described in this section or with knowledge of its wrongful acquisition receives, uses, handles, sells or otherwise disposes of information obtained as a result of the commission of such an offence, shall likewise be guilty of the said offence.

Liability for damages.

7. An operator of a data bank to which this Act applies who causes or permits inaccurate personal data to be supplied from the data bank as a result of which the person to whom the data refers suffers loss, shall be liable in damages to such person.

Rules.

8. The Registrar may make rules relating to the implementation of any part or parts of this Act and in particular relating to:

(*a*) the keeping of the register and records referred to in Sections 1 and 2 above;

(*b*) access by the public to the register referred to in Section 1 above;

(*c*) procedure on hearing objections and argment on a proposal to alter or expunge from the register under subsection 5 of Section 1 above;

(*d*) procedure on application to alter the register under Subsection 6 of Section 1 above;

(*e*) verification of the identity of a person demanding a print-out in accordance with Section 4 above.

Appeals.

9. An appeal shall lie to the High Court from any decision made by the Registrar under this Act.

Definitions.

10. In this Act, the following terms shall have the meanings hereby respectively assigned to them, that is to say:

'data' means information which has been fed into and stored in a data bank;

'data bank' means a computer which records and stores information;

'operator' means the person responsible for the operation of a data bank and for the introduction into and extraction from it of data;

'owner' means the person who owns the machinery comprising the data bank;

'print-out' means a copy of information contained in the data bank supplied by the computer and translated into normal typescript.

Expenses.

11. *There shall be paid out of moneys provided by Parliament any expenses incurred by the Registrar attributable to the provisions of this Act.*

Short title, commencement and extent.

12. (1) This act may be cited as the Data Surveillance Act 1969.

(2) This Act shall come into force on the first day of July 1970.

(3) This Act shall extend to Northern Ireland.

Appendix II

ACM CODE OF PROFESSIONAL CONDUCT

INTRODUCTION

This set of guidelines was adopted by the Council of the Association for Computing Machinery on November 11, 1966, in the spirit of providing a guide to the members of the Association. In the years to come this set of guidelines is expected to evolve into an effective means of preserving a high level of ethical conduct. In the meantime it is planned that ACM members will use these guidelines in their own professional lives. They are urged to refer ethical problems to the proper ACM authorities as specified in the Constitution and Bylaws to receive further guidance and in turn assist in the evolution of the set of guidelines.

PREAMBLE

The professional person, to uphold and advance to honor, dignity and effectiveness of the profession in the arts and sciences of information processing, and in keeping with high standards of competence and ethical conduct: Will be honest, forthright and impartial; will serve with loyalty his employer, clients and the public; will strive to increase the competence and prestige of the profession; will use his special knowledge and skill for the advancement of human welfare.

1. *Relations with the Public*

1.1 An ACM member will have proper regard for the health, privacy, safety and general welfare of the public in the performance of his professional duties.

1.2 He will endeavour to extend public knowledge, understanding and appreciation of computing machines and information processing and achievements in their application, and will oppose any untrue, inaccurate or exaggerated statement or claims.

1.3 He will express an opinion on a subject within his competence only when it is founded on adequate knowledge and honest conviction, and will properly qualify himself when expressing an opinion outside of his professional field.

1.4 He will preface any partisan statement, criticisms or arguments that he may issue concerning information processing by clearly indicating on whose behalf they are made.

2. *Relations with Employers and Clients*

2.1 Am ACM member will act in professional matters as a faithful agent or trustee for each employer or client and will not disclose private information belonging to any present or former employer or client without his consent.

2.2 He will indicate to his employer or client the consequences to be expected if his professional judgement is overruled.

2.3 He will undertake only those professional assignments for which he is qualified and which the state of the art supports.

2.4 He is responsible to his employer or client to meet specifications to which he is committed in tasks he performs and products he produces, and to design and develop systems that adequately perform their function and satisfy his employer's or client's operational needs.

3. *Relations with Other Professionals*

3.1 An ACM member will take care that credit for work is given to those to whom credit is properly due.

3.2 He will endeavour to provide opportunity and encouragement for the professional development and advancement of professionals or those aspiring to become professionals with whom he comes in contact.

3.3 He will not injure maliciously the professional reputation or practice of another person and will conduct professional competition on a high plane. If he has proof that another person has been unethical, illegal or unfair in his professional practice concerning information processing, he should so advise the proper authority.

3.4 He will co-operate in advancing information processing by interchanging information and experience with other professionals and students and by contributing to public communications media and to the efforts of professional and scientific societies and schools.

Appendix III

DAILY SURVEILLANCE SHEET

From a Nationwide Data Bank

(Reprinted with permission from *Computers and Automation*, October 1969, copyright 1969 by and published by Berkeley Enterprises, Inc., 815 Washington St., Newtonville, Mass. 02160., U.S.A.)

Dennie Van Tassel
Head Programmer
San Jose State College
125 S. 7th St.
San Jose, Calif. 95114

The 'Daily Surveillance Sheet' below is offered as some food for thought to anyone concerned with the establishment of the proposed 'National Data Bank'. Hopefully, it will help illustrate that *everyone* should be concerned.

NATIONAL DATA BANK
DAILY SURVEILLANCE SHEET
CONFIDENTIAL
July 11, 1987

SUBJECT *Dennie van Tassel*
San Jose State College
Male
Age 38
Married
Programmer

PURCHASES	*Wall Street Journal*	*.10*
	Breakfast	*1.65*
	Gasoline	*3.00*
	Phone (328–1826)	*.10*
	Phone (308–7928)	*.10*
	Phone (421–1931)	*.10*
	Bank (Cash Withdrawal)	*(120.00)*
	Lunch	*2.00*
	Cocktail	*1.00*

Lingerie	*21.85*
Phone (369–2436)	*.35*
Bourbon	*8.27*
Newspaper	*8.10*

COMPUTER ANALYSIS

Owns stock (90 per cent probability).
Heavy starch breakfast. Probably overweight.
Bought 3.00 dollars gasoline. Owns VW. So far this week he has bought 12.00 dollars worth of gas. Obviously doing something else besides just driving the 9 miles to work.
Bought gasoline at 7.57. Safe to assume he was late to work.
Phone No. 328–1826 belongs to Shady Lane – Shady was arrested for bookmaking in 1972.
Phone No. 308–7928. Expensive men's barber – specializes in bald men or hair styling.
Phone No. 421–1931. Reservations for Las Vegas (without wife). Third trip this year to Las Vegas (without wife). Will scan file to see if anyone else has gone to Las Vegas at the same time and compare to his phone call numbers.
Withdrew 120.00 dollars cash. Very unusual since all legal purchases can be made using the National Social Security Credit Card. Cash usually only used for illegal purchases. It was previously recommended that all cash be outlawed as soon as it becomes politically possible.
Drinks during his lunch.
Bought very expensive lingerie. Not his wife's size.
Phone No. 369–2436. Miss Sweet Locks.
Purchased expensive bottle of Bourbon. He has purchased 5 bottles of Bourbon in the last 30 days. Either heavy drinker or much entertaining.

OVERALL ANALYSIS

Left work at 4.00. Since he purchased the Bourbon 1 mile from his job at 4.10. (Opposite direction from his house.)
Bought newspaper at 6.30 near his house. Unaccountable 2½ hours. Made 3 purchases today from young blondes. (Statistical 1 chance in 78.) Therefore probably has weakness for young blondes.

A SELECTED BIBLIOGRAPHY

Section 1. Complete Publications

Acheson, E. D. (ed.), *Record Linkage in Medicine*, E. & S. Livingstone, London, 1968.

Proceedings (papers and discussion) of a conference. Contains some useful material on ensuring that the 'right' computer record is obtained; also thoughts on confidentiality and medical ethics.

Bingham, Harvey W., 'Security Techniques for E.D.P. of Multi-level Classified Information', Burroughs Corporation, Paper RADC–TR–65–415, AD 476557, December 1965.

Report of an eight-month study. Very detailed and highly technical description of a proposal for a secure environment. 'Should definitely be read by all who plan to design or configure a computer system, in which secure information must be protected' – Hoffman.

Boruch, Robert F., 'Educational Research and the Confidentiality of Data', American Council on Education Report, Vol. 4, No. 4, 1969.

Specific aspects of the privacy issue are examined with respect to the 'Ace' data bank – biographical and other data on college freshmen. Leaves some questions unanswered.

Brenton, Myron, *The Privacy Invaders*, Coward-McCann, Inc., New York, 1964.

The ways privacy is invaded today. Tiny electronic devices, secret cameras, mailing lists, etc. Easy reading; somewhat terrifying.

Emery, F. E. (ed.), *Systems Thinking*, Penguin, London, 1969.

This is an anthology of journal articles on general systems theory, and how it relates to organizational analysis.

Fogarty, Michael S., *Issues of Privacy and Security in the Urban Information System*, Northwest Regional Educational Laboratory, Oregon.

A good paper for making urban officials, etc., aware of the costs and benefits of large computer data banks. Problems of privacy considered. Contains bibliography.

Harrison, Annette, *The Problem of Privacy in the Computer Age: An Annotated Bibliography*, Rand Corp. RM–5495–PR/RC, December 1967.

A 300-entry bibliography covering all aspects.

Hoffman, Lance J., *Computers and Privacy: A Survey*, Computing Surveys, Vol. 1, No. 2, June 1969.

Extremely valuable review of the problem by an expert in computing. Summarizes readably Petersen and Turn's technical protection suggestions (q.v.). Useful bibliography, though brief.

Hsaio, David K., *A File System for a Problem Solving Facility*, Ph.D. Thesis, Univ. of Pennsylvania, 1968.

An important concept of 'authority items', protecting individual items of data rather than merely whole files, has been introduced and implemented.

Jacob, J., 'Data Banks, The Computer, Privacy and the Law.' National Council for Civil Liberties, News Release, 1968.

This short, but thorough, paper examines the threats of computer systems, and makes proposals for legislation on the grounds that existing legal concepts are inadequate. Essential reading.

Kahn, David, *The Codebreakers*, Macmillan, New York, 1967.

A copiously documented book on cryptology, cryptanalysis, and codes. Shows ciphering schemes.

Kahn, Herman and Wiener, Anthony, J., *The Year 2000: A Framework for Speculation*. Collier Macmillan, New York, 1968.

An exhaustive review of the trends discernible in our times, in business, industry, society, etc., amply illustrated with statistics. Extrapolates from these to suggest pointers for the way things may go, emphasizing that alternative choices continuously arise.

Long, Edward V., *The Intruders: The Invasion of Privacy by Government and Industry*. Praeger, New York, 1967.

A study of the broad problem of the invasion of privacy in the USA, treated in a topical, readable manner. Foreword by Hubert H. Humphrey.

Madgwick, Donald., *Privacy Under Attack*, National Council for Civil Liberties, London, 1968.

A pamphlet as part of the N.C.C.L. privacy campaign. Covers the computer as well as other intrusive devices, and makes proposals for legislation. Thorough and very readable.

Packard, Vance, *The Naked Society*, David McKay, New York, 1964.

The best-selling expose of snooping methods, surveillance, so-called 'personality tests', etc., said to be threatening American's privacy in the early sixties.

Parker, Donn B., *Privacy in Resource-Sharing Computer Systems*, C.D.C. (internal) Report TER–06, November 1967.

Good statement of the reasons for protection of computer systems, and what the manufacturer (i.e. Control Data Corp.) should be doing both internally and in his products. Emphasises that simple safeguards are inadequate.

Rosenberg, J., *The Death of Privacy*, Random House, New York, 1969.

Privacy, computers and data banks. A review of the US discussion, action, and present situation. Most topics are covered in more detail in other publications, but this is a readable general book.

Sjoberg, Gideon (ed.), *Ethics, Politics, and Social Research*, Routledge and Kegan, Paul London, 1969.

This is a book of papers on the ethics of social science, which is of interest to specialists.

Stone, M. G., *Computer Privacy*, Anbar Monograph No. 13, London, 1968.

Designed deliberately to alert managers to their responsibilities, this short paper outlines the problem generally, in a rather flamboyant style.

Westin, Alan F., *Privacy and Freedom*, Atheneum, New York, 1967. Bodley Head, London, 1970.

This remains the classic exposition of the whole subject, covering not only the technological threats of the present and future, but also delving into the concepts implied in the title with examination of the necessary controls of any society. Copiously documented, with four separate bibliographies. Essential reading for anyone concerned with the problem.

Yavitz, Boris, and Stanback, Thomas M., *Electronic Data Processing in New York City*, Columbia University, New York, 1967.

Belies its title. The research was amongst N.Y. firms, but the result is a thorough presentation of just how and why organizations have turned to computer methods. An easy to read book for the layman wanting to understand the use of the new tool in the modern office.

Anonymous, *Computers and Freedom*, Conservative Research Department, December 1968.

A group of Conservative Party lawyers discussed the issue, and produced this pamphlet. Some of the things it said were new at the time; nothing has developed into Party policy.

Anonymous, *The Considerations of Data Security in a Computer Environment*, I.B.M. Corp., New York, 1969.

Some general security considerations and methods of providing safeguards. An excellent introduction to the technical problems for any installation reviewing its privacy situation.

Granbard S. (ed.) 'Towards the Year 2000: Work in Progress', special issue of *Daedalus – Journal of American Academy of Arts and Sciences*, Vol. 96, 3, Summer 1967.

The meetings of the Commission on the Year 2000; transcripts of discussions, and contributed papers. The distilled wisdom of many eminent futurists, presented unemotionally.

Section 2. Government Documents

NOTE: The U.S. Congressional and Senate Hearings, referred to throughout this book, are described in the Acknowledgements preceding Chapter 1. They are published by the US Government Printing Office.

California: Assembly Bill 1381, 1968 Session. The Bill recognizes: (1) an individual's right of privacy as a direct right, and (2) computerized data as 'public records'.

Canada: Data Surveillance Bill – Ontario Bill No. 182, 2nd Session, 28th Legislature.

The British Data Surveillance Bill (q.v.) was based on this, to a large extent – and was introduced a month earlier! The Bill was introduced by Mr T. Reid (Scarborough East), MP.

Haringey Borough: Long-term computer study, Initial Report. London Boroughs Management Services Unit, 1969.

A thorough presentation of the interrelationship between functional departments of a local authority, showing clearly how a central data bank would be beneficial. Details all the probable files, right down to actual record content. Also costs out a proposed computer system.

Westminster: Hansard, House of Commons, May 6, 1969.
Mr Kenneth Baker, MP, introduces his Data Surveillance Bill.

Westminster: Hansard, House of Lords, December 3, 1969.
Lord Windlesham initiates a lengthy (and notably wise) debate on computers and privacy.

Section 3. Papers in General Publications

Bachi, R., and Baron, R., 'Confidentiality Problems related to Data Banks', Invited paper, International Statistical Institute, London, September 1969.
This paper is written to alert statisticians, and discusses various 'Administrative Registers' – e.g. Census, Directories – in depth. Large bibliography.

Batty, C. D., 'On Computers, Privacy, and Human Judgement', Proceedings 5th Annual Colloq. on Information Retrieval, USA, May 1968.
A reasoned argument for the computerization of personal information in a large file, which too blandly assumes that the privacy situation will be better, not worse.

Benn, Anthony Wedgwood, 'Maintaining Human Supremacy', *New Scientist*, August 7, 1969.
A general piece by the Minister of Technology on the problem of man *v.* the machine. It touches on the privacy problem, in part.

Butler, David, 'Impact of Computers on the Industrial Power Structure', *B.C.S. Computer Bulletin*, October 1969.
Suggests that social and political power resides with those who run the major (economically) industries of the land, and that since computers are 'running' more and more organizations the whole of our power structure is in flux.

Calder, Nigel, 'Computers On Tap', *New Statesman*, April 21, 1967.
This is a general article on the possible use of computers and raises the problem of privacy to a useful degree, if a trifle complacently.

Clarke, A. H., and others, 'Practis', *Journal of Royal College of General Practitioners*, Vol. 17, 60. 1969.
The brief report of an experimental introduction of computerized recording within the GP's surgery; the trial proves that on-line systems are a workable proposition.

Comber, Edward V., 'Management of Confidential Information', in Proceedings of Fall Joint Computer Conference, USA, November 1969.
Poorly put together, but nonetheless useful to perhaps broaden the horizons of those designing a data bank that is to contain sensitive information.

Curran, W. J., Stearns, B., and Kaplan, H., 'Privacy, Confidentiality, and

Other Legal Considerations in the Establishment of a Centralized Health-data System', *New England Journal of Medicine*, July 31, 1969.

Recognizing that *the* major issue in using computers for medical data is absolute confidentiality, the authors make specific proposals for the protection of information.

Douglas, William O., *et al.*, 'The Computerization of Government Files: What Impact on the Individual?' *U.C.L.A. Law Review*, Vol. 15, 5, September 1968.

Good, easily-read summary of file computerization, and the related laws and concepts of privacy. Appendices describe data held in California State files, with such statute as applies to them. Various safeguards mentioned.

Fisher, Arthur, 'Computers – Tools for Terror or Progress?' *Science World*, October 25, 1968.

A short three-page article for the layman.

Gallati, R. R. J., 'Criminal Justice Systems and the Right to Privacy', Proceedings of 5th Annual Conference, Urban and Regional Information Systems Association, USA, 1967.

Increasing crime rates demand modern information systems for law enforcement – but there must be complete security of the data. Worthwhile reading for *anyone* setting up personal files, but especially those working on the National Crime Centre.

Gill, Stanley, Presidential Address, *B.C.S. Computer Bulletin*, November 1968.

The retiring President tells British Computer Society members, in no uncertain terms, that they have an ethical responsibility for the consequences of their work.

Goodman, Lord, 'The Decay of Liberty', the *Spectator*, May 12, 1968.

A broad polemic concerning the erosion of freedom, by a Labour peer in a Tory weekly.

Gribbin, August, 'Insurance Firms Maintain Secret Data Repository', *National Observer*, USA, October 3, 1969.

Describes the Medical Information Bureau, a data bank owned by insurance companies, which contains very much sensitive and subjective personal data, and is about to be computerized.

Hall, Peter, 'Computer Privacy', *New Society*, September 31, 1969.

The inevitability of integrated computer systems is accepted, and the threats scorned – by reference to the (quite inapposite) social structure in Sweden.

Hanlon, Joseph, 'Need Seen for Ombudsman to Regulate all Data Banks', *Computerworld*, USA, August 13, 1969.

A review of Rosenberg's book (q.v.), and a useful summary thereof for those who cannot take the full story.

Hardin, Garrett, 'An Evolutionist Looks at Computers', *Datamation*, USA, May 1969.

The view is advanced that computers are leading society down a road where the clever will get cleverer ('Eloi') and the average will sink lower

('Molochs'). Only the best people understand computers, and they will use its power to increase their own knowledge and, therefore, power. A somewhat horrifying prospect.

Lickson, Charles P., 'Privacy and the Computer Age', *I.E.E. Spectrum*, Vol. 5, 10, October 1968.

A non-technical paper attempting a definition of privacy, and looking at the law, past and prospective. Well referenced.

McCarthy, John, 'Information', *Scientific American*, September 1966.

The very early prophetic warning, and proposal for a new Bill of Rights to meet the Computer Age.

McDermott, John, 'Technology: The Opiate of the Intellectuals', *New York Review of Books*, July 31, 1969.

An excellent, original polemic aimed at the facile acceptance of technological innovations by the intellectual mandarins, now comprising the American Establishment.

Merton, Robert K., 'Bureaucratic Structure and Personality', *Social Forces*, Vol. XVII, 1940.

An original, seminal article of interest to sociologists only, concerning the effects of bureaucracy.

Miller, Arthur R., 'The National Data Centre and Personal Privacy' *Atlantic Monthly*, December 1967.

A professor of Law formulates strong criticism of the plan for a single computer centre, and states the case against data banks.

Miller, Arthur R., 'Personal Privacy in the Computer Age: The Challenge of a New Technology', *Michigan Law Review*, Vol. 67, 6, April 1969.

First-rate article, showing the inadequacy of existing law, and how information can be used in unintended ways. 'A frightening panorama of existing and possible future surveillance activities' – Hoffman.

Mindlin, Albert, 'Confidentiality and Local Information Systems', *Public Administration Review*, Vol. 28, Nov.–Dec. 1968.

Shows how the local government 'mini-dossier', used by planners, administrators, etc., gives rise to confidentiality problems. Non-technical.

Moss, Judith, 'Confidentiality and Identity', Presentation to A.C.M. Symposium, New York, October 18, 1968, and published as Lockheed Government Information Systems Report GIS–83.

Considers the practicalities of identifying information with a particular person. Criticises use of Social Security numbers, and also allowing individuals to see their own record. Some methods of attack on the identity problem are proposed.

Petersen, H. E., and Turn, R., 'System Implications of Information Privacy', Proceedings of Spring Joint Computer Conference, USA, 1967.

The paper summarized by Hoffman (*supra*). Detailed scrutiny of threats and technical protections, covering the computer processor, the files, the terminals, and the communications lines. Good bibliography. 'A must paper' – Hoffman.

Pilpel, Harriet F. 'What Price Privacy?' *Civil Liberties*, No 225, April 1965.

This discusses the law of privacy in the U.S.

Prosser, William L., 'Privacy', *California Law Review*, Vol. 48, 3, August 1960.

A comprehensive review of court cases involving privacy. Well written and interesting.

Robens, Lord, 'People and Computers', *B.C.S. Computer Bulletin*, April 1969.

An extremely interesting lecture on the changes to be feared and welcomed from the use of computers, with a warning to experts to moderate their enthusiasm for 'progress'.

Ruebhauser, Oscar; and Brim, O. G. Jnr., 'Privacy and Behaviour Research,' *Columbia Law Review*, 65 (November, 1965) pp. 1184–1211.

A useful guide to the problem for the social science researcher.

Schaar, John H., and Wolin, Sheldon S., 'Education and the Technological Society', *New York Review of Books*, October 9, 1969.

A general piece on recent US trends in education as it is affected by technology, with some reference to computer advances.

Shannon, C. E., 'Communication Theory of Secrecy Systems', *Bell Technical Journal*, Vol. 29, 4, October 1949.

A classic paper which develops the mathematical theory of ciphering systems, and introduces methods for constructing systems that will be very hard to break. *Not* for the non-mathematician!

Warner, M., and Stone, M. G., 'Politics, Privacy, and Computers'. *Political Quarterly*, Vol. 40, 3, July–September 1969.

A brief general introduction to the subject, by the present authors.

Anonymous, 'Data Strips on Passport Called Threat to Privacy', *Computerworld*, Vol. III, 29, July 23, 1969.

A proposed machine-readable passport is attacked on the grounds of assisting dossier-type movement records, and dubious accuracy.

Anonymous, 'Computers and Privacy – It's the Feeder's Fault', Editorial in *San Jose Mercury-News*, September 28, 1969.

The citizen should be required to tell Government less, not more, about himself. Then computers will only hold innocuous data, so there will be no problem.

Anonymous, 'Data Banks Revisited', *Computerworld*, August 20, 1969.

An editorial which views with alarm a new data bank to hold records of 300,000 children of migrant farm workers, 'with not a safeguard in sight'. Calls for Ombudsman protection.

INDEX